Family Stress Management

Third Edition

In 1988, I dedicated the first edition of Family Stress
Management *to my parents who survived the stress of immigration
and the Great Depression; in 2002, I dedicated the second edition
to my son and daughter who balanced work and family so well.
I dedicate this third edition to my four grandchildren, each studying to
ease 21st-century family stressors in the context of global warming
and space travel.*

—Pauline Boss

*For my sister, Barlynda, and my husband, Richard Walker, who
explore the wonders of the world with me through multiple lenses and
with open hearts, and for my parents, Elvis and Delores, who instilled
in me the power of family.*

—Chalandra M. Bryant

*With appreciation for my parents, Giulio (Jay) and Vetra Robinson
Mancini, who showed me how to live a resilient life, and for the love
of Deborah, Nathan, David, and Suzanne Mancini, who are the joys
of my life.*

—Jay A. Mancini

SAGE was founded in 1965 by Sara Miller McCune to support
the dissemination of usable knowledge by publishing innovative
and high-quality research and teaching content. Today, we
publish over 900 journals, including those of more than 400
learned societies, more than 800 new books per year, and a
growing range of library products including archives, data, case
studies, reports, and video. SAGE remains majority-owned by
our founder, and after Sara's lifetime will become owned by
a charitable trust that secures our continued independence.

Los Angeles | London | New Delhi | Singapore | Washington DC | Melbourne

Family Stress Management

A Contextual Approach

Third Edition

Pauline Boss
University of Minnesota, Twin Cities

Chalandra M. Bryant
University of Georgia

Jay A. Mancini
University of Georgia

Los Angeles | London | New Delhi
Singapore | Washington DC | Melbourne

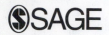

FOR INFORMATION:

SAGE Publications, Inc.
2455 Teller Road
Thousand Oaks, California 91320
E-mail: order@sagepub.com

SAGE Publications Ltd.
1 Oliver's Yard
55 City Road
London, EC1Y 1SP
United Kingdom

SAGE Publications India Pvt. Ltd.
B 1/I 1 Mohan Cooperative Industrial Area
Mathura Road, New Delhi 110 044
India

SAGE Publications Asia-Pacific Pte. Ltd.
3 Church Street
#10-04 Samsung Hub
Singapore 049483

Acquisitions Editor: Nathan Davidson
Editorial Assistant: Heidi Dreiling
Production Editor: Bennie Clark Allen
Copy Editor: Michelle Ponce
Typesetter: C&M Digitals (P) Ltd.
Proofreader: Jennifer Grubba
Indexer: Jean Casalegno
Cover Designer: Scott Van Atta
Cover Photographer: Amy Parish
Marketing Manager: Shari Countryman

Copyright © 2017 by SAGE Publications, Inc.

Printed in the United States of America

Library of Congress Cataloging-in-Publication Data

Names: Boss, Pauline, author. | Bryant, Chalandra M., author. | Mancini, Jay A., author.

Title: Family stress management / Pauline Boss, University of Minnesota, Twin Cities, Chalandra M. Bryant, University of Georgia, Jay A. Mancini, University of Georgia.

Description: Third edition. | Los Angeles : SAGE, [2017] | Includes bibliographical references and index.

Identifiers: LCCN 2016009992 | ISBN 9781452270005 (pbk. : alk. paper)

Subjects: LCSH: Families—United States—Psychological aspects. | Stress (Psychology)

Classification: LCC HQ536 .B674 2017 | DDC 306.850973—dc23
LC record available at https://lccn.loc.gov/2016009992

This book is printed on acid-free paper.

16 17 18 19 20 10 9 8 7 6 5 4 3 2 1

Brief Contents

Detailed Contents

Preface

Mission of Book—Purpose of Revision

As the original author of *Family Stress Management* (1988, 2002) and the Contextual Model of Family Stress (CMFS)—and now in my eighth decade of life—I have invited two younger and eminent family science scholars to join me in writing this third edition. They added immensely to this new edition.

This third edition continues the original commitment to understanding the external and internal contexts in which distressed families are immersed. But in this new edition, we highlight even more the multicultural differences in families. By using a universal stressor—a death in the family—we illustrate the vast diversity in beliefs and values in families, all of which can be found in American society. As we focus on differences as well as commonalities, the topic of family stress management becomes more complex with fewer pat answers or binaries. This lack of absolute answers is what provides a thoughtful excitement in this third edition of *Family Stress Management*.

The signature lack of jargon in *Family Stress Management* makes it a useful textbook (1) across disciplines, (2) for practitioners as well as researchers, and (3) for either undergraduate or graduate students. This is essential because today, the topic of family stress belongs to numerous disciplines: family social science, social work, nursing, human development, family psychology, sociology, pastoral studies, and military studies. With its more accessible writing style, *Family Stress Management* will enhance any course addressing individuals, couples, or families experiencing stress and trying to cope and regain their resilience.

Overall, the major features of the book and the benefits of these features are its inclusiveness and thus its usefulness for researchers, practitioners, and educators working with any family stressor in any context or culture.

While we discuss families within an external context of culture, history, economy, development, and heredity—contexts not often amenable to change—we also discuss the more malleable inner context comprised of the structural, psychological, and philosophical aspects of a particular family and its beliefs and values. Why is this contextual approach beneficial? It allows the readers to apply the framework to their own particular cases, their particular disciplines, and the particular families with whom they are working at a particular time.

Major Features of New Edition

How is this edition similar to previous editions? First, the core questions of *Family Stress Management*, first and second editions, remain: Why do some families survive stressful situations while others fall apart? Can a family's beliefs and values be used as a predictor of vulnerability to stress—or resilience? While these questions are similar to those asked earlier, our answers in this edition are much more nuanced. There is no one right answer for all families, even those living in the same neighborhoods, hence the need for a more open and inclusive CMFS.

Second, as in previous editions, the core framework for understanding family stress and the prevention of crisis remains the CMFS. It is meant to be a heuristic map to guide one's thinking when working in diverse cultures and with diverse stressors. Because the CMFS is an inclusive and interdisciplinary framework, it helps researchers and practitioners develop a better understanding of the complexities of family stress and resilience processes today.

What is different in this edition? Aside from an update in research literature, and an almost total reorganization and rewrite, we have now clarified the essential differences between ambiguous loss and boundary ambiguity, coping and resilience, and family versus community. Also, by emphasizing family function over family structure, we point out the wide range of ways families cope and remain resilient. Finally, in this new edition, there is more emphasis on resilience and community, the latter often being a support system that also helps individuals and families gain their resilience.

Pedagogical Aids

Stories

Each chapter (except for the first and last) begins with a story illustrating the main concepts in the chapter. The stories are intended to capture the attention of readers, facilitate critical thinking, and help them apply the context of each chapter to real life. Within some chapters, there are additional stories that bring to life the concepts covered.

Summary and Points to Remember

The "Summary" and "Points to Remember" provide a quick review of key issues in the chapter. "Points to Remember" highlight the main theme and core ideas for each chapter.

Discussion Questions

"Discussion Questions" provide an opportunity to process and apply information, in effect to extend learning. Many of these questions also provide an opportunity for self-reflection, thereby helping students develop a better understanding of themselves and how they are shaped by their own familial, cultural, and social contexts. The "Discussion Questions" (when used in a group or class setting) are also intended to spark the exchanging of ideas and sharing of experiences, so that individuals can learn about each other's similarities and differences. This is critical for those students (undergraduate or graduate) in any type of clinical or counseling programs. Finally, the questions can be used to assess students' understanding as instructors consider these two overarching questions: Can the student explain the basic concepts presented in the chapter? Can the student answer the questions by applying the concepts and ideas presented in the chapter?

Additional Readings

Each chapter contains a list of additional readings—academic books, chapters, journal articles, and novels. These are not the books/chapters/journal articles that are cited in the chapter. Those readings are provided in the reference list. We wanted to go beyond the reference list. The "Additional Readings" can be used by individuals or classes as supplemental materials that (1) illustrate or build upon the concepts covered or (2) demonstrate how a theory covered in the chapter can be integrated into a research study. In a few chapters, a film or video is even suggested. When students are presented with the same concept in different ways (chapters in this book, then "Additional Readings"), their ability to comprehend and apply the concepts (rather than simply memorize) increases. Everyone learns in different ways. The "Additional Readings" are intended to facilitate the learning process. Graduate students and upper level undergraduates can use the research articles (from journals) to develop their own studies, because we count on them to push the study of family stress management forward in the future.

Acknowledgments

Special Recognition

As coauthors, we all join in thanking Carol Mulligan for her skill and competence in finalizing the manuscript for this third edition of *Family Stress Management*. Her help has been invaluable to all three of us, as we reorganized, updated, and added new information.

Additional Acknowledgments

Pauline Boss: I thank the Department of Family Social Science at the University of Minnesota for the use of an office during the summer of 2015. Thanks to Evin Richardson for her help in gathering literature; to Carol Riggs for reading the final manuscript; to the professors whose responses helped shape this edition; and to my husband, Dudley Riggs, for his understanding and support during the nearly 2 years spent on this revision.

Chalandra M. Bryant: I extend a heartfelt thank you to National Council on Family Relations Board President (2015–2017) and family therapist Dr. William (Bill) Allen for providing advice and thoughtful critiques. Few colleagues push us to become better. He does so because he cares. *Thank you, Bill!* I would especially like to thank the person who gave me this amazing opportunity—Dr. Pauline Boss. The opportunity to write creatively and collaboratively, as well as exchange ideas, openly and analytically, subsequently led to the development of friendship that I will forever cherish.

Jay A. Mancini: For reviewing chapter drafts, I thank my colleagues Gary L. Bowen, Kenan Distinguished Professor at the University of North Carolina at Chapel Hill, School of Social Work, and Lawrence Ganong, professor at the University of Missouri, Department of Human Development and Family Science. I would like to acknowledge the assistance from the following University of Georgia students who gathered literature and read drafts of my chapters: Evin Richardson, Jacquelyn Mallette, Kristen Arp, and Alycia DeGraff. I appreciate their commitment to excellence and to family science.

SAGE Publishing also wishes to thank the following reviewers for their kind assistance:

Angie M. Giordano, *California State University Northridge*

Teri M. Henke, *Weber State University*

Heather R. McCollum, *Louisiana Tech University*

Lynette D. Nickleberry, *SUNY Empire State College*

Amanda Duffy Randall, *University of Nebraska at Omaha*

Jacqueline R. Roe, *Bowling Green State University*

Barbara H. Settles, *University of Delaware*

Jessica Troilo, *West Virginia University*

Venus Tsui, *Our Lady of the Lake University*

Amy Conley Wright, *San Francisco State University*

About the Authors

Pauline Boss, PhD, is professor emeritus of family social science at the University of Minnesota and a fellow in the National Council on Family Relations (NCFR), the American Psychological Association, and the American Association for Marriage and Family Therapy. She was visiting professor at Harvard Medical School (1994–1995) and the Moses Professor at Hunter School of Social Work (2004–2005). She is a former president of NCFR and a family therapist in private practice. In 1988, Dr. Boss wrote the first edition of *Family Stress Management* with a subsequent edition in 2002. For the third edition, she invited Chalandra Bryant and Jay Mancini to be her coauthors. Each edition has considerably advanced the Contextual Model of Family Stress.

With groundbreaking work as scientist-practitioner, Dr. Boss is the principal theorist in the study of family stress from ambiguous loss, a term she coined. Since then, she has researched various types of ambiguous loss, summarizing her work in the widely acclaimed book *Ambiguous Loss: Learning to Live with Unresolved Grief* (Harvard University Press, 1999). In addition, *Loss, Trauma, and Resilience* (Norton, 2006) presents six therapeutic guidelines for treatment when loss is complicated by ambiguity. These guidelines are based on her years of work with families of the physically missing during the Vietnam War, after 9/11, and in Kosovo, as well as in clinical work as a family therapist. For families, Dr. Boss wrote the book *Loving Someone Who Has Dementia* (Jossey-Bass, 2011), which outlines strategies for managing the ongoing stress and grief while caring for someone who is both here and not here, physically present but psychologically absent. For more information, see her website, www.ambiguousloss.com.

Chalandra M. Bryant is professor of human development and family science at the University of Georgia (UGA) where she teaches courses in family development, intimate relationships, and family theories. Before moving to Georgia, she served as a faculty member at Iowa State University (1998–2003) and Pennsylvania State University (2003–2010). Her research focuses on close relationships and the ability to sustain close intimate ties. She is particularly interested in the manner in which social, familial, economic, and psychosocial factors are linked to marital and health outcomes. After earning her PhD at the University of Texas, she completed a 2-year National Institute of Mental Health (NIMH) postdoctoral fellowship. She serves on the editorial board of the *Journal of Family Theory and Review*. The International Association for Relationship Research presented her with the New Contributions Award (honoring significant contributions to personal relationships research) in 2002. In 2004, she received the National Council on Family Relations Reuben Hill Research and Theory Award (presented for an outstanding research article in a family journal). In 2005, she received the Outstanding Young Professional Award from the Texas Exes Alumni Association of the University of Texas. In 2015, she was recognized as a Faculty Member Who Contributed Greatly to Career Development of UGA Students. Her favorite hobby is hiking. Her nature photographs have been published in a hiking guide.

Jay A. Mancini is the Haltiwanger Distinguished Professor of human development and family science at the University of Georgia and emeritus professor of human development at Virginia Tech. Mancini was the 2013 Ambiguous Loss Visiting Scholar at the University of Minnesota. He received his doctoral degree in child development and family relations from the University of North Carolina at Greensboro. Mancini is a Fellow of the National Council on Family Relations. His theorizing and research focus on the intersections of vulnerability and resilience; his research projects have focused on families and time use, family gerontology, psychological well-being in adulthood, sustainability of community-based programs for at-risk families, community context effects on families, and quality of life among military families. He received the 2007 Alumni Distinguished Service Award from the University of North Carolina at Greensboro and the 2008 Alumni Distinguished Research Award from the College of Human Ecology at Kansas State University. His research and program development activities have informed federal programs directed toward at-risk children and families (U.S. Department of Agriculture and U.S. Department of Defense). In 2014 he was presented the Spirit of Military Families Coin by Defense Canada, Military Family Services/Services Aux Famillies Des Militaires.

1

Family Stress

An Overview

The Russian novelist Leo Tolstoy began his book *Anna Karenina* with these famous words: "All happy families are all alike; each unhappy family is unhappy in its own way" (1877/2001, p. 1).

Unlike Tolstoy, we focus on stress, not unhappiness; yet, our core premise about *difference* is the same. That is, distressed families are different in their own way, even within one community or culture. Each family's process has unique qualities. Values and beliefs often vary so that what distresses one family (or family member) may not distress another. While there are similarities among families, we focus, as did Tolstoy, on the differences that exist among troubled families.

In this chapter, we introduce and define the concept of family stress and its linkages, which comprise the Contextual Model of Family Stress (CMFS) conceptual model introduced in Chapter 2. When providing the fundamentals of any theoretical model, our assumptions must be stated at the outset:

1. Even strong families can be stressed to the point of crisis and thus immobilized.

2. Differing cultural values and beliefs influence how particular families define what is distressing and how those families derive meaning from what is happening.

3. The meaning people construct about a stressor event or situation is often influenced by gender, age, race, ethnicity, and class.

4. Mind and body are connected. Psychological stress can make people physically sick. This process can affect whole family systems.

5. Some family members are constitutionally stronger or more resilient in withstanding stress than others.

6. It is not always bad for families to fall into crisis; someone may have to hit bottom in order to recover; those who fall apart may become strong again, even stronger than they were originally.

7. Not all families with high stress are in trouble. Some enjoy and seek high stress if, for example, they enjoy competitive sports, risky work, or living on the edge.

8. Not all family stress is bad; stress can keep family systems alive and exciting.

Given these assumptions, we proceed to define family stress, explain the challenge of defining "family," followed by personal accounts from each of the coauthors. Who is our family? What is the context in which we live? You will see differences between the three of us, but those differences enable us to shed a broader light here on the topic of family stress management. We begin with definitions.

Defining Family Stress

Extrapolating from medical, sociological, engineering, and psychological disciplines, we define *family stress* as a disturbance in the steady state of the family system. Such disturbance may emerge from the family's external context (e.g., war, unemployment, hurricane), from the internal context (e.g., death, divorce), or from both simultaneously. In any case, the family system's equilibrium is threatened by change. Such destabilization can have a positive or negative impact on families, often influenced by the types of stress (e.g., volitional or unwanted, clear or ambiguous, predictable or unforeseen). Each influences the valence of impact in a different way. Even with unexpected catastrophes, many families have the capacity to bend with the pressure and grow stronger from the experience. Boss observed such resilience in New York City after the September 11, 2001, terrorism that demolished the Twin Towers of the World Trade Center; in the Gulf States after Hurricanes Katrina and Rita in 2005; and in Fukushima, Japan, after the 2011 triple disaster of earthquake, tsunami, and atomic meltdown.

Using the engineering metaphor, family stress is likened to a force pressing, pushing, or pulling on the family structure. Although this force can originate either inside or outside the family system, it is the pressure inside the family system that indicates the level of stress. Like an engineer inspecting a bridge for stress from the increased weight it must bear, or a physician checking an individual's health for an increase in blood pressure, a family therapist or researcher assessing family stress searches for (1) lowered performance in the family's usual routines and tasks and (2) the occurrence of physical or emotional symptoms in individual family members. If just one pillar of a bridge is weak, the whole bridge is strained. The same is true for families. When the level of stress increases on the family's structure, the lowered performance in family roles and increased psychosomatic symptoms signal danger.

To repeat, family stress does not have to result in trouble. A high-tension bridge, for example, is intact and functional despite the tension. Some high-tension families also remain solid and functional. Like the bridge, such families have flexibility and "sway" so they are able to avoid collapse. In highly stressed but functional families, we see flexibility in family rules, roles, and problem-solving skills. They are able to change often to adapt to the situation at hand. There is continuing assessment and negotiation between pressures and supports. Such flexible family systems can withstand high pressure because in addition to having supports and strength, they also have the ability to sway under pressure. This bridge metaphor should be kept in mind to better understand family stress management.

In addition to being flexible and resilient, many families may simply enjoy more stress than others. They may become bored without a constant string of stressful events to excite them or thrive on the challenge of facing and solving difficult problems. Such families may seek out new stressful activities. They may like to move frequently, travel often, seek out competition, and participate in a variety of challenging activities and do so without negative effects. We think of families of Olympians who encourage and enjoy the high competition of risky sports, like snowboarding. They thrive on competition. We see a competitive spirit in the arts as well, but added stress comes when life-threatening risk is involved, such as with astronauts or adventurers who dare to explore new frontiers. This characteristic of proactively seeking stress indicates the importance of assessing the family's perception or appraisal of a stressor event or situation. We must value rather than pathologize such people because society often benefits from their daring risk taking and desire for change.

"OF COURSE IT'S STRESSFUL! THATS WHY I DO IT!!"

Source: Gordon Smuder.

Overall, stress in couples and families is normal and, occasionally, as the cartoon with the trapeze artist shows, even fun and desirable. Stress is also inevitable because people (and therefore families) develop, mature, and change over time. With any change comes disturbance—what we call stress. Family routines change, patterns of interaction change, and people enter and exit the family system (Boss, 1980a; also see Table 5.1). Some are born, some die, some marry, some divorce, and some simply leave or return home. Others may uproot to faraway places or transition to another gender. In the larger social context, change also happens. The Great Depression, World War II, the civil rights movement, the women's movement, the searing polarization caused by the Vietnam War, the Gulf War/Operation Desert Storm, War on Terrorism campaign, domestic terrorism, school shootings, the financial crash of 2008 with unemployment lasting for years, the housing crash, 9/11, Hurricane Katrina, murders, and the increasing division between rich and poor—all create changes in families. Stress results—some positive, some negative, or both—but in any case, the steady state of the family is disturbed and requires coping and managing to remain resilient.

Defining Family

In this book we continue to define family as a continuing system of interacting persons bound together by processes of shared roles, rules, and rituals, even more than shared biology. While Ernest Burgess (1926), one of the original family social psychologists, defined family as "a unity of interacting personalities" (p. 5), we add that these personalities must have a history and future together. In our definition of families, we place as much (and sometimes more) emphasis on the sharing of family rituals and celebrations (weddings, birthdays, graduations, holidays, funerals, etc.) as on the sharing of genetics. Why? Because we recognize that, in our mobile society, biology is not the single determinant of who is family. Children of divorce and remarriage; foster children; adopted children; lesbian, gay, bisexual, and transgender (LGBT) family members; and family caregivers may be most aware of their need for what Boss calls a "psychological family" (Boss, 2006, 2011)—a family of choice comprised of people you care about and want to be with for the rituals and events of joy as well as sadness. In addition, children of divorce and remarriage may be comforted by not having to choose between mom or dad's families with what divorce researcher Ahrons calls the binuclear family (Ahrons, 1994; Ahrons & Rodgers, 1994). As you can see, our definition of family emphasizes process and function more than structure (Boss, in press). Researchers find that "what matters in families is what family members do and how they relate, rather than how they are composed" (Arnold, Lucier-Greer, Mancini, Ford, & Wickrama, 2015, p. 16). In military families, for example, adolescents "thrive in a variety of family forms" (Arnold et al., 2015, p. 18) if there are healthy family processes. It appears that family process trumps family structure.

Clearly, our definition of the family runs counter to the definition of family that was popular in the 1950s. (For review, see Coontz, 1992, 1997, 2006.)

Back then, the normal American family was the isolated nuclear unit with a father and mother, married, living with their offspring under one roof, with father earning the living and mother at home caring for children and in charge of meal preparation and housekeeping. That form of family is now in decline, so some are reluctant to continue calling it the keystone of American society. On the contrary, it is a diversity of family structures that allows the adaptability and flexibility necessary for the *survival* of families across cultures.

An Example of Diversity in Family Structure: Grandparents Parenting Grandchildren

However families define themselves, most are flexible enough to find solutions to their problems. Yet, sometimes, narrow definitions of family prevent such coping. For example, in 1973, Inez Moore, a 62-year-old grandmother in East Cleveland, was actually arrested for violating the city's housing ordinance because she took into her home her divorced son and his little boy, plus her other grandson from her widowed son. Although this absorption of two nuclear families by a grandmother helped to relieve the stress caused by death in one family and divorce in the other, it did not fit the city's narrow definition of family.

Today, the U.S. Census recognizes that many grandparents are parenting their grandchildren. In 2013, about 2.7 million grandparents were responsible for one or more grandchildren (U.S. Census Bureau, 2015). New York offers Grandparent Family Apartments (a housing project provided by Presbyterian Senior Services, West Side Federation for Senior and Supportive Housing, and New York City Housing Authority), designed specifically for grandparents raising their grandchildren. To use the program, the grandparents must be at least 62 years old and have legal custody of their grandchildren (PSS/WSF Grandparent, 2016). Although this is a very unique housing program, it does reflect society's changing views of what defines a family.

Social work researchers Jan Backhouse and Anne Graham (2013) found that grandparents in Australia who are fully parenting their grandchildren experience high levels of stress as they grieve over losses: (1) the loss or incapacitation of their adult child, causing feelings of sadness, frustration, fear, and disappointment and (2) the loss of their dreams of being traditional grandparents with traditional grandparent-grandchild relationships. Thus, instead of playing the role of confidant or friend, they are providers and disciplinarians. Their dreams of indulging and spoiling their grandchildren and then handing them back to their parents are lost. One grandparent explained that handing them back is not an option, nor is taking a break (Backhouse & Graham, 2013). Instead, these grandparents are trying to help their grandchildren cope with the loss of a parent or parents, and some of these grandparents are coping with guilt regarding their failure to raise well-functioning adult children. Many grandparents taking care of their grandchildren reported the loss of their dreams for the future such as retirement plans, as well as the loss of friends and previous social activities. Such social isolation did not characterize those grandparents living in the Grandparent Family Apartments in New York. On the contrary, grandparents there felt as though they were part of a community.

One stated during an interview with CBS News (2011, April 4) that "we take care of one another" and "stick together" like a big family.

In 2012, Deanne Stein, a reporter from News 9 in Oklahoma, interviewed a grandmother on Grandparents' Day. The grandmother raises six grandchildren (3 to 10 years old) and was playing in the park with them while being interviewed; she pushed a granddaughter in a swing and caught a grandson as he slid down a pole. She said that hers was not a grandmother role. It was challenging because every minute was for her grandchildren, and they did not seem to rest so she used a lot of energy keeping up with them. She said, "They don't go home; they are at home." She embraces her role with no regrets ("Many Oklahoma Grandparents," 2012).

Defining the family only structurally, and as a nuclear structure, does not fit the reality of many American families who must find their own way to manage stress and solve their problems. We cannot support the idea that only one kind of family is normal and only one way of managing stress is right. We thus present here a less monolithic view of the family and a more inclusive family stress theory to account for the rich diversity in American families. Families today are defining themselves in multiple ways, so instead of one normative structure, we focus on family function; that is, what families actually do in their daily lives in relation to themselves and in relation to their surroundings. Are the children being fed and taken care of, socialized, educated? Is a safe place for growth and development provided? Are there close yet appropriate generational relationships with caring and support for one another? You may know of other functions. Researchers and clinicians now see that families can perform these essential functions in more than one way, thus explaining why we define families by their function and process (what they do) more than by their structure.

What Were Our Own Families Like?

As the three of us began this third edition of *Family Stress Management*, we became aware that for each of us, family has meant more than an isolated nuclear family. We each have a very different story about what family was for us:

Pauline Boss grew up in an immigrant family in the midst of the Great Depression. She writes,

I grew up in a Swiss American extended family living on a farm in southern Wisconsin. Everyone in our rural Wisconsin neighborhood was poor, so there was no stigma. In the evening, my parents sang or played games with us; kids played ball and helped with chores during the summer—and went skiing on skis my father made in the winter. Our one-room country school served as the community-gathering place for holidays and special occasions. In addition to my parents and siblings, our family included my grandmother who did not speak English, uncles, hired hands, and even the country schoolteacher if there was a blizzard. We all lived in a big white farmhouse—with no electricity until in 1938 the Rural Electrification Act finally reached us. Yet my childhood was happy. When we moved to town, I loved school, did well, and my parents borrowed money to send me to university. In the fall of 1955, just before the Salk vaccine came out, tragedy struck our family: My little brother, Eddie, died of bulbar polio, spending his last days in an iron lung. I shall never forget this loss. More will be said about this family crisis in Chapter 2.

When my remaining two siblings and I married and left home, we continued to live within a 5-mile radius of the family home. Crossover between households was frequent. Children played with cousins, sisters cared for each other's babies, and grandparents helped out and welcomed grandchildren after school. Meals were often shared, and modest amounts of money were exchanged as gifts or rarely, given as a loan. In other words, my family's boundaries stretched into a modified extended family system so that although not all members lived under one roof, all were inside the family symbolically and by self-definition. Today, weddings, graduations, and holidays are still celebrated together even though family members are now scattered across the United States.

Chalandra Bryant, born 2 years before President Lyndon B. Johnson signed the Civil Rights Act of 1968, grew up in a tight-knit African American family—mom, dad, one sister. She writes,

While my father was stationed in Vietnam, my mother and I lived with my maternal grandmother in Florida. My mother's brothers (my uncles) filled in for my father while he was gone. They played games with me, took me on trips, met my teachers, and picked me up from school. I don't want to say that they babysat, because they did so much more. They were an extension of my father. The time that I spent with them during my early years of life helped us forge a very strong bond, and that bond has lasted through my adult years. After my father returned home from the Vietnam War, the three of us moved to Biloxi, Mississippi. My father was stationed at a military base there. When Hurricane Camille hit, we lost everything . . . everything. We sought shelter with an older African American couple who had befriended my parents. The husband, Mr. Dan, cut a hole in the ceiling of his home so that we could sit up in the rafters as the floodwaters rose. Mr. Dan and his wife felt like family, but I knew we weren't related.

My uncles helped us move back to Florida after Camille. My parents bought a mobile home, and we started over. My sister was born shortly thereafter. She and I spent a lot of time at my grandmother's house while my parents were at work. My grandmother's house was always filled with family. Every Easter egg hunt, backyard barbecue, fish fry, and Thanksgiving celebration was centered around her home until her death. Losing her was devastating; she was the family storyteller, the keeper of our history. My uncles still take care of her house. They still grow vegetables in her backyard and share them with the neighbors. It is just much quieter now.

Jay Mancini was raised by a father who was a Bronze Star recipient in World War II and a mother who spent her career supporting college faculty and their students. His extended family was comprised of Italian-Americans and family members of Scot-Irish descent. He writes,

I was born in 1949 to an Italian father and a Scot-Irish mother (she was a Robinson). I am an only child. My father lived until I was 12, and my mother until I was 55. For the first 7 to 8 years of my life we lived in Marcus Hook, Pennsylvania, a modest town along the Delaware River (and about 12 or so miles from Philadelphia), where my father owned a barber shop (his father was a barber who arrived in the United States around 1911, from the village of Veroli, Italy). For a time, my mother ran a candy shop next to the barber shop. So the shop was on Market Street on the first floor, and we lived in the apartment above it. Several years ago, the apartment/shop was condemned and razed.

Among the other Italian families in the neighborhood, in addition to the Mancinis, were the Iaccones and the Montellas. My father, Giulio (later called Jay), was one of seven children, so there were many cousins. My mother, Vetra, was one of two living children, so there were fewer relatives by blood and two first cousins. My mother was born in Elliott Island, Maryland, not far from Cambridge. I was very close to my mother's mother, Lillian ("Maw," one of those curious words we call our grandmothers), and my mother's grandfather, Geary ("Pop" Gray). During my early years, parts of every Sunday were spent with my father's parents (Vincenzo, called "Jimmy the barber," and Concetta, at their row home), siblings, and the cousins, and those times were memorable because of the Sunday and holiday feasts and the attraction of hearing Italian spoken. I was also close to my father's younger brother, Joseph (who was called Ben).

Along the way, I had several other "relatives," defined by closeness and interaction rather than by birth. I grew up in an environment where we took people in on occasion and treated them as kin and also were taken in by others on occasion and treated as their kin. Until I went to New York to college in 1967, my geographic world was about a 20-mile radius from where I was born. I recall an upbringing where we did things for others.

These are our stories. What is yours? Families today are diverse, so we now use the term *family* to mean an extended system even if members do not all live under one roof. Parents, grandparents, sisters and brothers, aunts and uncles, nieces and nephews, and cousins, as well as persons not biologically related— friends, in-laws, steprelatives, godparents, foster parents, foster children, and even unrelated persons who live and grow up within a family (e.g., nannies) or who join in later life (e.g., caregivers)—all may be considered family.

While generations of family members may be spread throughout the United States and beyond, living in single-family homes, condos, dormitories, apartments, or in the military, they continue to keep in touch via telephone, e-mail, and social media, or visits by airplane, train, or automobile. Despite distance, happy events can be shared immediately via Twitter, Facebook, or telephone, and if there is a crisis, such messages often result in regrouping for support, in person or psychologically. These are common means of family stress management, and they overcome the challenges of geographic separations. Surprisingly, however, recent data show that the typical American lives 18 miles from his or her mother (Bui & Miller, 2015). What these data suggest is that the modified extended family is alive and well today in the United States.

General Systems Theory: The Family as System

Hans Selye (1978, 1980), a Canadian physician, was the first and most prolific researcher to study stress from a systems perspective. He focused however on the system *within* the human body. In groundbreaking research, he found stress to be "the common denominator of all adaptive reactions in the body" (1978, p. 64). In this book, however, we focus on a larger system—the family system.

Families are living organisms. This means that they are systems with interdependent parts. They have a structure with boundaries to maintain and functions to be performed, thus ensuring the system's growth and survival.

Systems theory states that the system is greater than the sum of its parts. In families, this means that the collection of family members is not only a specific number of people but also an aggregate of particular relationships and shared memories, successes, failures, and aspirations. Each family has a special unity of its own. The unique systemic strength that mobilizes a family is often observed when one of its members is in trouble. That family becomes more than the sum of its individual parts, taking on an extra power, like strands of steel bound together in one huge cable that holds up a suspension bridge. Joining forces and pulling in the same direction helps many families through adversity.

Sometimes sharing the same vision can be destructive rather than constructive. This is illustrated in the 2006 movie *Bug*, where Agnes, a lonely waitress, has escaped her abusive exhusband but now faces the stress of losing her young son, who has gone missing. Agnes's coworker tries to be helpful by introducing Agnes to Peter. They become a couple—of sorts. Peter tells Agnes that while he was in the Army, he was subjected to horrific scientific experiments that left him infected with bugs. He informs her that she, too, is probably infected and fills the room with fly catchers and bug zappers. He constantly slaps his body as if swatting bugs that only he sees. He uses sharp objects to extract them from his body. Unfortunately, Agnes also begins to see bugs that no one else—except Peter—sees. Given that she was already in a fragile state when they met, she has joined in his delusion. Both die when they set the room on fire in an effort to destroy the bugs (Anderson, Burns, Huckaby, & Friedkin, 2006).

While this is just a movie, it illustrates that systemic views can become pathological—and deadly. Family therapists see this more often in families where there is incest, eating disorders, addictions, violence, and abuse. For the most part, however, families' systems as a whole are not that delusional. Someone in the system is likely to have a different perception or vision—and then revolt. Practitioners and researchers must therefore use a systemic view of the family to see the full picture. This means that we assess families as a whole, as well as assessing their members, individually.

In family stress theory, a systems view helps us understand why one person has a particular response when he or she is alone but another when the kids come home from school, or dad comes home from work, or a noncustodial

parent arrives for a visit. In other words, the stress level of the whole is qualitatively different from the sum of its parts—the stress levels of individual family
members. Alone, each person in the family may act cheerful and in control;
together, they may create an atmosphere of tension tinged with anger, anxiety,
or sadness. That is why holiday gatherings often end up more stressful than we
expect. The whole is more (in this case, more tense) than the sum of its parts.

Family therapists, social workers, psychologists, nurses, and other medical
professionals witness this powerful systemic quality when a seriously ill child
becomes a parent's total focus. There is a ripple effect for the sibling or mate
who now feels left out. A family member who feels neglected begins to distance
himself or herself and perhaps act out to gain attention. A sibling may run away,
or a mate may indulge in self-destructive behavior with alcohol or drugs or have
an affair. Often, professionals and researchers examine only the person who is
acting out, when in fact the stress is present in the whole family system.

All too often, the family's stress is vented in the behavior of one person, who
becomes the scapegoat for a troubled and anxious family. To scapegoat one family
member as the source of trouble is one way families protect themselves from having to recognize impending loss and change. Indeed, human systems tend to resist
change, but stability is not always functional. A family may appear to be stable,
but if even one member is depressed or anxious, the system needs to change. We
thus face the dilemma of individual versus familial perceptions and meanings.

Symbolic Interaction as a Basis
for Studying Perceptions and Meanings

The perceptions and meanings of a stressor event are central constructs in our
contextual approach for working with family stress. The conceptual perspective
is *symbolic interaction,* a school of thought in social psychology.[1] It focuses on
interaction within a family and on symbols of interaction, such as language or
rituals (Bowen, Martin, & Mancini, 2013; LaRossa & Reitzes, 1993). The idea
is that a distressed family constructs a symbolic reality based on shared meanings
and role expectations inside the family. Those shared meanings, however, are
influenced by the world outside the family: the community, society, and culture.

This larger context provides the "shoulds" and "oughts," which are technically the norms and mores for communities and individual families. From the
symbolic interaction perspective, a family's rules reflect the rules of its larger
community context. But when a family belongs to a larger group that defines
the family differently than they do, the family experiences even more stress
because they cannot solve their own problems, as the Tolstoy quote at the
beginning of this chapter suggested, "in their own way." While "believing is seeing" makes the point that meaning-making shapes all that is to come in the
stress process, we also make the point that while perception matters, it is not *all*
that matters (Boss, 1992). Realities come to families in the form of diagnoses,
medical documentation of illness, disability, or abuse; arrests for drunken driving; death certificates; school grades; employment and income—or lack
thereof—and so on. These are realities, not perceptions, that families often face.

In addition to the CMFS, the work by researchers Patterson and Garwick (1994) in the area of chronic illness and disability remains useful for practitioners today. These researchers conceptualized a family's meaning of a stressor on three levels: situational, identity, and worldview. While Boss focused on perceptions and meanings already in the 1970s, and Patterson and Garwick did in the 1990s, there is now increased acceptance of subjective data (perceptions, meanings, and appraisals), as well as increased value in the qualitative data gleaned from family stories and narratives. We are optimistic about this shift to meaning-making because often, especially when a stressor cannot be fixed (e.g., terminal illness, missing persons, death in the family, a lost job), the only window for change and management of stress lies in the family members' perceptions of that event—and the meaning they attribute to it.

The internal context of perception is difficult to measure empirically, but scholars have made progress in describing how people across cultures uniquely perceive and manage their troubles (Boss, Kaplan, & Gordon, 1995; McCubbin, McCubbin, Thompson, & Thompson, 1998; Robins, 2010; Zimmerman, Ramirez, Washienko, Walter, & Dyer, 1998). For this challenge, positivist methodologies and postmodernist inquiries are needed. See Chapters 4 and 5 for lists of quantitative and qualitative research articles.

Is There a Family Perception?

One of the arguments in family research, and thus in family stress research, is whether families have a distinctive quality apart from the individuals who comprise the family. Is there such a thing as a "family perception" or a "family response"? Is the family only a collection of individual perceptions or appraisals?

Researchers and clinicians report observing the phenomenon of a family perception (Garwick, Detzner, & Boss, 1994) or "family paradigms" (Reiss, 1981). Evidence indicates that families do indeed have unique systemic characteristics, and this unity produces a "family perception." Family perception, as a variable, means that family members think collectively, that is, they see stressors in the same way and cope with stressors in the same way.

For the purposes of family stress management, a *family perception* is defined as the group's unified view of a particular stressor event or situation. One cannot get such a collective view without the family meeting together. Their collective voices and views must be analyzed as one. Garwick (1991) did this by analyzing family conversations as a whole, discovering that there was indeed a family-level perception of the situation. David Reiss (1981) was the first researcher to identify family paradigms (views of the world). Since then, the idea has persisted, especially with family therapists, nurses, and other family-centered practitioners who use family paradigms as a means of understanding how clients/families value and view their goals and resources for coping (Hidecker, Jones, Imig, & Villarruel, 2009; Paré, 1995). Today, the need for evidence-based therapy is benefiting from Reiss's early family paradigm approach (Stevens, 2013).

Knowing the collective paradigmatic view, however, does not preclude paying attention to each family member's individual perceptions. Both are needed. When, for example, a loved one dies from a catastrophic disaster or terminal illness, suicide, or murder or in war, family members' views often diverge. Each has his or her own private interpretation of what happened. The goal, however, is that eventually, there will be some convergence of perceptions about what occurred and what it means, even if that meaning is that the loss will never make sense. That, too, is a meaning (Boss, 2006).

Sometimes, however, a collective family meaning is never reached, and such families often splinter after tragedy. In the book (and film) *Ordinary People*, written by Judith Guest (1976), Conrad's mother is unable to accept the fact that one of her sons drowned and the other has tried to commit suicide because he blames himself for his brother's death. The mother finally leaves because she cannot perceive the situation in a way that will move the family from crisis to coping and then change. She cannot grieve because she wants the family to stay as it has been; she makes her dead son's room into a shrine. His death was real, however, and has to be recognized and grieved. With the help of a wise therapist, the father and son move from crisis to change and even growth. But the mother, who refuses therapy, remains frozen in grief.

Problematic Perceptions

We also see entire families that remain rigid with troubling views, such as when a family denies the needs of a hearing-impaired family member, saying "He can hear when he wants to," or when a family makes the excuse, "Dad isn't an alcoholic; he just drinks to relax from his high-stress job." Or when a wife denies that her aging husband is experiencing symptoms of Alzheimer's and chastises him by saying, "You only remember what you want to remember." We also see such denial in families where there is an implicit agreement to ignore sexual abuse. No one speaks the truth about what is occurring. In such family systems, there is an implicit agreement, systemically, about what is considered real or normal, what is perceived as right or wrong, and the rules for what can and cannot be talked about. Sometimes, some family members change their perceptions of what is happening and the denial (or delusion) explodes into reality. This is when healing can begin.

Systems therapy can help formerly intolerant families change and become more inclusive. In other cases, if the family as a whole remains intolerant, the person who begins to see more options may have to leave. Some LGBT youth, for example, leave home (Cochran, Stewart, Ginzler, & Cauce, 2002). One study indicated that the top five reasons LGBT youth are either homeless or at risk of becoming homeless are that they (1) ran away because their family members rejected their gender identity or sexual orientation; (2) were forced out of their homes by their parents because of their gender identity or sexual orientation; (3) endured emotional, physical, or sexual abuse in their homes; (4) aged out of foster care; or (5) endured financial or emotional neglect in their homes (Durso & Gates, 2012).

What this means to family researchers and practitioners is that the focus on the family system should not come at the expense of bullying and extricating individuals from that system. Both individual and family data are needed if we are to understand family stress. While we strive overall for families as a whole without abuse, incest, battering, or violence, we must also strive for individuals without depression, anxiety, suicidal ideation, addictions, or psychosomatic illnesses. Both levels—the family as a whole and family members individually—are critical to a meaningful family stress theory.

Sometimes, signs of everyday stress appear in an individual first and serve as an early warning that something is amiss with the couple or larger family system. A wise student wrote the following:

> I know that I ride the stress-induced adrenaline rush only so long. I have been paying attention to my stress levels for a year now. I know that I start sleeping more, eating more, and just lounging around my house instead of running errands and getting things done. I am more prone to migraines, and I get muscle aches. When I notice myself experiencing these things, I take an hour or so to journal and I talk with my partner. I think that part of couples and families managing stress is for them to find out what their individual warning signs are and then deal with them.

Such personal self-reflection helps people to manage individual stress so that it does not spill over into systemic stress.

Other issues in family stress management that belong in an overview are two areas where cultural differences in beliefs and values can add to family stress. They concern racial and ethnic diversity and gender diversity. We begin with the former.

Diversity and Multiculturalism in Family Stress Management

The United States is a diverse society composed of people who have come from someplace else, voluntarily or involuntarily. The "melting pot" has not occurred in many areas of the country (Garreau, 1982). Consequently, American society is a collection of diverse family units creating a mosaic more than total assimilation. When family therapists, educators, and researchers work with distressed families, diversity and pride of heritage emerge. In the sections that follow, we explain biculturalism, minority stress, and acculturative stress.

Families may hold on to their cultural values and traditions while also finding themselves immersed (by choice or lack thereof) in the culture of the larger population or even in the various cultural contexts in which they live (Romero & Roberts, 2003). This brings us to the notion of biculturalism, which, although defined in multiple ways (Benet-Martinez & Haritatos, 2005; Berry, 1997; Schwartz & Zamboanga, 2008) is most typically defined as comfort and proficiency with (1) the culture of the region in which one resides and (2) one's heritage culture. This does not simply apply to immigrants who moved from other countries. It pertains to the offspring of those immigrants. Even though those offspring may have lived in the receiving region their entire lives, they could still be rooted in their heritage culture, especially if their parents or other family members have steadfastly instilled in them their heritage culture (Portes & Rumbaut, 2006). Biculturalism also applies to people residing in ethnic enclaves, because in such environments the preservation of heritage culture might be encouraged and supported. Other groups to whom biculturalism applies are people belonging to or self-identifying with discernable minority groups, such as ethnic or racial minorities (Schwartz & Unger, 2010). Some believe that simply being a minority can be stressful.

Minority Stress

The term *minority stress* is used to describe psychological stress developed as a result of being subjected to minority status (Brooks, 1981; Meyer, 1995). More specifically, it refers to the juxtaposition of minority and mainstream values and the subsequent struggle that occurs between the social environment and individuals in the minority group (Meyer, 2003; Mirowsky & Ross, 1989; Pearlin, 1989). Not only must members of minority groups contend with negative social attitudes, but they are also stigmatized; as a result, they are subjected to chronic stress. Minority stress can be explained by theories such as *symbolic interaction* and *social comparison*, which view the social environment as the avenue through which individuals attain meaning and understanding of their world and their experiences (Stryker & Stratham, 1985).

Social psychological theories can also be used to explain the impact of stigma and negative social attitudes on individuals. Stigmatized individuals develop adaptive and maladaptive responses to cope with the stigma, and these responses may include the development of poor mental health. The angst between individuals and the manner in which they experience their society has been described as the essence of all social stress (Lazarus & Folkman, 1984). This, too, lends credence to the concept of minority stress. High levels of minority stress have been linked to acculturation (Saldana, 1994). One just needs to pay attention to the daily news to see evidence of it still today.

Acculturative and Bicultural Stress

Acculturative stress is stress resulting from the process of adapting to a new culture (Berry, 2005, 2006). It was through research on acculturative stress that the idea of bicultural stress emerged (Berry, 1980, 1997, 2003). In light of the melting pot notion perpetuated in the early 1900s in the United States, it was assumed that a person assimilating (or melting) into a new culture should/would give up his or her heritage/native culture (Keefe & Padilla, 1987). It was also assumed that assimilation would be hindered if an individual attempted to hold on to his or her specific culture, and that, in turn, would result in increased cultural stress and mental health problems for immigrants; essentially, good mental health was associated with assimilation (Keefe & Padilla, 1987; Pena, 2003; Stonequist, 1961).

The Stress of Discrimination and Racism

These are salient issues because discrimination has been, and remains to be, a pervasive component of life for a number of racial and ethnic minorities in the United States and other parts of the world (Alamilla, Kim, & Lam, 2010; Brody et al., 2006; Major, Quinton, & McCoy, 2002; Murry, Brown, Brody, Cutrona, & Simons, 2001; U.S. Surgeon General, 2001). Experiences of discrimination and racism contribute to poor mental and physical health (Brondolo et al., 2008; Hilmert et al., 2014; Lukachko, Hatzenbuehler, & Keyes, 2014; Moradi & Risco, 2006). Thus, experiences of discrimination are a form of stress (Bryant et al., 2010; Peters & Massey, 1983).

Families of color, targeted ethnicities, or same-sex or transgendered couples are often pressured by a hostile external context and by internalized perceptions of less worth. Prejudice, intolerance, and bigotry are external stressors that exacerbate stress, creating needless vulnerability. The additional and chronic stressor of living in a hostile, stigmatized, and biased environment influences both individual and family perceptions of everything they experience. Regardless of class, this extra layer of stress is experienced by many today, as recounted here by real persons:

Person A: A Middle-Class Professional Black Male

Each day discrimination presents itself to me in the form of ongoing "double marginalization," first as a member of the Black race, then as a Black male. When not confronted by direct violence, I feel as though I'm walking along that line painted down the center of a highway—dealing with two sides of discrimination experienced by Black men. One side simply ignores my presence, because to acknowledge me is to admit I exist. These behaviors involve interacting with me but only after long delays—long delays in getting service in public establishments or businesses and getting cut off as I'm walking or even having people cut in front of me as I stand in line. On the surface these behaviors simply seem rude—until you see patterns. Then it seems purposeful . . . intentional. Historically, rude behavior toward Black men always had a level of social acceptance and even political correctness.

On the other side of that line painted down the center of the highway, I go from being invisible to overly visible. Call it the "What is that Black man doing here?" effect. This behavior involves overtly monitoring me when I enter a public establishment, to the extent that whoever is with me will notice as I/we are followed in stores. This extends to not getting a taxi. I watched a taxi cab drive past me two blocks, pull over, and pick up a White woman. Profiling lives.

What did I do? Kept hailing a cab until I got one, because persistence and insistence are my weapons of choice.

Sadly, and to the detriment of my health, my discrimination radar is always on.

Person B: A Middle-Class Black Female

When I was in grade school, perhaps fifth or sixth grade, I became close friends with a girl named Annie. Annie and I just clicked, and we frequently ate lunch together and often worked on in-class assignments as a team so that we could be with one another. One Friday, I suggested to Annie that we hang out over the weekend some time. Annie said, "I would like to, but you can't come over to my house. A long time ago, two Black guys broke the windows out of my parents' front porch. They hate Blacks. My parents wouldn't allow you to come over to my house." My young mind knew that that was wrong, but my solution to the problem was that Annie could just come over to my house. So, that evening, I approached my mother. "Mom, can Annie come over this weekend? I can't go to her house, so can she come to ours?" My mother asked, "Why can't you go to Annie's house?" I recounted the story Annie had shared with me. My mother admonished me for being friends with her, saying, "Her parents won't welcome you into their home to play with their daughter because you're Black. We're certainly not going to pretend that's okay. The answer is no. You don't keep friends that make who you are an issue. We've taught you better than that." I continued to be friends with Annie, but eventually, we grew apart. Our friendship was limited to inside the school walls. She could never attend a birthday or slumber party at my home; I could never be welcomed in her home.

That Same Middle-Class Black Female Further Noted

While in college, I worked a part-time job at a local shipping store. After approximately 2 years on the job, I was working a shift on a Saturday afternoon with a coworker. He noted that he had something to do right after work, so I offered to complete the closing process for him. He hesitated in his response and said, "No. I should do it. The owner asked me not to have you finish closing." I looked at him oddly and wondered what could explain this. I had been trusted to complete the closing process on plenty of previous occasions. I could sense from his nonverbal actions that something was amiss. He confided that the owner felt some concern about my race and asked him to always finish out the closing process. I was shocked and started to cry. I was confused. I had a stellar track record on the job for 2 years and thought I was a trusted employee. In the end, I allowed him to complete the closing process, as the owner had requested. After speaking with my parents who validated my concerns about the issues, I decided to quit the job and walk away from the situation. On the next business day, I approached the owner about the matter and informed her that I was resigning from my job. She tried to explain her decision, but I was not receptive to her reasoning. It simply did not make sense. The next day, my coworker who had confided in me also quit.

In terms of responding to discrimination, I normally weigh the situation at hand and decide whether to try to work the matter out with the person, stay silent about the matter and just keep that person at a distance in my interactions, or to cut my losses and walk away from the situation.

Person C: A Black Female Student

One of my first memories of discrimination was in the eighth grade. There was a Caucasian girl in my class who I thought was my friend. We were having a conversation one day about some topic involving school work. I think I made a better grade on a test or something along those lines. She then made the statement, "You will never be as good as me. No Black person will ever be as good as me." I didn't understand because we were from the same neighborhood. I was so shocked and hurt that I said nothing to her. Those words have stuck with me since then. For years, I cowered in my classes because I was often the only Black person. I believed that all of my Caucasian classmates thought the same way as that girl, and I would never be smart enough. I continued to try to prove her and all of "them" wrong, but a large part of me still believed her. It wasn't until I entered college at [a historically Black college and university], surrounded by other Black achievers like myself, that I started to rebuild that confidence. It took a long time. Fast forward to 2012, immediately following the reelection of President Obama. I was at a park enjoying the day and reading for one of my classes. A big SUV comes down the road and someone in it yells the N-word. I knew they were talking to me because I was the only [person] there. I will never forget that moment either but for a different reason. I never thought for one second that racism was dead or that it couldn't happen to me anymore, but that moment let me know that no matter who I am or what I accomplish, some people are still going to see just another N-word.

These accounts are striking and provide vivid portrayals of the dynamics within the Contextual Model of Family Stress. As family experts, we strive to reduce such family stress, but we must begin with ourselves—our own biases and prejudices. As you read the narratives, did they surprise you? Or have you lived it and know it all too well in similar or other situations? In either case, we need to acknowledge and develop a better understanding of the stress of discrimination and racism before we can be of use to all families. Only after we see stressors through the eyes of families unlike our own, can we effectively assess and support without bias.

Gender and Family Stress

Studies about gender and family stress have historically found that women experience higher stress in marriage and family life than men. To learn if this is still true today, we briefly review research findings over time. Note how the changing social and historical context influences stress for women and men.

Trends in the 1970s

In the 1970s, sociologists Jesse Bernard (1971, 1972) and Gove and Tudor (1973) found women's social roles to be more stress producing than those occupied by men. Researchers studying acute stressors found that although men and women did not differ greatly in number of undesirable life events experienced, women were significantly more affected emotionally (Kessler, 1979). This greater female vulnerability may also have been caused by post World War II strains in the social roles of men and women. Gove and Tudor (1973) argued that after working outside the home during the war (e.g., Rosie the Riveter, a U.S. cultural icon that represented roles women assumed in factories and shipyards during World War II), women's position in U.S. society became less meaningful—and actually more stressful because they were now expected to return to the home. Based on evidence that more men than women were admitted to mental hospitals *before* World War II, and more women than men admitted *after* the war, it was proposed there was a *social construction of gender roles* that was influencing gender differences in stress outcomes (Gove & Tudor, 1973; Kessler, 1979).

Trends in the 1980s

In the 1980s, researchers continued to find that women's stress was primarily due to sex role socialization and the division of labor with women's roles restricted to the home. Sociologists Radloff and Rae (1981) found that women's socialization experiences produced susceptibility to depression through the learning of a "helpless" style of coping with stress. Other researchers found that women reported significantly higher rates of psychological distress than men (Al-Issa, 1982; Kessler & McLeod, 1984; Wethington, McLeod, & Kessler, 1987). According to Wethington and colleagues (1987, p. 144) this was because "the stresses in women's roles are more intense and persistent," and that "women are exposed more than men to acute life stresses which are centrally associated with their nurturant roles, and that this role-related difference is one important source of the mental health advantage of men" (Kessler & McLeod, 1984, p. 629). Women were "more affected emotionally than men not only by their own stressful experiences but also by the stressful experiences of the people they care about" (Wethington et al., 1987, pp. 144–145). This research pointed out the stressful bind for women in that "women's roles *obligate* them to respond to the needs of others" (Wethington et al., 1987, p. 145).

Sociologists also found married women to experience higher levels of stress than previously married women or women who have never married (Cleary & Mechanic, 1983; Fox, 1980; Gove, 1973). Sociologists Kessler and McRae (1982) and Pearlin (1975) attempted to understand what causes a social role to produce more or less psychological distress, but this was challenging because measures of chronic social role stressors and resources tended to be perceptual and thus subjective. Also, when outcomes and stressors were measured simultaneously, typical in cross-sectional studies, it was impossible to establish which came first—the stressor of a homebound role or its outcome of depression (Kessler, 1983; Seligman, 1975/1992). It was the classic chicken and egg question.

Indeed, the stressor may not have been the role per se, but rather, the conditions of feeling unappreciated, bored, fatigued, and isolated. Having little control over what one perceives as an important role was found to decrease longevity in women and men ("The Importance of Doing What's Important to You," 2001). These conditions, most severe for single mothers and those with young children, were considered the culprit. Women were also more likely than men to experience stress from receiving inadequate compensation for their work, lack of security, inadequate fringe benefits, and few opportunities for advancement (Pearlin & Lieberman, 1979).

Trends in the 1990s

For the 1990s, we purposely limit our review to the work of family psychologist, John Gottman, who conducted the first experimental research with couples. He induced disagreement within the couple and then measured their psychological stress reactions. Gottman and colleagues found that females in stressed relationships were more likely to seek out connection with their partner, whereas males were more likely to stonewall, enacting a flight response (Gottman, 1999; Gottman, Carrere, Swanson, & Coan, 2000; Jacobson & Gottman, 1998). This innovative research involved couples who were deliberately stressed in a laboratory setting by asking them to problem solve or setting them up to argue (See Babcock, Jacobson, Gottman, & Yerington, 2000; Jacobson & Gottman, 1998; Jacobson, Gottman, Waltz, Rushe, Babcock, & Holtzworth-Munroe, 1994).

Current Trends

Today, gender roles in families are more flexible, especially in families where women earn much of the income. We have "stay-at-home fathers" and "breadwinning mothers," though fewer of the former and many of the latter. Women may still be feeling more stress than men due to a perceived flexibility that is not real inside the family. Or the problem may be outside the family, in the larger community that has no affordable child care or transportation for both mothers and fathers.

Increasingly in the United States, women are the family breadwinners (Rampell, 2013). More than 4 in 10 American households include a mother who is the sole earner or the primary breadwinner in the family. As is true of most issues regarding families and family dynamics, there are multiple reasons for the increasing numbers of women becoming family wage earners. These include changes in women's roles within and outside of the family, changes in job opportunities for both women and for men, whether there are children in the family as well as their ages, and how educated women and men are.

A number of questions spring from these demographic changes and include how men's roles are changing. For example, do we expect more men to be stay-at-home fathers? Some philosophical and pragmatic elements are operating here. In the former case, when fathers are less in the economic-providing role, this requires a shift from traditional thinking about who is responsible for fulfilling the role toward family economic stability or success.

While patterns of who plays the role of breadwinner are changing, questions remain about the extent to which cultural and societal values are changing. In some families, if the family is to function, it is necessary for a wife or mother to be employed outside the home. This need for women to be breadwinners, fully or partially—precedes societal and even couple attitudes and values about shifting gender roles. When people still believe breadwinning is primarily a "man's job," there may be increased marital conflict—and sometimes violence against the woman earner. With such couples, there is need for a safety plan, anger management training, individual therapy, and if all goes well, couple therapy and learning resolution skills for areas of disagreement about changing roles.

Indeed, this situation is an example of how external and internal factors intersect to create high family stress and crises.

In 2013, Sheryl Sandberg, chief executive officer for Facebook, documented in her book *Lean In* a major family stress issue today that concerns gender. Summarizing her documentation, nearly 50% of mothers earn either all or most of the family's income, with another 23% earning at least a quarter of the family's income (Glynn, 2012). In addition, one in five families (20%) is headed by a single mother (Boushey, 2009) with rates much higher in Hispanic families (27%) and African American families (51%) (Mather, 2010). Although the number of stay-at-home fathers has risen slightly, it is worrisome that "family" may become the sole responsibility of women. Too much stress is placed on one person.

To exacerbate the issues of women's stress, findings still suggest that gender differences exist in stress levels—and they begin early. Depressive symptoms are more likely to develop in adolescent girls than adolescent boys, due in part to girls' greater sensitivity to stressful life events, especially the interpersonal (Oldehinkel & Bouma, 2011). In addition, females are still found to have higher incidence rates of major depressive disorder and slightly longer depressive episodes than males (Essau, Lewinsohn, Seeley, & Sasagawa, 2010).

More research is needed on this disparity in stress levels but focusing on the work-life balance, according to Sandberg (2013), is too narrow. The anxiety for women who are sole or primary breadwinners is not about having it all; it is, instead, according to Bravo (2012), their worry "about losing it all—their jobs, their children's health, their families' financial stability because of the regular conflicts that arise between being a good employee and a responsible parent" (Sandberg, 2013, p. 23). Focusing only on work-life balance makes the issue binary and misses the nuances of a middle ground. Based on a comprehensive review, gender researchers Meers and Strober (2009) found hopeful news: "The data plainly reveal that sharing financial and child-care responsibilities lead to less guilty moms, more involved dads, and thriving children" (Sandberg, 2013, p. 24). In addition, women's studies' researchers Barnett and colleagues (Barnett, 2004; Barnett & Hyde, 2001; Barnett & Rivers, 1996) surprisingly found that "women who participate in multiple roles actually have lower levels of anxiety and higher levels of mental well-being" (Sandberg, 2013, p. 24). Although this may be a class issue, employed women have "greater financial security, more stable marriages, better health, and, in general, increased life satisfaction" (Sandberg, 2013, p. 24; cited in Barnett, 2004; Bennetts, 2007; Buehler & O'Brian, 2011; Coley, Lohman, Votruba-Drzal, Pittman, & Chase-Landsdale, 2007; Cooke, 2006).

Clearly, families and the individuals in them can all flourish when mothers are employed outside the home, but there are still societal barriers for women working outside the home. The major obstacle is the lack of affordable quality day care for their children—which every other developed country already has in place. Another barrier is the lack of affordable quality day care for the frail elderly who live with families where both adults have outside jobs. If a working mother has to give up her paid employment to be the sole caregiver of a sick or frail family member, she not only loses her job and her coworkers, but the family loses her income. Given such systemic complexities, the larger society must become aware that if families are to survive and remain resilient, then we simply cannot expect women and girls to do it all. Just as we need to become more accepting of diversity with racial minorities, we also need to become more accepting of different choices regarding how to be a family. In the end, the goal is twofold: the functioning of the family system as a whole and the functioning of the individual within that family.

Summary

We began this chapter by defining both stress and family. Understanding each term requires understanding systems theory and symbolic interaction. A family is a living system of interdependent parts, with structure, boundaries, and functions. Members of a family often (but not always) have similar expectations, perceptions, and meanings. This shared understanding helps create the family's symbolic reality. With a stressor, the steady state of the family is disturbed, but it does not mean that this disturbance or change will automatically result in negative outcomes. Stress is inherently neither good nor bad. It depends upon the family. A family can experience tension, yet remain intact and functional. Some families are simply able to endure—or dare we say, "enjoy"—more stress than others. Such families see difficult situations not as insurmountable but as challenges.

Points to Remember

1. Family stress is inevitable, but not all stress is bad. Stress happens not just to individuals but also to families as a whole. The family as a whole can be threatened by an event that creates a situation that is beyond its control at the moment. The effects ripple through the system.

2. By definition, the family is a continuing system of interacting personalities bound together by shared rules and rituals even more than by biology. There is no such thing as one kind of normal family.

3. Systems theory holds that the system is greater than the sum of its parts. If even one member of a system is in trouble, then the whole system needs to change. Many families, however, maintain their equilibrium by having a family scapegoat—one person whom all members agree is the cause of the stress. We must not be pulled into the family's delusion that if this one person would go away or straighten up, there would be peace.

4. Perception affects the level of stress the family experiences. A family system has a character of its own, and this unity produces the family perception variable.

5. Symbolic interaction focuses on the interaction within a family as indicated by symbols of interaction (e.g., language, rituals, rules, and roles). A family constructs a symbolic reality on the basis of members' shared meanings (or lack thereof) about the stressful situation they are experiencing.

6. Perception is an important variable in family stress theory. It determines how an event is viewed by a family (as a unit) and by individual members in that family. It gives us a window through which to support or challenge the family.

Remember, although perception matters, it is not all that matters. This means that although perception is central, it is not the only important variable to consider in assessing family stress.

7. The same event is not viewed in the same way by all persons in one family, by all families in one community, or by all communities in one society. Perceptions among families differ, and perceptions among family members differ. Differences do not have to create crisis but can bring richness to family life.

8. Because families are diverse, we cannot say that there is ONE way for family therapists, educators, health care professionals, and researchers to help distressed families.

9. Selye (1978) was the first to show that the stress of life often leads to illness. He viewed stress within the human body, a biological system, as a state induced by change. Selye's ideas remain useful for understanding stress within a family system. The family's degree of stress results from events or situations that have potential to cause change. Stress is change and by itself is neither good nor bad. It depends on how the organism (in this case, the family) perceives it and reacts to it.

10. The focus on meaning and perceptions is now recognized as central to the understanding of family stress management and resilience.

Note

1. Wesley Burr, a family sociologist who takes this perspective, has written more technically about symbolic interaction, which is also known as interactionism, role theory, self theory, and social behaviorism: "Whatever label is used, it is the brand of social psychology that emerged from the writings of William James, C. H. Cooley, and George Herbert Mead. Technical readers will recognize that there are slight variations in emphasis in some of the different traditions in this theoretical orientation. For example, the dramaturgical approach used by Goffman (1959) differs from the more formal approach used by Biddle and Thomas (1966), and the more quantified methodology used by some is different from the more qualitative approach suggested by the older University of Chicago approach, typified by the work of Strauss and Blumer. These subtle differences can be ignored for the purposes of a text that focuses on the application of the basic ideas of this school of thought rather than the discovery and justification of new ideas" (Burr, Leigh, Day, & Constantine, 1979, p. 102).

Discussion Questions

1. Identify a stressful event that occurred in your family. How did you perceive the event? What meaning did the event hold for you? Think of someone in your family (or even a friend) who perceived the event very differently. Explain how that person perceived the event. Why do you think the two of you perceived the event so differently?

2. Think about your personal life. What is your primary or biggest stressor? How does that stressor affect you? Do your feelings or behaviors change when you experience that stressor? If so, how do your family members and friends react to those feelings and behaviors? Has your stressor indirectly affected them?

3. What stressors seem to cut across all socioeconomic levels; that is, what stressors seem to be present regardless of one's socioeconomic level?

4. What stressors do children today experience compared to children 50 years ago?

Additional Readings

Driscoll, M., & Torres, L. (2013). Acculturative stress and Latino depression: The mediating role of behavioral and cognitive resources. *Cultural Diversity and Ethnic Minority Psychology, 19*(4), 373–382.

Folkman, S. (2013). Stress, coping, and hope. In B. I. Carr & J. Steel (Eds.), *Psychological aspects of cancer: A guide to emotional and psychological consequences of cancer, their causes, and their management* (pp. 119–127). New York, NY: Springer.

Gradus, J. L., Smith, B. N., & Vogt, D. (2015). Family support, family stress, and suicidal ideation in a combat-exposed sample of Operation Enduring Freedom/Operation Iraqi veterans. *Anxiety, Stress, & Coping: An International Journal, 28*(6), 706–715.

Hatch, S. L., & Dohrenwend, B. P. (2007). Distribution of traumatic and other stressful life events by race/ethnicity, gender, SES, and age: A review of the research. *American Journal of Community Psychology, 40*, 313–332.

Irwin, J. A. (2014). Lesbian, gay, bisexual, and transgender stress. In *The Wiley Blackwell encyclopedia of health, illness, behavior, and society* (pp. 1288–1290). Hoboken, NJ: Wiley-Blackwell.

Lavee, Y. (2013). Stress processes in families and couples. In G. W. Peterson & K. Bush (Eds.), *Handbook of marriage and the family* (3rd ed., pp. 159–176). New York, NY: Springer Science.

White, R. M. B., Liu, Y., Nair, R. L., & Tein, J-Y. (2015). Longitudinal and integrative tests of family stress model effects on Mexican origin adolescents. *Developmental Psychology, 51*(5), 649–662.

2

The Contextual
Model of Family Stress

In April of 2008, Jenifer, mother of two children (12 and 9 years old), lost her home (a six-bedroom house nestled on an acre of land) in Georgia because she couldn't afford the monthly mortgage payments after medical bills and a divorce. Her salary as a day care center director simply was not enough. She and her children moved to a two-bedroom apartment. Now, even her children worry about money. While grocery shopping, her 9-year-old son, noticing the price of milk, told her that they shouldn't buy it. He gets up after she goes to bed and checks all the doors to make sure that they are locked. Then he goes to her room and tells her that everything is safe so it's okay to sleep. He must have noticed that she no longer sleeps well. This child now worries not only about money but also about his mother. (Armour, 2008)

During the Great Recession of 2007 to 2009, stories about foreclosures, bankruptcies, job loss, and homelessness dominated the news media across the United States. For families, this crisis took its toll. Although the exact figures vary, most sources indicate that millions of people lost homes to foreclosure during this economic downturn (Bernard, 2014; CoreLogic, 2012; Schoen, 2010). According to a professor of economics at Princeton University and a professor of finance at the University of Chicago, between 2007 and 2009, about 8 million jobs were lost, and over 4 million homes were foreclosed (Mian & Sufi, 2014).

There are countless stories like this of family stress where the external and internal contexts of family life merge to increase family stress and also sometimes cause a crisis. In Chapter 1, we defined family stress as a change or disturbance in the steady state of the family system and illustrated family stress with a bridge metaphor. In the preceding story, the structure of the family's support was not a bridge but a house—the family home—which fell away. The family became disorganized, with a child now taking care of his parent. With all highly distressed families, a framework like the Contextual Model of Family Stress (hereafter referred to as the CMFS) helps practitioners and researchers to more fully understand how to assess and intervene with troubled families.

Here, in Chapter 2, we define and discuss all the constructs upon which the CMFS is built. Consider this chapter a glossary for a theoretical map. As you read, you may want to refer back to this chapter because definitions will not be presented again in such detail.

Family stress terms are notorious for their inconsistency. Our aim is to clarify definitions so that family therapists, educators, social workers, nurses, family psychologists, and researchers can all understand each other in their mutual goal of helping couples, families, and communities to manage stress. First, let us explain why a contextual model is essential for helping families in stress.

Why a Contextual Model?

All families, worldwide, experience stress, but not all are in trouble. Other factors in addition to the stressful event influence family vulnerability or breakdown. The end result of the stress process, whether the family and its members manage to avoid or survive crisis, is influenced by their internal and external contexts. The *internal context*, over which the family may have some control, is composed of structural, psychological, and philosophical dimensions, as well as the family's chosen beliefs and values and way of life. The *external context* consists of dimensions over which the family has little or no control—culture, history, economy, development, and heredity (including race, class, gender, age, sexual orientation, and physical constitution). This includes unemployment, terrorism, war, military deployment, financial recessions, illness, aging, natural catastrophe, and when and how one dies. Unique stories of coping and managing are less often in the newspapers and on the evening news than are catastrophic stories of disaster and loss. Family and community narratives about strength are only recently being documented to help us recognize and understand the processes of resilience and overcoming adversity.

On *20/20*, Barbara Walters once told the story of an African baby who was accidentally dropped into a fire by her 13-year-old mother (who was having a seizure). The baby girl, named Lydia, was taken to a hospital and given up by her parents. She miraculously survived, and today she lives a comfortable upper-middle-class life in the United States. After 38 years, married and a mother of three, she returned to the interior of Africa to visit her birth mother who could not believe the beautiful woman her nearly dead baby daughter had become. Such stories of resilience may help to balance the many stories of victimization that the media broadcast (Neufeld, 2001).

A family's external context influences how families and the individuals in them perceive what they experience. Those contextual factors play a role in determining whether families give the stressor a positive or negative valence. In the case of Lydia and her mother, their definition of the event and their interpretation ebbs and flows. Lydia's mother had been sold into marriage and poverty when she was 12 years old, so she had little power to influence her situation; Lydia, however, did. She had grown up in safety and comfort.

She obtained an education and resources to search for her birth mother. Paradoxically, the daughter who almost died in the fire and who had to have her legs amputated, had more mastery and control over her life than did her healthy but impoverished and oppressed mother. Knowing the great variations that exist in the family, we gain a broader repertoire for working with distressed individuals and families. For this reason, we contextualize this model of family stress. Whether in the time of Tolstoy or today, families are both alike and different, and the differences yield for us the most knowledge about how to strengthen families. We now move on to the CMFS and its definitions.

To define and describe terms that comprise the CMFS, we begin with the outside of the model in Figure 2.1 and move toward the middle. That is, we move from external context to internal context to the recursive ABC-X process of family stress management.

The Family's External Context

Individuals and families do not live in isolation. They are part of a larger context or environment, which is critical to understanding their ability (or inability)

Figure 2.1   The Contextual Model of Family Stress

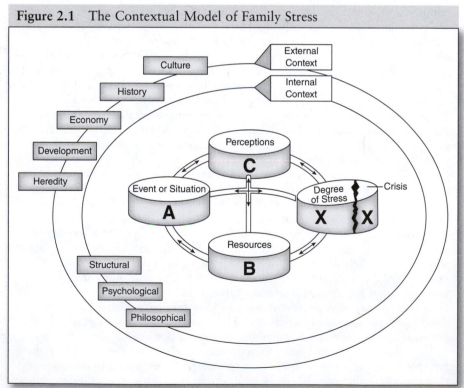

Source: Adapted from Boss (2002).

to manage stress and recover from crises. Of the two different contexts in which family stress can be shaped—the external context over which the family has little or no control and the internal context over which they do have control—we discuss the external context first. The external context is composed of five dimensions that influence family stress management: culture, history, economy, development, and heredity (see Figure 2.2). The external context is the environment or ecosystem in which the family is embedded. It can, for example, include global politics, macroeconomics, and catastrophes caused by nature, war, political terrorism, or ethnic annihilation. It can also include societal pressures from discrimination and poverty.

Because the five dimensions are imposed on families from outside their system, the external context is a macro pressure over which the family has little or no control. It also includes the limits of time and place, in which a troubled family, through no volition of its own, finds itself.

Cultural Context

Culture refers to the beliefs and behaviors of a group of like-minded people who share unique characteristics such as race, religion, nationality, or ethnicity

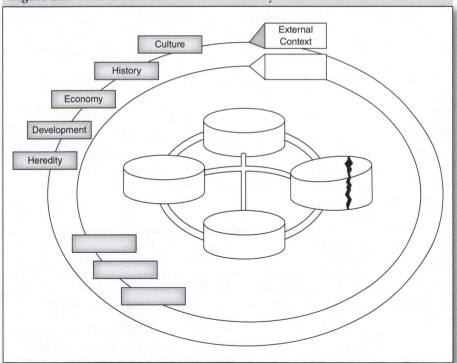

Figure 2.2   The Contextual Model of Family Stress: External Context

Source: Boss (2002).

(e.g., Native Americans, African Americans, Asian Americans, Latin Americans, Pacific Islanders, etc.). (To differentiate from community, we note that while culture refers to customs, arts, religions, foods, and sports of a particular group of people, community often refers to where people live or meet—e.g., military base, religious convent, West Side neighborhood, parish church, etc. Of course, community has psychological elements. For more information on communities, see Chapter 8.)

Although the family's private beliefs and values are, for most of us, under our control and therefore part of the internal context, the larger society's *cultural context* may still provide the canons and mores by which families live. Culture defines the rules for problem solving and coping with prejudice and stigma and defines how to do this with accepted and legal methods for managing stress. The larger culture, then, provides the meta rules by which families at the micro level find their way to coping and managing.

Sometimes, however, a family belongs to a subculture *or* community whose rules conflict with those of the prevailing culture. In such subcultures, problems are often solved by group leaders or elders. When, for example, the Hmong tradition was for older men to marry 13-year-old girls, there was incongruity between our larger society's laws and Hmong cultural values, mores, and rules; the two competing models could not coexist. Cultural prescriptions and proscriptions conflict until rules and values shift to fit the law of the land. Hitting one's wife is another example. It may be accepted in one culture but not legal in the larger society. Also, on college campuses, perhaps another subculture, there had been a similar mismatch between cultural behavior and the law when it was found that about 25% of students felt it was okay to slap around a partner "if they needed it" (Grant, 2015). Such attitudes are clearly at odds with the laws of larger society. But imagine if you are part of a subculture where a number of people endorse hitting or abuse. What do you do? Accept it? Head to the authorities? Which authorities?

Historical Context

The *historical context* of family stress is the time in history during which an event or situation occurs to the family or a family member (Elder, 1974/1999; Elder & Giele, 2009). A past event may influence the family's meanings and ways in which members manage stress and crises today. When we try to understand family stress, we have to know what historical events have been influential (Bengtson & Allen, 1993; Bowen, Martin, & Mancini, 2013). For example, if the stressful event was loss of a job, it would mean one thing if the loss happened at a time of job scarcity and it would mean another at a time when jobs were plentiful. Other important historical events that influence meaning and perceptions about family stressors include human-caused events of prejudice (slavery, the Holocaust, uprooting and forced education of Native American children in government boarding schools to eradicate their Indian identity, the fight for civil rights, continued ethnic cleansing worldwide [from Cambodia in the 1970s to Syria today]). There are natural disasters (floods, droughts, earthquakes, tsunamis, and fires) and human-made disasters (war, terrorism, murder, torture, and abuse). At identifiable times in history, these traumatic events leave their mark on the cohort that manages to live through them and, often, on subsequent generations.

When we ascertain the historical context of a particular family in stress, we then know more about whether the event occurred in an environment of choices versus one of powerlessness, captivity, or discrimination or in an environment of vast resources, privilege, and empowerment versus limited resources. The environment gives us clues to understanding the problem and shaping more effective interventions, but the historical time of the stress also provides clues. Both the environment and time reflect context. Like a pebble tossed into the water, contextual time markers leave their traces through a ripple effect, from the external contextual level to the family level. For example, a military couple may have a marriage problem, but to deal with it, they must acknowledge their separate experiences: namely, the soldier's experience in battle and the spouse's experience at home. Furthermore, the historical period in which the war takes place may also make a difference in perception; for example, what couples took from the Vietnam and Gulf Wars versus World War II is very different. Subsequent generations may still reflect some of the previous generation's coping behaviors. We think of many films that illustrate ancestral trauma: *Schindler's List*, *Ten Years a Slave*, *Roots*, *Amistad*, *The Diary of Anne Frank*, and *The Hurt Locker*.

Economic Context

The community or society's economy forms the family's *economic context* at a macro level and influences how the family reacts to a stressful event. For example, during a strong economic period, being laid off from a job is not as stressful to a family as it is when the economy is weak, with high unemployment and scarcity of jobs. When the chance of getting another job is slim, losing one's job becomes a crisis. During the Great Recession in the United States, unemployment was high, family incomes plummeted, and middle-class families everywhere, and especially in Detroit, faced foreclosures and lost their homes. Yet, some couples and families remain strong despite loss of employment. For example, Elder (1974/1999) and other family scientists Conger and Rueter (Conger, Reuter, & Elder, 1999) and Kwon, Rueter, Lee, Koh, and Ok (2003) studied couple resilience to economic pressure and found that high marital support was a protective factor against loss of income. Family researchers Dew and Yorgason (2010) found this strength as well in retirement age couples.

Overall, however, the management of stress within a family is not only complicated by the fluctuating state of the larger economy but also by unexpected changes in family income. Boss, a family therapist, has worked with a family in which the stress of the husband's job loss was erased by an unexpected inheritance, but then marital and family stress increased because the husband began spending most of his time gambling and became addicted. More money is not always a solution for reducing stress.

Developmental Context

Here, development refers to the human maturation process controlled by biology. For the most part, it is not under the family's control. Children grow up and leave—or return home; grandparents become primary caregivers for grandchildren when parents are unable to function in that role. Elders become frail and die; one's parents grow older and may need help.

While the *developmental context* includes the individual's and family's place in the life cycle when a stressful event occurs (Aldous, 1978; Carter & McGoldrick, 1999; Papalia, Olds, & Feldman, 2001), we propose a less linear and less normative-based model (Boss, 1980a). Marriage and divorce, for example, can occur at any age, not just during young adulthood; families can be new even if the people in them are old. Today, pregnancies occur within a wider range of the developmental context as technology now makes it possible for women well into their 40s to have children. Nevertheless, the different levels of family stress caused by the same event (in this case, pregnancy) cannot be explained by theories of development without looking at developmental nuances that can occur. That is, a 16-year-old girl could be deeply distressed to find out she is pregnant, while a 40-year-old woman, more mature psychologically as well as more financially stable, could be elated to finally be pregnant. Such contextual differences in development often explain why people have different perceptions and coping strategies for the same event.

Other developmental milestones can create and exacerbate family stress. Having elderly parents, for example, may be more stressful today because technology has made it possible for them to live longer, thus increasing the number of people with dementia and other frailties needing full-time care. Unfortunately, family and societal policies have not adapted adequately to this new longevity of our elders. Most of us expect our parents to take care of us when we are young, but fewer of us are prepared to care for our parents when they are old and frail. To complicate matters, caregiving families may not have adequate resources to care for their elderly parent in their own homes if they so choose. Moreover, the cost of having a frail parent in a long-term care facility is incredibly expensive.

When elderly parents are chronically ill and frail, the burden of caretaking falls predominantly on adult daughters or daughters-in-law (National Alliance for Caregiving & AARP Public Policy Institute, 2015). The increased stress this presents for individuals in the middle generation, who may concurrently be launching adolescents, supporting adult children, or even preparing for retirement, places them in a generational squeeze. With pressure from both above and below, they have been called the "sandwich generation." Midlife families, and especially midlife women, are now considered high risk for not only stress but also mortality, because of simultaneous stress stemming from the needs of frail elderly parents, children, housework, employment demands, plus their own retirement plans (Navaie-Waliser, Spriggs, & Feldman, 2002; Yee & Schulz, 2000).

Hereditary Context

The family's *heritable* and *genetic context* affects the health and physical strength of the family members. Because of genes and strong constitution, some people, and even some families, are simply physically healthier than others. Such people and families have more stamina and resilience when under pressure. They not only have more energy to deal with an event but also have the strength to persevere when the stressful situation is of long duration. A strong constitution makes it easier to cope when pressure continues over an extended period of time such as with unemployment or a chronic illness.

Perhaps the most prolific body of research about heredity and stress was produced by social psychologist and epidemiologist Ernest Harburg, spanning the late 1970s to 2003. To determine the effects of heredity on stress as indicated by blood pressure and cortisol levels, he developed a "family set" research method, in which he used a primary family member, plus his or her sibling or first cousin as the "set." He also used a randomly selected unrelated individual for comparison (Harburg, Erfurt, Schull, Schork, & Colman, 1977). In a classic series of studies, Harburg and colleagues found that for both Black and White participants, environmental variables, such as neighborhood, contributed more to variations in blood pressure than did their genetic differences (Chakraborty, Schull, Harburg, Schork, & Roeper, 1977).

Much more research is needed to determine the effects of heredity and genetics on individual and family stress. Family scientists have already joined scientists from other disciplines to conduct research (D'Onofrio & Lahey, 2010; Salvatore & Dick, 2015), showing that environment strongly influences the survival of the human body, perhaps despite genetic makeup. The important point is this: We can change our view of a stressor even if we cannot change our heredity. It is on this premise that we place the hereditary makeup of family members in the *external* context of the CMFS.

Historically and still today, people tend to describe those who have lived long enough to reach an old age as "coming from good stock." They saw a strong constitution, such as, in the late comedian George Burns, who lived to be 100 years old despite smoking cigars daily. On the other hand, people worry about youthful deaths such as that of Steve Jobs, the creator and chief executive officer of Apple, who died at age 56 in 2011 from cancer. While anecdotally, many of us rely on having a strong constitution and genetic makeup, much more research needs to address if or how heredity helps distressed individuals and families.

Summary

The external context of the CMFS consists of culture, history, the economy, development, and heredity, each of which constrains the management of stress because each is outside of the family's control. For this reason, we encourage family professionals, policymakers, and researchers to work for change in this larger arena (Ungar, 2012). The family is expected to be the keystone of society, but policymakers do little to strengthen the family for that larger societal role. In 2001, family psychologist Nadine Kaslow documented global trends and problems in families, most of which are influenced by the external context: shifting sociopolitical borders; changing male-female relationships; increasing domestic violence; increasing divorce rates; longing for greater spirituality; growing addictions; proliferating wars, starvation, and persecution; escalating crime and violence; more missing family members; growing numbers of homeless and throwaway children; increasing waves of immigration; rising incidence of uprooting; and increasing multicultural diversity (Kaslow, 2001). Sadly, the list remains much the same today. The external context needs to become more family friendly—family safe, actually. Asking families to be resilient is not enough.

While families are active reactors to the macro events of the external context, they are active shapers within the internal context. There, families have more volition, control, and mastery to not only react but also to shape their processes of coping and resilience. We now explain the internal context.

The Family's Internal Context (Structural, Psychological, and Philosophical)

The *internal context* of the family is composed of three micro dimensions that are classified as structural, psychological, and philosophical. Change in the family's internal context is more readily possible because the family has relatively more control over it.[1] It comprises the family's values and belief systems and broadens the multicultural application of the contextual stress model. Note that in Figure 2.3 these dimensions comprise the inward ring around the core that is the family stress process.

Unlike the external context, which is composed of elements over which the family has little or no control, the *internal context* is composed of elements that the family, at least its adult members, *can* change and control (Figure 2.3).

Figure 2.3   The Contextual Model of Family Stress: Internal Context

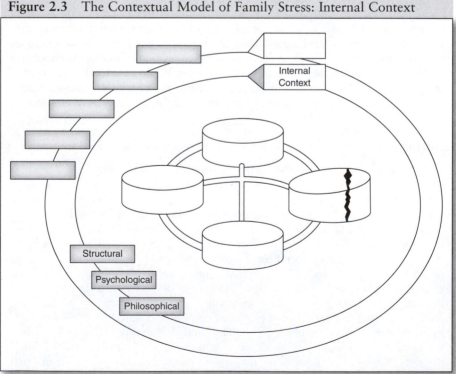

Source: Boss (2002).

Maintaining some control allows some choice about how and whether to shift gears and change; thus, even highly stressed families can change to survive, even thrive.

First, the *structural context* refers to the form and function of the family's structure: its boundaries, membership, role assignments, and rules regarding who is within and who is outside these boundaries. When the boundary of a family remains unclear (boundary ambiguity) (Boss, 2002), there is unclear support in the structural context and thus more stress in the system. More is said about boundary ambiguity in Chapter 5.

Second, the *psychological context* refers to the perception, appraisal, definition, or assessment of a stressful event by the family as a whole, as well as by its individual members. Here, we prefer the term *perception* because it embodies both cognitive (thinking) and affective (feeling) processes. How the family and its members perceive an event, mentally and emotionally, determines their ability to mobilize defense mechanisms and problem-solving strengths.

Third, the *philosophical context* of the family refers to its values and beliefs at a micro level. This is under the family's control. A particular family, for example, can live by rules that are different from those of the larger culture to which it belongs. Many immigrant and minority families in American culture still experience this incongruence. For example, when the larger culture provides government support for the institutional care of elderly parents but not for care within the family home, the external and internal contexts are brought into conflict and even more stress is created. Another example is the military subculture that sometimes imposes rules on family dependents that are inconsistent with those of the larger culture with secrecy about the whereabouts of a spouse or parent who is on a dangerous military mission. This leads to additional stress for families already worried about deployment. Such cultural incongruence may be even greater for military families living on installations in foreign countries. They must intermittently know and follow the rules of American mainstream culture, the military subculture, and the foreign culture in which they reside. It takes a strong family to synthesize such complexity into its private philosophy.

Population mobility also creates pockets of philosophical diversity and complexity. In almost any American city or town, there is a range of family beliefs that often directly oppose each other. For example, some families may believe that illness can be overcome by modern science and technology, other families put their trust in homeopathic remedies, and still others look to the healing powers of religion and prayer. As another example, some families believe that fighting back actively is the appropriate response to a stressor event while others believe in passive acceptance of whatever happens to them. Thus, even within the same cultural context, families may differ in their private philosophies.

Although such family beliefs and values are influenced by the external context, we note that a family's internal synthesis of beliefs and values (which become the family's own philosophy of being) directly influences the family's perception of a stressor event and how to deal with it. Consequently, we focus heavily in this book on the internal context—not because it is more important than the external context but because it is malleable. While both external and internal contexts are critical in determining which families remain strong, the internal context provides a more feasible window for change. It contains a possible set of leverage points that can be activated by family members themselves. It is for this reason that the internal context is of interest to family therapists and counselors who work with distressed and traumatized couples and families.

As we work with and study stressed families, we must ascertain their internal context before we can understand how the family sees the problem and whether change is possible. To further complicate matters, the family's internal context often shifts over time, with individual family members often disagreeing in their perceptions of the situation. Thus we need to ask family members, "What does this situation mean to you now?" (Boss, 2006).

Some families try to change their external context, but many remain powerless in the face of international politics and the devastation of war or plague. Although such families may try to eradicate such external stressors, they are rarely successful, at least in the short term. Often, the only option left is to change their perception of what is happening to them, which brings us back to the internal shift that they can control.

This ends our definitions of the CMFS's external and internal contexts. Keeping in mind that the following constructs are context-laden, we now move deeper into the model to define the ABC-X dimensions. We discuss them one at a time, beginning with the A factor, then B, C, and finally, X.

The ABC-X of Family Stress: A Frame for Definitions

When Reuben Hill (1958) formulated his ABC-X model, he provided a heuristic model for the scientific inquiry of family stress. He presented this model to a group of social workers in 1957, thus linking the work of family sociologists to that of practitioners. His framework for family stress theory focused on the following independent or intervening variables, which remain the foundation of family stress theory today:

A—the provoking event or stressor

B—the family's resources or strengths at the time of the event

C—the meaning attached to the event by the family (individually and collectively)

X—the outcome (coping or crisis)

Boss (1987, 1988, 1991, 2002) built upon Hill's heuristic ABC-X model but adapted it to be less linear, more contextual, and more focused on meaning and perception. With these major changes and additions, the CMFS was born. While other family stress models were developed, for example, the Double ABC-X model (Lavee, McCubbin, & Patterson, 1985), we find the parsimony and usefulness of the CMFS to be especially easy for practitioners and researchers to apply. Hill's work remains the heuristic core (Figure 2.4), but now the C factor is emphasized, which is what makes the theory a useful guide for intervention.

From a clinical perspective, the family's perception of an event is often the most powerful—or only—window for change. Perception, however, is difficult to measure, which may explain why the C factor was the least investigated in earlier decades. Since 1973, the focus for Boss has been on the C factor, for which we encourage continued study.

Because developing family stress theory is an interdisciplinary endeavor, you will see that we have merged constructs and definitions from family science, child development, social work, and nursing literatures, among others, because all have contributed directly or indirectly to understanding the processes of family stress management and resilience. In addition, using a general systems perspective, we include both individual and group indicators. Moving now to the inside of the model, we define the components of its ABC-X core.

The A Factor: Stressor Event (Stressful Event)

A *stressor event* is an occurrence that is of significant magnitude to provoke change in the family system. A stressor event is not synonymous with stress. It is an event that marks a possible starting point for the process of change and subsequent stress in the family system. It disturbs the family's status quo.

The stressor event also has the potential to increase the family's level of stress, although it does not necessarily do so every time. Stressors may be positive, normative, or toxic. The degree of stress depends not only on the actual magnitude of the event but also on the family's perception of that event. Families often

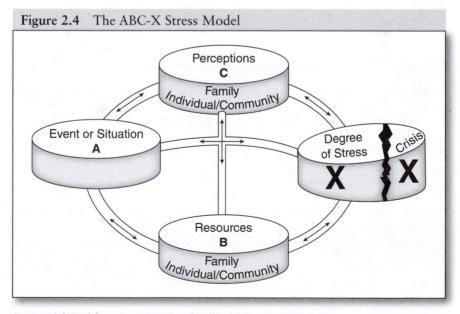

Figure 2.4   The ABC-X Stress Model

Source: Adapted from Boss (2002) and Hill (1958).

view the same event differently (e.g., one family is ecstatic over a move to a new country, whereas another is panic stricken or angry) or may perceive an event differently over time (e.g., the first time a family moved it was exciting, and small children were not disturbed, but after the 12th move in 15 years, the mother feels defeated, and high-school-aged children are angry).

The Danger of Circular Reasoning

Because a stressful event is only a stimulus, it cannot be synonymous with the outcome of that stimulus. This means that a stressor event is not the same as the degree of stress the family experiences (see Figure 2.4). Were they the same, this would be a tautology (circular reasoning). A *tautology* is an untestable hypothesis because obviously "stress equals stress" or "change equals change." The correlation would be 100%. A researcher would be wasting his or her time trying to test such hypotheses. It would not provide an explanation or help us to understand nuance or complexity or move our thinking to action.

To avoid the danger of tautologies, we propose that the *type* of stressor event influences the *degree* of stress experienced. Thus, in the model in Figure 2.4, "type of event" equals "degree of stress" (rather than stress equals stress). This is a very important point. Not only does it avoid circular reasoning, but it also aids in parsimony and conceptual clarity. You will see how this equation becomes even more complex (but still testable) when we add "the family's perception of that event." Were we to add "community perception of the event," as recommended by family psychiatry researchers Reiss and Oliveri (1991) and Reiss (1981) and more recently by Mancini and Bowen (2009, 2013), there would be no danger for tautology.

Classification of Family Stressor Events

Stressor events are varied and multiple. Because it is essential to be able to identify them, the basic types are classified and defined in Table 2.1 for quick reference and better understanding. Here's the point: It is more useful to classify stressor events or situations by their characteristics and intensity than by the name of a particular event or disease.

When an individual is faced with a stressor event, either as a professional who works with stressed families or as a family member, it is important to identify the type of event before assessing or responding to the situation because the type will influence the entire process: the family's perception of the event, the degree of stress experienced by the family, and the managing strategies used or not used. In fact, the type of event may be highly correlated with the family's ability or inability to manage stress or recover from crisis. Certainly, the type called "ambiguous stressor events" has been identified as a major predictor of family stress that is difficult to resolve (Boss, 1999, 2006).

The types of stressor events in Table 2.1 provide a template for assessing the characteristics of stressor events, some of which will be problematic and others that are normative. Rather than focusing on a specific disease or event,

Table 2.1   Classifications of Stressor Events and Situations

Source	
Internal: Events that begin with someone inside the family, such as addiction, suicide, violence, or running for an election	**External:** Events that begin with someone or something outside the family, such as floods, terrorism, or loss of job
Type	
Normative, Developmental, Predictable: Events that are expected during the life course, such as birth, puberty, adolescence, marriage, aging, menopause, retirement, and death	**Catastrophic, Situational, Unexpected:** Unforeseen events or situations, such as a young child dies
Ambiguous: Events or situations that remain unclear, such as facts about the status of a family member remain unclear or are unavailable	**Clear:** Facts are available, such as the family knows what is happening and how it will turn out
Volitional: Events or situations that are wanted and sought out, such as freely chosen job changes, college entrance, or a wanted pregnancy	**Nonvolitional:** Events or situations not freely chosen, such as being laid off, fired, divorced, or being given up for adoption
Duration	
Chronic: A situation of long duration, such as diabetes, chemical addiction, or discrimination and prejudice	**Acute:** Event that lasts a short time but is stressful, such as a broken leg
Density	
Cumulative: Events or situations that pile up, one after the other, so there is no time to cope before the next stressor occurs, such as families worn down by multiple unresolved stressors	**Isolated:** One event that occurs by itself or alone with no other stressor; it is easily pinpointed

Source: Adapted from Boss (2002).

Table 2.1 expands our thinking to include the nuances of what is stressful and why.

As you can see, we categorize stressors by source, type, duration, and density. To assess, we ask, Did the stressor originate inside the family or from the external context? Was it expected, clear, and volitional or the opposite? Is the stressor now chronic, becoming a situation and not just an event? Was it made more dense by piling on other stressors? While some of the subcategories in the table are more positive than others, all have the potential to disturb the family's status quo. We now discuss each subcategory.

Normal, Developmental, and Predictable Stressor Events

While normative stressors are usually expected events (e.g., children grow up), the normal and expected development of a child to adolescence, for example, tends to increase family stress, especially if the parents do not acknowledge the maturation and change. Retirement can cause a crisis in an older, traditional couple when the husband and wife continue to interact as if the husband still has a full-time job. To avoid conflict and dissatisfaction in the family, he may have to take on a new role, such as sharing the household duties with his wife, and she may have to adjust her activities to adapt to his increased presence at home. With many normative developmental events, a family must change at every transition point. Who is in the family and how? We define normative stressor events in terms of family boundary changes across the family life cycle; with each event, the family either loses or gains a member, and this means that its boundary is disturbed. When the physical presence of family members increases or diminishes, there is a ripple effect that causes stress at various degrees of the entire family system.

Catastrophic, Situational, and Unexpected Stressor Events

Catastrophic types of stressor events (Table 2.1) initially interested family stress theorists such as Reuben Hill more than 4 decades ago. They are unexpected (nonnormative) events, the result of some unique situation that could not be predicted and is not likely to be repeated. As a result, such events are usually highly stressful.

Negative examples of unpredictable and unique events include disasters and catastrophes such as the March 11, 2011 Fukushima triple disaster in northeastern Japan (earthquake, tsunami, and subsequent nuclear disaster); the Newtown, Connecticut school shooting of 20 grade school children; the disappearance of the Malaysian airliner and its 239 passengers; the BP oil spill; the AIDS epidemic of the 1980s; and other major earthquakes, volcanic eruptions, tornadoes, fires, and floods.

Unexpected events that are not catastrophic may also be stressful for families. Examples include finding lost relatives or receiving unexpected job offers or promotions. Such events are positive, but they create a disturbance in the family's routine and thus have a potential for increasing the family's level of stress.

Ambiguous Stressor Events

Ambiguity is created when facts can't be obtained about an event or situation. The whereabouts or fate of a kidnapped boy—even a lost pet—remains unclear for a long time, or an illness takes away the mind or memory of a family member. For example, a grandfather with advanced Alzheimer's disease is no longer the person he was and is now unrecognizable. The ambiguity lies in his being here but not here. An ambiguous stressor may be an event that is predicted but no one knows if and when it will really occur (e.g., tornado, hurricane, earthquake, Alzheimer's disease). In any case, with ambiguous stressors, facts are unclear or nonexistent. Families are pushed to the limit of what they can withstand. Many find resilience in surprising ways. When Microsoft scientist and Turing Award Winner Jim Gray was lost at sea in 2007, with no trace of his boat anywhere, his family and his colleagues searched the sea for a long time but found nothing to clear up the ambiguity (Boss, 2008). Eventually, his wife found new meaning through writing poetry, which allowed her to move forward with a new kind of life (Boss & Carnes, 2012). The pain of such stress is the ambiguity of losing a person who has disappeared. Categorizing such painful stressors as "ambiguous" and naming the culprit as "the not-knowing" is more effective than attributing blame to those who are, through no fault of their own, at the mercy of the ambiguity.

Clear Stressor Events

When clear facts are available about an event—what is happening, when, for how long, and to whom—a family is in a better position. There is no question about what is happening to them, the prognosis, and what will help to reduce their stress. If the event, such as a hurricane, cannot be changed, the family is at least clear about the duration of the storm, its logical progression, and what they must do to protect themselves.

Volitional Stressor Events

Volitional events are those that a family controls and implements. Making a move willingly or planning a pregnancy are examples of volitional stressor events. Thus, these events are classified by the degree of choice and control of the family members and the system as a whole. Other examples of volitional stressor events are a desired marriage, a wanted divorce, or a deadline that a family has chosen to meet. Some families actually enjoy challenge and thus choose vacations that include some stress; for example, white-water rafting, climbing mountains, running marathons, bicycling hilly terrain, or simply taking a road trip with small children.

Typically, in our culture, volitional stressor events are associated with lower degrees of family stress because the events are purposefully selected. The family remains in control of its destiny. Stories about some immigrant families, such as those of former U.S. Secretary of State Madeleine Albright (part of the Clinton Administration, 1997-2001) and the family of President John F. Kennedy, reflect a constant search for challenge and high-stress situations. The problem, however, is that not all members of a family may enjoy a high degree of stress all the time. Not everyone may be an adventurer or enjoy competition. There may be a shy person in a family devoted to public service. When we work with families, we have to be sure that all family members want an event to occur before it can validly be classified as volitional for the entire family.

Nonvolitional Stressor Events

Nonvolitional events are events that are thrust on a family. They originate in the outside context and are not a result of action by anyone inside the family. The key point is that the family has no control over the occurrence. Examples of nonvolitional family stressor events are family breadwinners being laid off from their jobs or a family member being robbed. Disastrous events that are called "acts of God," such as volcanic eruptions or earthquakes, are also categorized as nonvolitional. Even human-made disasters such as the nuclear bombings in Hiroshima and Nagasaki in 1945 can, at least from the Japanese people's perspective, be classified as nonvolitional; there was no knowledge of the nature of the bombs before they were dropped.

Stressor Situations

A chronic stressor is defined as a stressful situation (rather than an event) because it is characterized by (1) a long duration; (2) the probability of occurrence with other events, especially normal developmental transitions; and (3) the potential for high ambiguity in its origin (etiology), progression, and conclusion. The situation is difficult to change—that is, the stressor persists. Such chronic stressors may be an illness (e.g., alcoholism or Alzheimer's disease), an economic situation (e.g., poverty), or a social condition (e.g., discrimination against race, gender, and sexual orientation). Other examples of chronic stressors are living in constant danger (e.g., terrorism, persecution, or high murder rate in neighborhood). Other chronic situations may not be dangerous but are nevertheless a constant irritation (e.g., noisy atmosphere for people living near an airport or in some college dormitories). The key point is that a chronic stressor is a long-term situation rather than a one-time event and thus, more problematic.

Chronic stressors have special characteristics that affect the degree of stress experienced in a family. The following questions define the characteristics:

1. Is there ambiguity rather than predictability in the event or situation—that is, is there uncertainty regarding facts about the onset, development, and resolution of the situation? The chronic stressor of Parkinson's disease, for example, has more predictability (due to a known medication) than does the chronic stressor of autism (about which less is known).

2. What is the context in which the chronic stressor event develops—that is, is the stressful event a result of the larger context (e.g., inflation, living near an active volcano, or the closing of a factory) or the result of an individual action (e.g., a lifetime of smoking that caused a persistent illness)?

3. What is the visibility or nonvisibility of the situation? Some chronic stressors, such as diabetes or heart disease, are not physically noticeable, whereas others, such as loss of a limb or being blind are more apparent to outsiders and family members.

Each of these characteristics may affect the family's perception of the event, which will determine the degree of stress experienced collectively and individually. Therefore, we must obtain answers to the aforementioned questions when we work with chronically stressed families.

Even more than with short-term events, the subtle characteristics of chronic stressor situations call for special consideration in research methodology, clinical diagnosis, and assessment of family stress. Instruments must have the capacity to measure perceptual variables that are influenced by the duration and ambiguity of long-term stressor situations. Tests and measuring instruments must be sensitive to the possibility that the family members are denying what is happening to them. For example, the family may deny the existence of a persisting illness in one of its members. Such denial occurs with many chronic illnesses, such as alcoholism, drug addiction, Alzheimer's disease, and end-stage renal disease.

Another characteristic unique to a chronic stressor situation influences research and therapeutic assessment: The family's perception of the situation may change during the family life cycle. According to Lynn Wikler (1981, 1986), a social work researcher, the painful reality of a chronic stressor such as severe intellectual disability is again inflated at each juncture of the life span when a developmental step would normally occur in the affected person. For example, when a child reaches the age of high school graduation and cannot graduate and attend college or obtain employment as other children do, the family is newly reminded of the constraints on the child's situation. If the family maintains normal expectations, their chronic stress may be increased to a higher level at each developmental point. Disability as a chronic stressor event is an added complication when combined with the normal stressor events of developmental family life transitions that occur naturally during the life span. Another example is when a caregiver and the family may not be able to deal with both the stressor situation (e.g., a chronically ill family member) and normal stressor events (e.g., the death of an aged parent and an adolescent leaving home) happening during the same period. Managing all of these changes may become overwhelming. Therefore, it can be predicted that a family will be highly stressed whenever a normal developmental transition occurs simultaneously with a chronic family stressor situation, even though the family managed the illness reasonably well before the transition point and will do so afterward.

Acute Stressor Events

Acute stressor events are those that happen suddenly and last only a short time. Their duration is usually predictable. Examples are a child breaking a leg and wearing a cast for 6 weeks or a family member undergoing emergency surgery and staying home from work for a few weeks to recuperate. The major distinction between a chronic and acute stressor event is that the latter happens suddenly and then is over. The duration of the acute stressor event is short and reasonably predictable. Note, however, that aftereffects are not predictable and also can be long lasting. An example is the acute stressor of heart surgery followed by the ongoing chronic heart disease itself.

Cumulative Stressor Events

The accumulation of stressor events is a phenomenon in which several stressor events or situations occur at the same time or in quick sequence, thus compounding the degree of pressure on the family. The phenomenon is also called cumulative disadvantages or adversity (Gerard & Buehler, 2004; Lucier-Greer, Arnold, Mancini, Ford, & Bryant, 2015). The idea of accumulation is the basis of the frequently used stress scale, Schedule of Recent Events, developed by psychiatrists Holmes and Rahe (1967), which quantifies self-reported stressors piling up or accumulating for individuals (Rahe, Veach, Tolles, & Murakami, 2000) and the Family Inventory of Life Events and Changes Scale developed by family social scientists McCubbin, Patterson, and Wilson (1981), which quantifies stress pileup as reported by a family member. The concept of stressor pileup is important because it is the accumulation of several stressor events rather than the nature of one isolated event that determines a family's level of stress, its subsequent vulnerability to crisis, or its ability to recover from a particular crisis. An event rarely happens to a family in total isolation; normal developmental changes are always taking place as family members are born, mature, grow older, and die. The pileup of stressor events and situations is highly influential in assessing a family's level of stress.

Isolated Stressor Events

Isolated stressor events are single events that occur at a time when nothing else is disturbing the family status quo. This single event can then be pinpointed as the event that is causing one's stress. Life is good, but one day, you mistakenly park in the wrong place. Your car is towed, you are very upset, you hitch a ride to the tow pound, pay a considerable fee, and have your car back. The stressor event is over, although there may still be a credit card bill to pay off. Or, you break an ankle, you go to the hospital, they treat you and put your ankle in a cast, you experience more stress for 6 weeks or so as you limp around, they take the cast off, and you can walk again as normal. Such isolated stressor events are more easily (though not happily) dealt with in a linear fashion. Although we may be deeply stressed or in pain, it is clear what happened and what we need to do to fix the problem.

With this brief discussion of each classification of stressors shown in Table 2.1, we reiterate the core point: Classifying stressor events and situations by source, type, duration, and density will reveal the nuances of why some events are more immobilizing than others. Classifying stressors in this manner is more revealing than classifying them by disaster or disease. Nevertheless, there are some cautions.

Cautions About Defining a Stressor Event

Keep in mind what we said earlier: What is defined as a stressor event is highly influenced by the family's external context—the time in their lives and the place in which they live. Community and cultural contexts influence what the family defines as a "stressor event." Marriage, pregnancy, an adolescent leaving home, the loss of a job, women working outside the home, failing an exam, or even winning the lottery are all viewed differently. We cannot automatically assess such events as stressful without first asking the family, and its members, how they define the event. There are times when military deployment is a stress reducer rather than a stressor event. The same can be said for death, if a family member has been in great pain or in a coma for a long time.

Although neutral, a stressor event has the potential to be either positive or negative—or a mixture of both. Winning a large amount of money has as much potential to cause stress in a family as losing money. However, when a stressor is transformative and leads to growth, it is an example of making lemonade out of lemons.

Stressor events do not always increase stress to a crisis point. They can occur, and the status quo of the family can be disturbed, but the family's stress level can be managed if the system finds a new equilibrium.

On the other hand, when a stressful event such as sudden loss of income occurs, a family can refuse to acknowledge the event or to change their behavior (habits of spending freely). They act as if nothing happened, using credit cards and going deeper into debt. Here, the denial of the event (loss of income) prevents change and thereby increases the probability of crisis in the family.

A family cannot begin to manage stress or solve problems until they recognize that they have a problem. Families cannot deal with a stressor event until, as a group, they recognize that the event has occurred. If only one family member sees the problem, there are few systemic options: the rest of the family has to change their perceptions of the event; the dissenting person has to change his or her perception; or ultimately that dissenter is isolated, shunned, and has to leave.

Throughout the time a particular family is experiencing a stressor event, their resources for coping and managing are hopefully gathered, assessed, and set in motion. Resources can influence how a family responds to stress.

The B Factor: Resources (Individual, Family, and Community)

We now move to resources, the B factor in the CMFS. Family resources are the individual, familial, and community strengths and assets available to the family at the time of stress or crisis. Examples include financial stability, good health, intelligence, education, employable job skills, proximity of support, spirit of cooperation in the family, relationship skills, network and social supports, and resilience—both individual and collective. Family resources then are the economic, psychological, and physical assets from which the family can draw upon in response to stressor events or situations.

A question remains about whether resilience is a resource or an outcome in the CMFS. In this book, we present resilience as a process so it occurs in multiple places—but not at the same time. That would be tautology. For the most part, we see resilience as an outcome of the family stress management process (see Chapter 7).

The C Factor: Perception

The C factor is defined as the family's collective perception of a stressor event or situation. It is how they think about or view what they are experiencing. Hill originally called the C factor the "definition of the event," but that term was too narrow (Boss, 1988, 2002). Boss preferred the term "perception" because it included more than the family's definition of the stressor; it included—and elevated—the value of a family's subjective interpretation and meaning of a stressful event. If families are expected to act on their own behalf, to change or to transform, then honoring the sense *they* make of their experiences is the first step.

With perception (and thus meaning) now the central construct, a major theoretical shift took place; the focus in the CMFS was now on the social construction of meaning. This continues today, as symbolic interactionism remains relevant. While Boss built her early work on the symbolic interactionism of pioneer sociologist George Herbert Mead (1956), family sociologist Sheldon

Stryker (1968), and especially sociologist Erving Goffman, (1959, 1974) (see Boss, in press for review), today, we also build on the social construction theory pioneered by Peter Berger and Thomas Luckmann (1966), David Reiss (1981), and psychologist Kenneth Gergen (1994, 1999, 2001), a major figure in the development of social constructionist theory and its applications to practices of social change. Like Boss (2006), Gergen agrees that loss is "a rupture in meaning" and "a relational disorder and not individual pathology" (2006, back cover). Meaning must be restored if a family and its individual members are to remain strong after loss. Today, we continue our emphasis on perception because it embodies both the cognitive (thinking) and affective (feeling) processes of family stress management.

The Primacy of Perceptions

In work with distressed families, it became apparent that unless we could identify, understand, and measure their perceptions, we would not have a valid view of what was happening to families or how to intervene (Boss, 1992). During Boss's initial studies with families of men declared missing in action in Vietnam and later with families in which there was Alzheimer's disease, she paid as much attention to qualitative narratives from family members as to quantitative data from questionnaires. The latter were often easier to analyze and much more acceptable as research data when she began in the 1970s, but it was the stories told by family members that informed her of the power of their perceptions of the situation. Hill (1949/1971) originally called this the family's "definition of the event," medical sociologist Aaron Antonovsky (1979) called it "appraisal," and Patterson and Garwick (1994) called it "levels of meaning." The latter reflects the growing consensus among family stress researchers that perception and meaning are central to understanding sometimes puzzling processes observed in distressed families.

For example, a student wrote:

> I work in a shelter for battered women and I am continually amazed and saddened by different women and children's perceptions of what is going on in their lives. Some women view the battering as just another event in their lives and take it in stride; others are unable to function from the hurt and shame. The meaning each woman attaches to her abusive situation is always different. It is often hard for me to understand their perception because mine varies drastically. Some women see abuse as normal stress, while others see it as a crisis. Most continue to function (going to work or school) while living in the shelter, while others are traumatized and barely able to take care of themselves. Some have to be referred to hospital or medical staff. My perception of their situation often differs from theirs. Even after I find out what their perceptions are, my values and standards block my ability to fully see where they are coming from. I am very sensitive to their situations and offer them several resources to become more self-sufficient and improve their lives, but I am still unable to totally view battering the way they do. My question is this: Is this a bad thing? Must

I constantly remind myself that I am perceiving it differently and try to perceive it in the way they do in order to help them? Or do I just need to know their perceptions in order to fully understand the premise they are coming from?

This student began to answer her own question by framing her last question. Where she is "coming from" is influenced by her community and cultural context. We need to know the premise or meaning that all family members have about the family's situation. How do they define it? What meaning does it have for them and their community? We would never agree that being battered was normal, but if this is what a woman believes, it helps us to know this as we work with her. If she believes it is normal to be hit by her partner, she needs information and group experiences to show her that other options exist. In such cases, we work cognitively and psychodynamically to change perceptions so that everyone in that group or family becomes intolerant of abuse and more able to express feelings verbally.

How a family perceives an event or situation and the meaning it embodies is critical in determining the degree of stress they experience (i.e., crisis or coping). For example, the death of a parent is described as a loss, but it might *mean* the end of someone's world—a repossessed home; no car; no money for education, food, or clothes; even homelessness. In another family, the death of a parent is also sad but may simply mean the end of a long and good life.

In sum, you see that we support the primacy of perceptions, but we must also add that perceptions are not *all* that matter (Boss, 1992). Sometimes, the family's perception can be distorted, so other views are needed—the teacher's, the nurse's, the doctor's, or the social worker's view. Multiple views are needed to validate assessments. This is true for research as well as for professionals who work with families who are in disagreement or denial.

Collective Versus Individual Perceptions

And that brings us to collective perceptions. This means that everyone in the family agrees with how the stressor event or situation is perceived. As in any system, the whole is greater than the sum of its parts; the family's collective perception can overpower the meaning that any individual family member might give to the same event. When even one family member begins to see things differently, change is on the way for the entire family system. To determine the degree of incongruence among individual members' perceptions, we recommend using both individual and collective assessment of the C factor. In effect, we are assessing the degree of family agreement in perceptions of the event versus their degree of disagreement.

The X Factor: Family Crisis

Family stress sometimes results in crisis (Figure 2.4). A family crisis is (1) a disturbance in the equilibrium that is so overwhelming; (2) a pressure that is so severe; or (3) a change that is so acute that the family system is blocked, immobilized, and incapacitated. At least for a time, the family does not function. Family boundaries are no longer maintained, customary roles and tasks are no longer performed, and family members can no longer function at optimal levels, physically or psychologically.

The following case from Boss's own family illustrates this point. She shares her family's story of crisis:

> In the summer of 1955, the summer before the Salk polio vaccine was discovered, polio was rampant, and many of the young were stricken. Eddie, my younger brother, was a strong 13-year-old and the predicted star of the freshman football team. Disaster struck, however. He played football one Friday and died the next. The young football squad carried his coffin at the funeral, and the whole school and community were in shock. Our family was immobilized. Friends and people from the community came to our home with food. My parents could not function or work, so friends and neighbors had to chauffer them, help plan the funeral, and fill in for them at work. I was at the university but could not study. None of us could perform our usual tasks. Each of us withdrew into our own private grief. Our family rule of "we take care of ourselves" had to give way as friends and neighbors took over to help. Our family system was in crisis. We were immobilized by Eddie's unexpected and terrible death from polio.

Figure 2.5   The Turning Point in Family Crisis

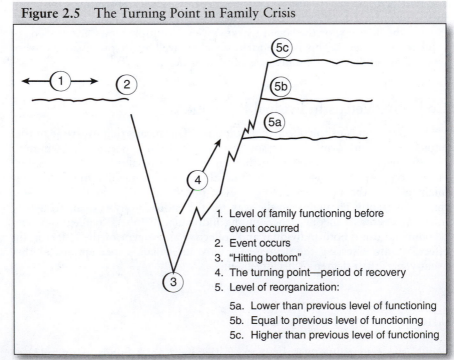

1. Level of family functioning before event occurred
2. Event occurs
3. "Hitting bottom"
4. The turning point—period of recovery
5. Level of reorganization:

   5a. Lower than previous level of functioning
   5b. Equal to previous level of functioning
   5c. Higher than previous level of functioning

Source: Adapted from Boss (2002), Hill (1949/1971), and Koos (1946).

When a family is in crisis, using the bridge metaphor means that the structure has collapsed. At least for a time, the family cannot function. Specific indicators of such family crisis are (1) the inability of parents to take care of themselves, their children, their work, or their business; (2) the inability of family members to make decisions or to solve problems (e.g., about the funeral, money, or work); (3) the inability of family members to perform daily tasks and roles so that outsiders are temporarily needed to do this; and (4) the care for each other as family members or spouses may retreat to private coping. In the case of Eddie's sudden death, the family was stunned and in deep grief, so it was others who drew them out to see the public support—the school community, the church congregation, the football team, relatives, and friends of all ages. As family members could no longer take care of each other, they were fortunate to have the support of the community to keep them going during this terrible time. When a beloved family member dies suddenly and all too young, the strongest of families can fall into momentary crisis and immobilization.

We want to emphasize that the terms *stress* and *crisis* cannot be used interchangeably. Whereas family stress is a state of disturbed equilibrium, family crisis is a point of acute disequilibrium. Therefore, family stress is a continuous variable (degrees of stress), whereas family crisis is a categorical variable (a family is either in crisis or it is not; see Figures 2.4 and 2.5). In crisis, the family system is immobilized and stops functioning. Like a bridge that collapses, a family crisis is determined by the point at which the family structure can no longer perform its intended functions. In a family, however, in addition to the pressures that outweigh the family supports, their perception and appraisal of what is happening can influence the point at which the break occurs or is avoided.

The Roller Coaster Model of Family Crisis

The roller coaster model of family adjustment after crisis developed by Hill in 1949 and adapted by others (Boss, 1987; Hansen & Hill, 1964) illustrates familial adjustment to crisis. According to the model, crisis is the period of disorganization and immobilization in which previous interactions and behaviors for managing and solving problems become inadequate, frozen, inoperable, or blocked. The system hits bottom. Depending on the amount of time needed to shift gears or change, the family reaches a turning point, begins to move again, reorganizes, and enters what Hill (1949/1971) called the period of recovery. The family reaches a new level of reorganization that is higher, lower, or equal to the one experienced before the onset of the stressor event (see Figure 2.5). Today we call this growth an indicator of resilience or post-traumatic growth (see Chapter 7). This means that a family does not have to be destroyed by crisis or immobilization.

Linking the ABC-X Model to the Roller Coaster Model of Family Crisis

While there is a difference between Hill's ABC-X model of family stress and his roller coaster model of family crisis, the two are linked. The roller coaster model (as adapted, Boss, 1988, 2002) illustrates the breaking point after increasingly wild gyrations of resisting until, finally, the family structure breaks under the pressure. Like an overloaded bridge, it is no longer functional. The family falls into crisis (as indicated by immobilization). Ideally, the family eventually reaches a turning point, which means they decide to start moving forward again, and they may function at a level lower than, equal to, or higher than before the crisis occurred (see Figure 2.5). We believe, however, that the roller coaster model represents only one portion of the broken X factor in Figure 2.4. There we show crisis as a state separate from high stress (note the broken line). Crisis is something other than simply the highest point of the stress continuum. That is, crisis is not a continuous variable: It is a categorical variable. You are either immobilized or you are not. Although hopefully temporary, crisis as indicated by immobilization is an outcome.

In contrast to the model of family stress shown in Figure 2.4, the roller coaster model in Figure 2.5 helps us to understand family recovery because it shows the disorganization and reorganization process in families. They are immobilized, hit bottom, and, hopefully, turn the corner to begin the process of recovery. Importantly, families often grow stronger after surviving crisis so that their levels of functioning can become even higher than before the crisis. Outcomes can range from low stress, meaning the family is managing, to high stress or crisis, meaning the family is still struggling.

The Turning Point: Family Recovery After Crisis

Crisis is painful and may debilitate the family, but the length of the debilitation may vary from hours to years. Given minor and some major crises, a family may often hit bottom, turn the corner, begin the recovery process, and repair itself (see Figure 2.5). This ability to recover marks the major difference between a mechanical system (the bridge) and an organic system (the family). A family system has the potential to grow and learn from a crisis, whereas a bridge does not. Therefore, for human systems, crisis may be simply a turning point, not an end point. This is a hopeful note for families in crisis.

When the ratio between the family system's support and the pressure on it shifts so that the pressure decreases and the support becomes stronger, recovery is occurring. Turning points result from (1) a change in the stressor event, (2) a change in the availability of resources for coping, or (3) a change in the family's perception of both factors. In the case of incurable illness or when the pressure of the event cannot be lessened, we can ease the stress level with the second and third factors. If, however, the family's resources cannot be increased, then we can intervene with only the third factor, changing the family's perception of what is happening to them.

Some families reach a turning point after the crisis by redefining the events that have been stressing them, or they redefine their existing strengths, resources, and supports. Even if nothing else changes, families may have changed their perception of what was happening to them or what resources and supports were available to them for coping. Clinicians call this process *reframing*. Such a change in perception can alter the ratio of family pressure to family support and thereby precipitate a turning point, which is the beginning of recovery for a family in crisis. This is important in crises in which the event, in this case, a loss, for Boss's family, cannot be changed. The family could not change the loss of Eddie, so they changed their perception and worked tirelessly to help others.

> After Eddie's death, our family took a long time to even begin recovering. While we began to work again, to eat, and even occasionally find a reason to smile, I never felt I recovered as such; rather I learned to live with the sadness. Perhaps that is what recovery means for some. Routines returned. Help from the outside was needed less and less. My parents met with others who had lost children. Perhaps what helped the most is that a year later, all of us in the family went door to door to collect donations for the March of Dimes, which at that time was funding research on preventing polio. We found a meaning in our sorrow and thus were no longer in crisis. After hitting bottom, we were on the way to becoming a new family system, one without Eddie, except in memory. The stress from that awful event of loss will always be with us, but we are no longer immobilized. Indeed, crisis does not have to permanently destroy a family. It can make them stronger.

Family Strain

Before we end this section on crisis as outcome, we need to clarify that not all families fall into crisis. Some are just highly stressed but managing; others are driven to the brink but holding on and still functioning. We call it *strain*.

Family strain can be likened to a bridge shaking but not collapsing. The structure is still functional—at least minimally—but it is bent out of shape, creaks, and shakes under pressure. Strain results from a mismatch at the point where pressures occur and the supports are grounded. In a family system, that means supports (resources and strengths) may exist, but they are not where they are most needed. For example, poor families who have seen trouble before and know how to survive may be more resilient than more privileged families who have not faced trouble before. Psychologically strong families are those who avoid the mismatch between the location of its strengths and pressures. Those families may still continue to function, albeit shakily, if there are some outside supports that come to help.

The danger of strain for a family is that if their structure begins to change at some time (which is quite likely because children grow up and parents grow older), the existing mismatch limits the family's degree of tolerance to adapt to stress. A strained family is brittle (the opposite of resilient). Thus, in an already strained family, the chance for total collapse (crisis) is high when an additional event occurs and even more pressure is added. The family becomes highly vulnerable.

Therefore, it may be more critical to avoid the mismatch of strain than to avoid the occurrence of stressor events. After all, a life without stress would be unusual. We need to know how much pressure we can handle and if we can handle more pressure at certain times than others. The family that is not strained can more easily manage and cope with everyday stressor events because resources can simply be directed to match pressures when and where they occur. In addition, although the mismatch that defines family strain does not always depend on the accumulation of stressor events, it is more likely to occur when events pile up persistently and exert increasing pressure at different points of the family structure, thus aggravating the dangerous mismatch.

For professionals working with families, the identification of vulnerable families may be easier if they search for this mismatch between stressors and strengths, pressures and supports, and rigidity and resilience to determine which families are fragile and which are strong. Some families can handle a lot of pressure, whereas others cannot. Strain, with its brittleness, more than stress or crisis, may be a distinguishing variable in identifying vulnerable families.

In the next chapter, we discuss a universal stressor—a death in the family. The responses, however, to the stress of losing a loved one to death vary across cultures and ethnicity. Focusing on this common family stressor through a multicultural lens, the following chapter shows us the urgent need for more inclusion of diversity in the study and practice of family stress.

Summary

Neither individuals nor families exist in a vacuum. They are a part of a larger context. Sometimes they have very little control over the context in which they find themselves embedded. Families generally have relatively more control over their internal context, compared to their external context. Thus, for example, although they cannot change their heredity (external), they can change their perceptions and appraisals (internal). Doing so can impact the outcome of a stressor event. Sometimes family stressors lead to crises, and crises can immobilize and incapacitate a family system.

Points to Remember

1. Elements of the external context of family stress are culture, history, economics, development (maturation), and heredity. The family has relatively little influence over these elements.

2. Elements of the internal context of family stress are the family's structure, its psychological defenses, and its philosophical beliefs. The family has some control over these elements.

3. The CMFS remains heuristically useful and is now presented with more emphasis on diversity and multiculturalism and on community as well as family. It is not a linear model; it is recursive, systemic, and contextual, and we hope useful for research as well as practice.

4. It is more useful to classify stressor events or situations by their characteristics and intensity than by the name of a particular event or disease. For example, in a family with the A factor stressor of a loved one with memory loss, the ambiguity is the stressor, not the patient or the family members who give care. Too often families miss that point and begin blaming each other for their exhaustion and ongoing stress.

5. The B factor represents resources that could aid in coping and resilience. Resources can emerge from an individual, couple, family, or community.

6. The C factor, the family's perception of the event, is the most important part of the CMFS equation for intervening with a situation that cannot be fixed. It is the most difficult to assess, however, because it is perceptual. Sometimes, the family's perception can be distorted, so other views are needed—the neighbor's view, the teacher's view, the nurse's view, or the social worker's view. Multiple views are needed to assess family stress and the functionality of coping and adaptive strategies.

7. Family crisis is caused by such severe stress that the family cannot function; it is immobilized. When a crisis occurs, the family hits bottom. Hopefully, the family will reach a turning point. This is the point at which the recovery process begins. The family may become even stronger than it was before the crisis occurred.

8. *Family stress, crisis,* and *strain* are different terms and cannot be used synonymously. Family stress means a change in the equilibrium of the family system. It may be a change the family enjoys and seeks out, or it may be a change they would prefer to avoid. In either case, family stress does not necessarily lead to crisis. Strain means the family and its members are approaching their limits for coping and managing, but they are still holding together.

9. The degree of stress is a continuous variable, whereas crisis is a categorical variable.

Note

1. The Serenity Prayer, written by St. Francis of Assisi, represents an attitude toward family stress management that has proven helpful to both men and women experiencing stress for many generations: "God grant me the serenity to accept the things I cannot change, courage to change those things I can, and wisdom to know the difference." People from many Eastern and Western cultures have found this approach to stress management useful.

Discussion Questions

1. Why are women typically responsible for taking care of elderly (or ailing) parents? What evidence suggests that this is, or is not, changing? Do you know of cases that involve men accepting that responsibility? Describe their situations.

2. Early in this chapter, we explained that a particular family can live by rules that are different from those of the larger culture to which it belongs. Provide four specific examples. Discuss the problems this "mismatch" (or incongruity) may cause.

	The Family's Rules	The Larger Culture's Rules	Problems This May Cause
1			
2			
3			
4			

3. Sue and Jim have been married for 40 years. They have two adult children who live nearby. Sue stopped working 5 years ago. Jim retires next month. What stressors might the family experience? What boundary issues might surface and why?

4. Think about a time when you experienced an accumulation of stressor events. Describe what happened. How close together in time were the events? Were they normative events? Why would or wouldn't you categorize them as normative? For each of the stressor events you experienced, identify A, B, C, and X.

5. Why can or can't families live in isolation?

Additional Readings

Berger, R. (2015). *Stress, trauma, and posttraumatic growth: Social context, environment, and identities.* New York, NY: Routledge.
Fiese, B. H., & Spagnola, M. (2007). The interior life of the family: Looking from the inside out and the outside in. In A. S. Masten (Ed.), *Multilevel dynamics in developmental psychopathology: Pathways to the future* (pp. 119–150). Mahwah, NJ: Erlbaum.
Gilligan, R. (2009). Positive turning points in the dynamics of change over the life course. In J. A. Mancini & K. A. Roberto (Eds.), *Pathways of human development: Explorations of change* (pp. 15–34). Lanham, MD: Lexington Books.
Maguire, K. C. (2015). Stress and coping in families: A review and synthesis of the communication research. In L. Turner & R. West (Eds.), *The SAGE handbook of family communication* (pp. 154–169). Thousand Oaks, CA: Sage.
McCubbin, H. I., & Patterson, J. M. (1983). The family stress process: The double ABCX model of adjustment and adaptation. *Marriage & Family Review, 6*(1–2), 7–37.
Moran, C. L. (2014). Stressors, primary and secondary. In W. C. Cockerham, R. Dingwall, & S. T. Quah (Eds.), *The Wiley Blackwell encyclopedia of health, illness, behavior, and society* (pp. 1–3). Chichester, UK: John Wiley & Sons.
Sullivan, K. (2015). An application of family stress theory to clinical work with military families and other vulnerable populations. *Clinical Social Work Journal, 43*(1), 89–97.
Walsh, F. (Ed.). (2012). *Normal family processes: Growing diversity and complexity.* New York, NY: Guilford Press.
Weber, J. G. (2011). *Individual and family stress and crises.* Thousand Oaks, CA: Sage.

3

Multicultural Perspectives of a Universal Stressor

I *was living hundreds of miles away. It had been about 2 or 3 months since I visited my family. It was a good visit, as always. At least twice a week I would communicate with someone in my family—either my sister, my parents, or uncles. Each time, everyone was doing well. We were, and still are, a tight-knit family. One night—and I remember this vividly—I had a peculiar dream. In the dream I heard a noise. I got out of bed, crept into the living room, and peered through the blinds of the patio door. A wolf—gray and white—was standing there scratching the screen. He stopped when he noticed me. We stared at each other for several seconds in silence until he nodded (as though he were nodding goodbye), turned, and slowly walked into the night.*

When I awoke the next morning, I could still clearly recall the dream. Later that day, my mother called and said that she had sad news. Before she spoke another word, I said, "Uncle Roe left us last night." Puzzled, she replied, "Yes, but how did you know? Did you get a call from someone else?" I described the dream to my mother and told her that somehow I knew the wolf was Uncle Roosevelt. I just knew. I knew as IT turned and walked away that HE was "passing on." Oddly enough, my mother was not surprised. She simply said, "Your grandmother used to have dreams like that when a close family member passed." Interestingly, during that conversation neither my mother, nor I, used the words "dead" or "died." Of all of my uncles, I was closest to him. When I was a little girl, he would pick me up from nursery school every day. He willingly stepped in to be my "dad" when my own dad was on active duty in Vietnam. Each afternoon, after I climbed into his huge old truck, he would take a piece of gum out of his shirt pocket and hand it to me—with a smile breaking across the unshaven gray and white stubble covering his face. He remained an active part of my life even after my dad returned home. He and my father (who is still living) were very close and quite similar in the quiet, unassuming way they supported each other and took care of family. (Chalandra Bryant, African American female, reared in a two-parent home that was both highly religious and spiritual.)

The stress from a death in the family is a universal family stressor. Almost everyone will experience this normal life course event, if only as a result of the death of one's parents. If we are truly interested in building resilience after such ubiquitous stress, we cannot limit our view to the individual. Family researchers and therapists have for some time called for a systemic approach to deal with loss and grief (e.g., Boss, 1999, 2002, 2006; Nadeau, 1998; Walsh & McGoldrick, 1991, 2004). Grief researchers also recommend that we improve our systemic approach so that we can work more effectively with families (Neimeyer, 2014).

Although grief is a universal experience, the manner in which it is experienced is not. That is because grief is embedded within a cultural framework. Cultural beliefs and values provide a lens through which our understanding of the world is filtered. There is a great deal of variation across cultures with regard to rituals, expected roles of family members, and types of emotional responses deemed appropriate/inappropriate. This chapter explores ways in which various cultures define death and grieve. Both Western and Eastern cultures are addressed. We highlight how culture may play a more defining role than just religion, because people who share the same religion but are of different cultures may not grieve in the same way. We also explain how culture plays a role in determining who is in and out of the family after a death has occurred. We are not able to cover every culture; however, the examples presented in this chapter should help you to be cognizant of the existence of differences—some stark, some not so stark—in grief across numerous cultural groups.

Although there are countless stressors, we chose to focus on a death in the family and the subsequent grief because we wanted to illustrate cultural differences using a universal stressor. Family stress practitioners and researchers need to know about death because it is perhaps the only universal stressor occurring across cultures, races, class, gender, and generations. Thus, it is critical that we understand the complexities of working with families that are distressed and possibly traumatized by grief. Understanding that our own culture affects our views and values, which, in turn, shape our professional work, is just as critical. For example, Western cultures tend to value individualism rather than collectivism and thus may resonate with individual interventions more than other groups. Wealth (income), status, and privilege have been linked to high levels of mastery (that is, the need to control); however, individuals who are used to being in control tend to have a challenging time dealing with events that are out of their control (e.g., death), despite access to external resources.

The Stress of Grief and Loss From Death

Before we move too far along in this chapter, we need to review a few basic definitions.

Loss implies a deficit. We had something—a close relationship—and now it is gone. If we were attached to the lost person, we ache from the loss. There is a feeling of emptiness whether it be a beloved grandparent, parent, partner, spouse, child, friend, or even a pet. We are bereaved and thus grieving.

What is the difference then between grief and bereavement, and does it matter? Grief is defined as "mental anguish or deep sorrow caused by bereavement" (Boss, 2011, p. 27; New Shorter Oxford English Dictionary,1993). Bereavement is defined as being bereft or deprived (New Shorter Oxford English Dictionary,1993). Thus, grief is the outcome of bereavement or being deprived of a loved one (e.g., feeling abandoned). The two terms are often used interchangeably, but if we pay attention to nuance, grief is an outcome (the feelings and behaviors after loss) while bereavement is the situation of being bereft—for example, losing someone you care about or love. In this chapter, we focus primarily on grief because it is the more universal term and more precisely describes the outcome: loss. Mourning reflects "culture-based practices of demonstrative sorrow observed by people emotionally connected to a person who has died—for example, wearing of black clothing, staying indoors and shading windows, or flying a flag at half-mast" (Schoulte, 2011 p. 12). Grief involves feelings (such as pain) and thoughts of those we have lost.

Grief manifests itself in various ways—as sadness, misery, melancholy, sorrow, and depressive symptoms, but it can also show itself as anger. While these are normal reactions to loss, sometimes clinical depression follows. In any case, however, loss and grief are challenging for families and their individual members.

Death is a common type of loss that causes family stress and grief (Boss, 2006), but because there are other losses that can distress or traumatize families, we emphasize the need to first clarify the *type* of loss in order to determine how to help families manage it and ease their grief. In this chapter, we conceptually clarify loss and grief and their fit within the Contextual Model of Family Stress (CMFS) (see Chapter 2) and provide guidelines to help you work more effectively with families to find meaning in loss rather than seeking closure (Boss, 2006, 2010, 2011; Boss & Carnes, 2012; Boss & Ishii, 2015; Boss & Yeats, 2014).

Cultural Perceptions of Death and Loss

Culture is a social construction that includes numerous factors: identity, beliefs, history, traditions, and religion, to name a few. It is important to note that within any given culture there is much variation in some of these factors. Our culture strongly influences our perceptions and understanding of the world. Because cultures are complex and grief occurs within the context of cultures, grief (coupled with its concomitant cultural nuances) is too complex to be described in a single statement. Truly understanding bereavement in a particular cultural context requires developing an understanding beyond the culture itself. One needs to also explore the juxtaposition between (1) how that culture dictates how an individual should grieve and (2) how the individual is actually grieving (Shapiro, 1996). Is there a good fit between (1) and (2)? Fit sheds light on the degree to which the individual's grief is regulated by others (Walter, 1999). Families even within the same culture can grieve differently, and family members have the power to positively or negatively regulate grief.

Families do not all respond to loss in the same way. Those families in which members provide mutual support, offer comfort, openly share thoughts/feelings, and are strongly bonded as well as highly committed to one another—indicative of cohesion—are likely to prevail during times of loss (Kissane, 2014). Some families block communication; in some families, the members blame one another for the loss or for their circumstances after the loss. Such actions impede natural mourning and ultimately hinder the grief process (Kissane, 2014). Beliefs about death also influence the grief process.

Definitions of Death

Grief varies because people across various cultures experience different realities. This suggests that the definition of death itself may differ across cultures. For example, in the United States, death is considered to have occurred when breathing stops; however, for the Matsigenka of Peru, someone can be considered dead before breathing stops (Shepard, 2002). Glenn Shepard (2002), a medical anthropologist, described an emaciated woman, surrounded by family as she lay bleeding and dying. He tried to explain to the family that a doctor diagnosed the woman with cancer. Shepard then offered to give her medication that would ease the pain. The woman's eldest son told Shepard that there was no point, because "she is already dead" (Shepard, 2002, p. 204). In Oman (the Middle East), just because someone stopped breathing did not mean that they were dead. Instead, they were believed to have been removed from the present by a sorcerer (Al-Adawi, Burjorjee, & Al-Issa, 1997). After the burial had taken place and mourning had ended, it was believed that life could be restored if the sorcery was neutralized.

The very manner in which the dead are viewed varies by culture. Some cultures believe that the dead are a presence among the living, which can be benevolent or malevolent. For example, the Australian Aborigines of the central Cape York Peninsula in northern Queensland believe that the dead are initially a threat because they are on a quest to bring a family member with them into the spirit world; then, over time, as the dead settle, they benignly watch over the living (Smith, 2008).

This notion of "watching" is not uncommon. Believing that the deceased are watching over their families is a way for individuals to resolve the loss. Think about Bryant's story that appeared in the beginning of this chapter. Her narrative account is as much about premonitions as dreaming. Although she was hundreds of miles away from family when her uncle died, she may have been able to resolve the loss and move past her inability to be there with him when he died, because she believes he visited her in a dream to say goodbye. Cultures do not all grieve in the same way. Boss's clinical experiences suggest that almost everyone dreams about loved ones after they are dead and often before, but not all cultures feel free to express and share those dreams.

Resolving Loss

Though definitions of death differ, there are some universals. Resolving loss (or attempting to resolve loss) is a universal (Boss, 2004a). In the 1960s and

1970s, psychiatrist Elisabeth Kübler-Ross wrote about the five linear stages of grief: denial, anger, bargaining, depression, and acceptance. (For more information, see Kübler-Ross, 1969, and Kübler-Ross & Kessler, 2005.) While Kübler-Ross intended these five stages for the dying person who was losing life and *not* the family mourners, the stages were usurped as a model for grieving that would lead to completing the work of grief. If you finished the five stages, your mourning would be finished. Your sadness would be gone. Regrettably, for many, it does not work that way. Kübler-Ross wrote in her last book that even for her, dying was a messy business (Kübler-Ross & Kessler, 2005). She knew that she was dying; as stated in the book's preface (aptly titled "I Am Done"), she alluded to that knowledge: "I know that if I stopped being angry and anxious of my situation and let go, my instincts tell me it would be time for me to die. I am halfway there" (Kübler-Ross & Kessler, 2005, p. xv). She died on August 24, 2004, before the book was published. Surely she would have agreed that for family members left behind, mourning would also be a messy business. It is not a linear process with a clear endpoint.

Although all families, regardless of cultural background, face the universal task of resolving loss (Boss, 2006), *how* this is achieved does, indeed, vary across cultures. Our cultural values guide our perceptions or understanding of the world (Morgan & Laugani, 2002), which can shape how we process information or even how we make decisions upon experiencing a loss (Schoulte, 2011).

Same Religion, Different Culture

While it is helpful to know how certain *religions* view death and grieving (because such knowledge provides insights about a person's grieving), individuals adhering to the major religions vary greatly not only culturally but also in their interpretations of religion, as well as how strongly they adhere to the tenets of their religion (Hays & Hendrix, 2008; Wikan, 1988). Therefore, we cannot assume that groups of people grieve in the same way because they are of the same religion.

Some argue that culture influences one's response to loss more than religion does (Rosenblatt, 2013; Wikan, 1988). Unni Wikan (1988), professor of social anthropology, addressed loss and bereavement among a sample of Egyptian and Balinese Muslims. Although both groups adhere to similar religious principles, their cultures are quite distinct. Religion is not independent of culture; rather, it is a part of culture (Wikan, 1988). Among the poor of Cairo, Egypt, the death of one's child elicits intense, heartfelt grieving. It is not uncommon for mothers to sit listlessly for weeks or months in mourning. This behavior is expected of them. An extreme case that was described to Wikan involved a mother whose child died in a train accident. That mother completely withdrew—no longer speaking, taking care of her other children, or sleeping with her husband—for seven long years. Even though her reaction was extreme, people understood. Different responses were observed in Bali when a child dies. Mothers typically try to hold back the tears. They are reserved, particularly when in the company of people outside of their closest family members and friends.

We cannot ignore culture, religion, family, or individual characteristics. These are core factors that shape beliefs and behaviors. Culture is intricately intertwined with multiple aspects of our lives. A discussion of death with respect to specific cultures follows.

African American

There are significant differences between Western (such as the United States) and Eastern cultures. However, even *within* the United States there are differences. This is not surprising given that so many cultures make up the U.S. population. Most notable are those differences in grieving between African Americans and White Americans. Identity is a salient part of those differences. Identity assessment, which is frequently observed as a component of grieving, refers to the identity of the deceased, the identity of other key individuals who are grieving the loss, and one's own identity. Identity is, in part, about discovering and understanding our history and how we are similar to or different from others, as we discover, accept, or come to terms with where we "fit" or "belong" and where we do not. (We are not suggesting that all African Americans share the exact same identity; there is much diversity within the African American population.)

Despite sharing a great deal of history and even culture in the United States, African Americans and White Americans differ. Experiences of racial discrimination and oppression have shaped the identities of African Americans. Living in a society where they have been historically mistreated and misunderstood has led African Americans to become more vigilant—that is, observant of others, as a protective mechanism (LaVeist, Thorpe, & Pierre, 2014). Thus, when asked to compare their grieving to White Americans' grieving, the differences noted were based upon their observations and experiences. Studies suggest that White Americans may be less open about their feelings, particularly during times of loss. For example, White Americans of Scandinavian descent are likely to adopt a stance of emotional control; similarly, those of Norwegian descent are likely to minimize expressions of excessive anger as well as pleasure (for review, see Tsai & Chentsova-Dutton, 2003). Research also suggests that compared to White Americans, African Americans exhibit greater outward emotional expression (e.g., weeping intensely) when death has occurred (McIllwain, 2002). This corroborates observations that African American funerals are typically longer and more expressive than those of White Americans. These differences are said to be rooted in racial discrimination that is intricately entangled in the grief process. Dealing with racism can be so distressing and consume so much energy that it can intensify or hinder grieving. This is consistent with the Mundane Extreme Environmental Stress (MEES) Model, which is discussed later.

During times of slavery, it was not safe for slaves to exhibit strong emotions. Grieving could not interfere with work because consequences were dire. Expressions of grief served only to let slave owners know how to more effectively exert pain. Moreover, identity was taken away with enslavement.

Paul Rosenblatt and Beverly Wallace (2005; social scientists with interests in family systems and loss) conducted a qualitative study of loss and grief that involved interviewing 26 African Americans (19 women and 7 men).

One study participant said:

> We never really been allowed as African Americans to do that whole [grief] process . . . In Africa we were able to mourn the loss and to grieve. But once we entered the ship and came across the ocean, we were stripped of that right . . . When we came to . . . this country, we lost our identity, and when you don't have an identity you can't associate the grief process . . . My great, great, great grandmother was sold . . . to a man in Mississippi, and she was allowed out of her six children to take three with her . . . Was she allowed to grieve the loss of her husband and her other three children? No . . . (Rosenblatt & Wallace, 2005, p. 162)

Grieving was limited for African Americans during slavery, and it appears that it continues to be limited by the larger U.S. culture. For example, African Americans have often been forced to halt the process of grieving. Outpouring of grief expressed by African Americans has made White police officers and hospital officials feel so uneasy that they have tried to quell it.

Another study participant from the same study said:

> Remember when the young African American man got shot off of West Broadway. His family, their grieving is very demonstrative, right then and there. And the police officers did not know how to handle it. "You better quiet down." Instead of knowing this person is grieving, and it's at the height, so you're telling somebody to quiet down, and they end up arresting the person.
>
>   Interviewer: Because they were crying too loud.
>
>   Right. And they can do that. They can. If some young man gets shot and kins and family are down at the hospital, the hospital staff gets nervous. "Call the police." And so then here you are in pain, and you've got to figure out a way to clamp this down so that you won't go to jail. Or if you want to grieve, you can't, because you gotta try and pull everybody together so that nobody goes to jail because they're hurting. So, that's the racism part. It's where folks don't know what to do, don't know how to treat it. They act like there's something wrong with you because you're hurt that somebody's gone. (Rosenblatt & Wallace, 2005, pp. 163–164)

Let's not dismiss these differences as stereotyping. Understanding these differences might explain and improve race relations. Understanding these differences might help a clinician treat a client or even intercede on behalf of a grieving client who is being asked to remain silent by hospital staff or other authorities. So, let's consider why African Americans experience grief in the manner described.

African Americans are less likely to distinguish between extended family members and nuclear family members; thus, the loss of what some cultures may have considered a peripheral family member elicits profound emotion among African Americans (Laurie & Neimeyer, 2008). African Americans are less likely to use hospice or palliative care services (Matsuyama et al., 2011); instead, they typically provide the required care for ailing family members.

The time spent together draws them emotionally closer, which can make the loss and grief more intense. The emotional and physical energy needed to provide the care also leads to a flood of emotions when the loss finally occurs. Knowing how deeply the dying family member suffered in life (experiences of unfair treatment, discrimination) can also intensify grief as remaining family members reflect upon what was and what could have been.

Interestingly, as alluded to earlier, racial discrimination is also a factor contributing to the stifling of emotions (Rosenblatt & Wallace, 2005). Perhaps these experiences can be explained using the MEES model, according to which racism is a continuous, contextual variable in the lives of African Americans (Peters & Massey, 1983; Pierce, 1970, 1974). Sometimes this stress is overt, and sometimes it is subtle. It is referred to as mundane (M) because this stress is very common in the lives of African Americans. It is extreme (E) because it has a severe impact on how African Americans view the world and themselves. It is environmental (E) because it is generated and fostered by the environment. Lastly, stress (S) refers to the energy-consuming efforts required to deal with racism. One interviewee (in Rosenblatt & Wallace's 2005 study) reported difficulties grieving the loss of her mother because dealing with racism was so distressing and all-consuming. Her description fits the MEES model.

Identity, which is rooted within a sociohistorical context, shapes how grief is experienced. Reactions we get from others can influence the grief experience. Being asked to quell one's weeping may lead to the quelling of emotions and thus the quelling of the grief process.

Asian

Generally speaking, Asian families are usually characterized by hierarchies, filial piety (respect for one's parents, elders, and ancestors), a strong concern about shame, and limited emotional expression (Mondia, Hichenberg, Kerr, & Kissane, 2012); however, like most groups, there is a great deal of within group variation among Asians. They differ in terms of ethnic origin (for example, China, India, Cambodia, Japan, Malaysia, Vietnam, Thailand, Philippine Islands, Pakistan), traditions, and religious practices and beliefs. Therefore, within each of the aforementioned groups, there is a great deal of diversity. In the sections that follow, a few specific groups are described.

Chinese

Practices involving and beliefs about death may vary greatly even across Chinese individuals in different communities (Chow & Chan, 2006). For instance, while the Chinese in Hong Kong would generally prefer to die in a hospital, those in Taiwan would generally prefer to die at home (for review, see Chow & Chan, 2006). Hong Kong is known as a point where "East meets West"; consequently, many death/dying/bereavement professionals infuse knowledge of the West in their practices. Some families hire Taoist monks or chanters to pray for the spirit of the departed in an effort to prevent the departed from going to hell (Lee & Chan, 2004).

Because immortality is a salient component of rituals, assurances that the departed will not exist in an impoverished spiritual world are made by burning paper houses and paper money as well as other material goods (Chow & Chan, 2006). Food (e.g., fruit, fowl) is offered to ward off hunger. Sometimes, professional mourners are hired as a means of showing how much family members are grieving. The children and spouse of the departed are expected to cry (Tanner, 1995).

Some sources (see Chow & Chan, 2006) suggest that people stop visiting after the burial, because the house in which the person died is believed to emit bad energy ("qi"). This suggests that network members avoid a family when that family is in need of support. Why? Chow and Chan (2006) explain that in "old rural communities in China, a significant number of deaths might have been caused by infectious diseases" (p. 5). Therefore, "the bad qi around the family of someone who died might have been bacteria and virus that may spread infection and illness" (Chow & Chan, 2006, p. 5). Although in modern Chinese cities, few die of infections, there is still reluctance to venture near a home in which someone died. Chow and Chan (2006) note that the 2003 Severe Acute Respiratory Syndrome (SARS) outbreak in Toronto was a reminder of the "possibility of infection at funeral services" (p. 5; also see Tyshenko & Paterson, 2010).

Many of the aforementioned practices are not espoused by Buddhists. Buddhists, instead, believe in karma and reincarnation (Lee & Chan, 2004). Monks gather and chant before a Buddhist dies; the chanting is believed to assist the dying.

Filipino

The notion of shame and losing face is evident in the Filipino culture. For example, *hiya* is a concept in Filipino culture denoting fear of perceived inferiority or embarrassment; this can impede the desire to share feelings (Tiu & Seneriches, 1995). Pride and a strong sense of masculinity are expected to characterize Filipino men (Nadal, 2009). In this case, mothers may instruct their sons to remain quiet rather than cry during bereavement.

Japanese

Among the Japanese, a vestige of "ie seido," the patriarchal family household system promoted by the Meiji government (1868–1911), is the existence of family graves in modern-day Japan. Traditionally, a gravestone bears a family name and one patrilineal line is the only successor to that grave. The wife of the successor is buried in her husband's family grave (see Nakamatsu, 2009, for review). A 2002 government survey revealed that over 75% of survey participants believed that ancestral graves should not only be protected but also handed down to a child; however, some members of younger generations are not as supportive of this custom.

Tomoko Nakamatsu, a professor of Asian Studies (2009), conducted a study of the custom. Twenty-three Japanese women in their 50s and 60s, from the semirural area of Wakayama, were interviewed in 2003. All of the women indicated that their religion was Buddhism. Nakamatsu focused specifically on grave-tending. Grave-tending (or gravesite maintenance) is a form of unpaid domestic labor tied to the role of wife, and it is also a religious practice. Because community members keep a close watch over this task, wives do not want to leave their sites untidy. One participant, a wife in her early 60s who goes to her husband's family grave once a week to clear the area and change the flower offerings, wants the obligation to end. She, therefore, wants her own ashes as well as those of her husband, scattered somewhere rather than being buried in the family grave.

Another participant, a woman who had been divorced for 15 years, obtained the right to use a gravesite in a community-owned cemetery, next to her biological family's ancestral gravesite. She could not use her family's grave even though she was using her maiden name again and served as caregiver for her elderly father. Instead, the grave will later belong to her brother and his line of descendants. At the time one applies for the use of a public cemetery, one must typically already have possession of the ashes in need of burial. This stipulation makes it challenging for childless individuals who want to plan ahead and prepare for their own burial (Makimura, 1996, as cited in Nakamatsu, 2009). There were also succession rules that applied even to public cemeteries in Tokyo Metropolis. This means that until the reform of cemetery laws in 1993, the first born son was granted priority (see Nakamatsu, 2009 for review).

Yet another participant in Nakamatsu's study, a woman in her 50s, and also a divorcee, expressed ambivalent feelings about the family grave. For several generations, members of her biological family "house" had been village leaders. She had been raised as the successor of the house because she had no male siblings. She was proud to serve in that role and was quite thankful to her ancestors, given her family's esteemed history; however, she was a feminist, and as such, she also felt burdened by the role. She understood that the practice of family grave-tending is embedded in a patriarchal system, but as an advocate for gender equality in other aspects of her life (i.e., work), she was left feeling conflicted. Her privileged heritage, as reflected by the family grave, had shaped her identity.

Korean

Soo-Young Kwon, a professor of theology, was prompted to write about funeral traditions when his father died while visiting him in the United States, and he had to transport the body back to Korea. Koreans prefer not to embalm the deceased, but Kwon had to forgo that tradition in order to abide by the regulations stipulated when shipping human remains to another country (Kwon, 2006). While describing the experience of burying his father, Kwon shared what typically happens in Korea.

In Korea, as soon as there is news of a loved one's death, mourners begin visiting the deceased's home for about 3 days (known as *samiljang*), eating and reminiscing (Kwon, 2006; Mills, 2012). An old custom involves the use of a Korean folk singer (called *sorikkoon*) who would take the lead singing dirges.

The funeral is not meant to serve as a farewell ritual. Koreans believe that the body of the deceased holds three spirits. The spirits separate from each other upon death: one stays in the body, one moves on to the "other world," and the third is symbolically kept in a box—a spirit box (Kwon, 2006; Kyu, 1984). The spirit box, along with an ancestor tablet (symbol representing ancestors) is traditionally placed in the mourning shrine at home (Kwon, 2006). The "other world" is believed to be an extended reality of our world; it is not a disconnected realm. Family members place some of their favorite items and some of the deceased's favorite items in the coffin. Although fewer Koreans keep a spirit box in their home today, some still feel that the spirits of their ancestors exist in this world with them.

Nepalese

For some cultural rituals, an actual body is needed. For example, in Nepal, the body must be buried or burned in order to ensure the passing of the soul. If proof of death (but no body) is provided, then among some cultures of Nepal, an effigy of grass can be used. Cultural rituals were not able to take place when the deaths of the disappeared were ambiguous (Robins, 2010). (See Chapter 4 for information about ambiguous loss.) The inability of wives (through no fault of their own) to comply with the aforementioned cultural rituals is stigmatizing. These women must learn how to cope with their loss while surrounded by individuals requesting proof of death.

The role one's sex plays in Nepal is significant in life and in death. The fate of a woman—that is, her position in a family after the death of her spouse and sometimes her burial site—is often in the hands of other people.

Although there are many differences between each of the aforementioned groups, there are similarities in beliefs, rituals, and traditions. Keep in mind though, that even within the same family, beliefs may differ.

Peruvian

According to anthropologists and archeologists (interested in pre-Hispanic mortuary rituals in Peru), native Andeans believed that the dead actively participated in the world, and consequently the living and dead were in close contact with each other (Klaus & Tam, 2015). In both early and contemporary Andean societies, the physical remains of ancestors are a crucial component of social functioning.

Let's take the inhabitants of Huaquirea, a district of Antabamba in Peru for example. There it is believed that the condition of the corporeal body is both a reflection of and reflects the condition of the soul. Kind and caring protectors (called *khuyaqkuna*) are a consequence of duly attended dry bones; whereas, a decomposing corpse is brought forth from (reanimated by) a sinful person (Allen, 2002; Nystrom, Buikstra, & Muscutt, 2010). The heat of the afterlife renders the soul into a hard, dry seed. That seed signifies agriculture, which signifies food, and that ultimately signifies life. The seed also reflects "the animating water of life expelled from the dead body in the heat of the afterlife that feeds the seed" (Nystrom et al., 2010, p. 478; cited from Gose, 1994). The connection between the living and the dead is symbolized by the creation of that hard, dry seed. Human remains, which are also hard and dry (as mummies or bones), are similar to the hard seed.

The strong belief in the connection between the living and the dead clearly cuts across many cultures. However, cultures differ in *how* the connection is manifested.

Irish

In 2013, about 33.3 million U.S. residents claimed Irish ancestry, reflecting more than seven times the population of Ireland, which is only 4.6 million (U.S. Census Bureau News, 2015). Irish is one of the most frequently reported ancestries in the United States, second only to German (U.S. Census Bureau News, 2015).

Some Irish still believe in the old customs. Traditionally, the Irish have believed that windows should be open at the time of death so the spirit can leave. Wake and funeral attendance were even expected of estranged individuals (Dezell, 2000; McGoldrick, 2004). The body was not left alone until burial; hence, nightlong vigils occurred, during which time jokes and stories about the deceased person were shared. Even during wakes, the Irish may express little sorrow and may instead engage in joking and storytelling. Thus, it was not unusual for wakes to be livelier or cheerier than weddings (Evans, 1957; Suilleabhain, 1967). (It is important to note that deaths of children or young adults or other traumatic losses were not dealt with in this manner.) As part of the funeral ceremony, usually mourners and the hearse would drive past various places the departed spent time, such as places lived and schools attended (McGoldrick, 2004).

A recurring theme across cultures is reminiscing and sharing stories about the deceased, which is a way to honor them. While most cultures honor their deceased, *how* they do so may differ across groups. Recall such examples as grave-tending, burning paper money and paper houses, and singing dirges.

Jewish

Although the level of religious observance varies within each of the major types of Judaism (Orthodox, Conservative, Reform, and Reconstructionist), many Jewish individuals engage in traditional mourning processes in similar ways (Petkov, 2004). Upon death, the departed is typically not left alone until burial (similar to the Irish) (McGoldrick, 2004). A *shomer*, or guardian, remains with the body reciting prayers (Getzel, 2000). Burial usually occurs within 24 to 48 hours. A prompt burial not only relieves strain for the mourners, it is also believed to help the soul separate from the body and find peace. A trained burial society, the chevra kadish, washes and dresses (in simple white garment or shroud) the body for burial (Ponn, 2001).

Cremation and embalming are typically avoided. Simple unlined wooden coffins are traditionally used to facilitate the natural effects of decomposition.

The coffin usually remains closed during the funeral, as gazing upon the departed is considered disrespectful; however, if a family member is having a difficult time coping with the reality of the death, viewing the body may be deemed beneficial. Viewing the body may also occur if several years have passed since family members have seen the departed, and they request a chance to say goodbye. After the graveside ceremony, 7 days of mourning, known as *shiva*, ensues. During this period, mourners remain in the house surrounded by the departed's belongings. To help promote deep mourning, no attention can be paid to physical appearance; hence, mirrors in the home are covered. The goal is to focus on the loss. Neighbors and friends provide food daily and visit. Generally, the setting is reflective and solemn (Petkov, 2004).

Again, we see the theme of honor; that is, honoring the deceased, as the focus is on the loss, not self—hence the covering of mirrors. Another theme that appears to cut across many groups is the sharing of food. As learned earlier, some cultures do not consider a deceased loved one as "out of the family" since some people still talk to their ancestors.

Identity and Status in One's Family After a Death

We defined *family* in Chapter 1 as a system of interacting persons bound together by shared goals, beliefs, and rituals; physical presence; psychological presence; and shared genes. Those are common elements used to define family. One's identity or status in one's family after the death of a family member can be influenced by one's culture. Let's explore how this can happen.

One of the most impoverished countries in Asia is Nepal. Many cultures and ethnicities reside there. The high caste Hindu culture influences and dominates the indigenous and lower castes, which has resulted in the conversion of non-Hindu groups to Hinduism (Robins, 2010). This is a place where people typically marry within caste as well as ethnicity, and multiple generations of family members share a home. Women are subservient; it is through marriage that women are granted social acceptance and access to property (Axinn, 1992). Married women typically put red powder (*sindhur*) in their hair and wear bangles, thereby making their status quite visible. Women as wives (and daughters) have clear positions in the highly codified Hindu society. Among higher castes, the death of a husband—widowhood—is viewed as a "social death" for a woman. Her sindhur is removed, and her bangles are broken (Chakravarti, 2006, as cited in Robins, 2010). In some indigenous groups, it is not unusual for widows to marry their husband's younger brother, but remarriage is shameful in Hindu tradition (Robins, 2010). True widows (husbands' deaths have been confirmed) typically must wear a white sari (Alexander & Regier, 2011); they have a clear status, but that status is low.

Deaths and disappearances elicit slightly different reactions. When a woman's husband disappears, the ambiguity of her position can cause problems. Some wives of missing husbands continue to wear the sindhur and bangles; they do so because since there is no body, they have hope—hope that their husbands will return. Younger women with no children are more likely to leave and remarry but face the "stigma of remarriage as a betrayal of both the family and her husband" (Robins, 2010, p. 260). Families often limit the movement of these women as a means of curtailing their ability to search for a new husband. This means that a wife of a deceased husband can be trapped in a family that not only does not want her there but also does not want her to leave because if she left, social stigma would befall the family. Thus, such a wife (if she has few alternatives) may be stuck in a hostile household as a result of a husband's disappearance. Although the status of widows (true widows) is low, women whose husbands are missing have no status.

Again, we see the impact that one's gender can have on one's fate. Upon death of a husband, a wife's position and identity itself within a family can change.

Contextual factors shape beliefs and practices. They may even influence the management of a stressor. When providing professional help to individuals who are experiencing a death in the family, their cultural context must be taken into consideration.

Applying the Contextual Model of Family Stress to This Universal Stressor

It is essential that professionals and scholars have a theoretical map that is inclusive of diversity. Of course, it cannot be a theory of everything, but it must be more than a theory for one group of people. Theory has to guide us in easing the stress of families from any culture, community, neighborhood, or family. It must help us ease the stress for any person, regardless of race or religion, color or creed, gender or generation.

When working with a grieving individual, couple, family, or group of families, professionals and researchers will find it useful to consider the CMFS as a heuristic map to guide their work. Whether one works preventively or clinically, educationally or therapeutically, or as a researcher, it is helpful to apply this mapping. Begin by specifying each of the factors in the model for a family *after a member has died.*

A Factor: Consider, as an example, the death of a loved one—specifically, an officially validated death with visible remains or DNA proof of death. The A factor then is listed as "a clear and verified death." Death is a stressor event, but stressor events are classified in different ways—for example, normative, predictable, unexpected, ambiguous, clear, and so on. (Recall Table 2.1, *Classifications of Stressor Events and Situations.*) Thus, the death of an elderly grandparent, while difficult, is usually more expected than the death of a child; the death of a loved one from a known terminal illness may be more easily understood than unexplainable and sudden deaths caused by murder or suicide. While this chapter does not deal with ambiguous loss (see Chapter 4), we make the point here that even when officially verified, some deaths are more ambiguous than others.

B Factor: This refers to a family's resources that may be called upon to help them cope with or manage the death and ongoing grief. Resources can reside in the individual, couple, family, or community. With a clear death, community and religious rituals and symbols are usually ready to help the bereaved family members know what to do and know who will be there to support them. Depending on the family's culture and beliefs, there is a script to follow that helps in times of death.

C Factor: This refers to perceptions of the stressor event or situation. These include individual as well as collective perceptions. Individual family members may see the loss differently—some may have been close to the deceased, while others not, so conflicting views often add to the family's stress. Yet the resource of support from others in the community (clergy, friends) may help assuage the stress of disagreement at this fragile time. Perceptions of the bereaved often differ from those of professionals or researchers who are observing them—as outsiders looking in—especially if the outsiders are of a different culture. The differing perceptions can lead professionals and researchers to misunderstand what keeps families resilient despite the pain of loss from death. Regardless of our training, we can miss the signs of human resilience in cultures other than our own.

X Factor: The X factor is the outcome of the stressor. The outcome of the stressor is expected to vary over time, as we hope to see the family gradually build its resilience to manage the stress of loss rather than continue to be immobilized by it. The goal of the outcome is not for the family to get over their grief but rather to learn to live with it, integrate it into their lives, and move forward with their lives.

The degree of stress (X factor outcome) depends primarily on the meaning the loss has for the family. The goal is to prevent family estrangement and cutoffs due to differing perceptions. For example, if the loss is due to unexpected murder or unexpected suicide versus the expected loss of a 90-year-old grandparent who lived a good life, finding meaning is more challenging, if not impossible. On the other hand, the loss of an elder, like a 90-year-old grandparent, may elicit more intense emotions among some cultures if he or she was seen as the elder guiding the family. For example, for Bryant, Uncle Roosevelt was one of the elder uncles, and as such, his counsel was sought and valued by nuclear and extended family members.

Where Is the Field Now?

For the researchers, therapists, and educators who focus on *the social and relational context of family loss and grief*, the following should be emphasized:

First, families can live with grief from the death of a loved one and still thrive. There is no need to "get over it" (Boss & Carnes, 2012). Grief has ups and downs across time, with the periods of sadness (downs) surfacing farther and farther apart but never vanishing completely (Bonanno, 2009; Kissane, 2003, 2011). Living with loss and grief is less stressful than trying to "get over it." Many family members dislike the term "acceptance." They say that they will never "accept" a loved one's death; instead, they eventually find some peace in it. Helping professionals should be mindful of offending language as they work with bereaved families. Ask rather than tell.

Second, the work of bereaved families lies in finding their natural resilience, a necessity for living with the inevitable losses that occur across the life cycle. The goal then is to gain enough resilience to manage the grief over time, as it resurfaces with varying levels of intensity. With this new focus on resilience, professionals look for flexibility plus growth. Families can actually grow stronger relationally and emotionally after having suffered the tragedy of loss. This is evidence of resilience.

The third emphasis involves using family and community approaches to ease the stress and pain of loss and grief. Family- and community-based interventions may ease family stress after crises and disasters (for overviews see Brymer, Steinberg, Watson, & Pynoos, 2012; Landau, 2013; Miller, 2012).

That is where the field is now. In our last chapter, we discuss where the field is headed, as well as factors researchers, therapists, and educators should consider when helping families that are experiencing stress.

Conclusion

We approached this chapter with caution and encourage readers to do so as well. That is, we do not want our description of cultural differences to be construed as rigid stereotypes, nor do we want to suggest that tendencies of any given group are observed only in that group, because those tendencies or characteristics could possibly be observed in other cultures or across individuals in other cultures. Our intent was to expose readers to various characteristics that may be encountered across a diverse group of families. Keep in mind that expressions of grief differ between groups as well as within groups. Factors such as acculturation, religion, gender/sex, age, ethnic/racial identity, family structure, and socioeconomic status (to name a few) may contribute to within-group variations. There are a number of ways that counselors may diagnose clients incorrectly. Be wary of these pitfalls: (1) neglecting to consider that there may be medical (psychological, physical) reasons for atypical grieving, (2) pathologizing culture-based behaviors, and (3) presuming too many of the behaviors are a consequence of cultural differences (Danieli & Nader, 2006).

Summary

This chapter addressed death and how death and grief are experienced across cultures. Death is a universal event that can generate family stress and grief. Grief is also universal and manifests itself in a variety of ways such as sadness, depression, misery, and even anger. Grief varies, however, as people across cultures experience it differently. For example, recall our introductory story—a dream. Most people dream about deceased loved ones, but the level of ease with which those dreams are shared differs across cultures. There is even variability across individuals who are of the same religion. Overall, neither culture, religious affiliation, family values, nor individual characteristics can be overlooked when helping people who have experienced the loss of a family member.

Points to Remember

1. Culture is intricately intertwined with multiple aspects of our lives.

2. Grief is embedded within a cultural framework.

3. Grief and bereavement are not interchangeable. Grief is an outcome (the feelings and behaviors after loss), and bereavement is the situation of being bereft or deprived.

4. Grief is mental anguish or sorrow caused by bereavement.

5. Rituals and beliefs differ across cultures, and members of a given culture are likely to hold similar beliefs and practice similar rituals, but that does not mean that all members of a given culture will agree with those beliefs or practices.

6. Family composition and where family boundaries are positioned are determined to a large extent by one's culture and ethnicity. Individuals adhering to the major religions vary in their interpretations of religion, as well as how strongly they adhere to the tenets of their religion.

Discussion Questions

1. What role does your identity play in your grief?

2. What words or phrases does your family or your culture use when a loved one ceases living (e.g., died, passed on, passed away, no longer with us)? What special meaning do those words or phrases hold for your family?

3. Think about your own cultural and familial background. What rituals did your parents and grandparents engage in when a close family member died? Do you still honor those rituals? Why, or why not?

4. Identify two or three different cultures. What funeral rituals or beliefs do they have in common? Are there more similarities or more differences?

Additional Readings

Agee, J. (1957). *A death in the family*. New York, NY: Penguin Books.

Burke, L. A., Neimeyer, R. A., & McDevitt-Murphy, M. E. (2010). African American homicide bereavement: Aspects of social support that predict complicated grief, PTSD, and depression. *OMEGA, 61*(1), 1–24.

Dose, A., Carey, E., Rhudy, L. M., Chiu, Y., Frimannsdottir, K., Ottenberg, A., & Koenig, B. (2015). Dying in the hospital: Perspectives of family members. *Journal of Palliative Care, 31*(1), 13–20.

Dyregrov, K., Dyregrov, A., & Johnsen, I. (2013–2014). Positive and negative experiences from grief group participation: A qualitative study. *OMEGA, 68*(1), 45–62.

Ghesquiere, A. (2013–2014). "I was just trying to stick it out until I realized that I couldn't": A phenomenological investigation of support seeking among older adults with complicated grief. *OMEGA, 68*(1), 1–22.

Hodges (IV), S. J., & Leonard, K. (2011). *Grieving with hope: Finding comfort as you journey through loss*. Grand Rapids, MI: Baker Books.

Ko, E., Cho, S., Perez, R. L., Yeo, Y., & Palomino, H. (2013). Good and bad death: Exploring the perspectives of older Mexican Americans. *Journal of Gerontological Social Work, 56*(1), 6–25.

Kübler-Ross, E., & Kessler, D. (2000). *Life lessons: Two experts on death and dying teach us about the mysteries of life and living.* New York, NY: Scribner.

Neimeyer, R. A., Prigerson, H. G., & Davies, B. (2002). Mourning and meaning. *American Behavioral Scientist, 46*(2), 235–251.

Randolph, A. L., Hruby, B. T., & Sharif, S. (2015). Counseling women who have experienced pregnancy loss: A review of the literature. *Adultspan Journal, 14*(1), 2–10.

Film

Doillon, J. (Director, Screen Writer), & Gozlan, C. (Executive Producer). (1996). *Ponette* [Motion Picture]. France: Les Films Alain Sarde, Rhone-Alpes Cinema, et al.

4

Ambiguous Loss

A Major Stressor

Pauline Boss coined the term *ambiguous loss*. Her earliest work was on "psychological father absence in intact families" (1973), then on boundary ambiguity in families of soldiers missing in action (1975b, 1977, 1980b; Boss & Greenberg, 1984), and finally on ambiguous loss (1987, 1991, 1999, 2004a, in press). While boundary ambiguity was operationalized by roles and membership in what family social scientists Kingsbury and Scanzoni (1993) called "neo-structure functionalism," since the 1990s, Boss and others have focused on the broader construct, ambiguous loss. To clarify each construct, we have devoted a chapter to each. We discuss ambiguous loss in Chapter 4, followed by boundary ambiguity in Chapter 5.

When a family member's absence or presence is unclear, the stressor event or situation is called *ambiguous loss*. It is the A factor in Figure 4.1. How the family as a whole and its individual members perceive the situation is called *boundary ambiguity*, a construct that belongs under the C factor in Figure 4.1.

While the goal of ambiguous loss is meaning, the goal of boundary ambiguity is structural. That is, the goal of work with ambiguous loss is to find some meaning in the absence of facts, whereas the goal with boundary ambiguity is to clarify family membership and roles, who is in or out of the family and who does what in the family. To decide which construct is of interest to you and relevant to your particular work, we recommend that you read both Chapters 4 and 5 and then decide which best fits your needs at this time. (Also see Boss, 1992, 2004b, 2006, 2007a).

***

Figure 4.1   Where Ambiguous Loss and Boundary Ambiguity Fit Into the Contextual Model of Family Stress

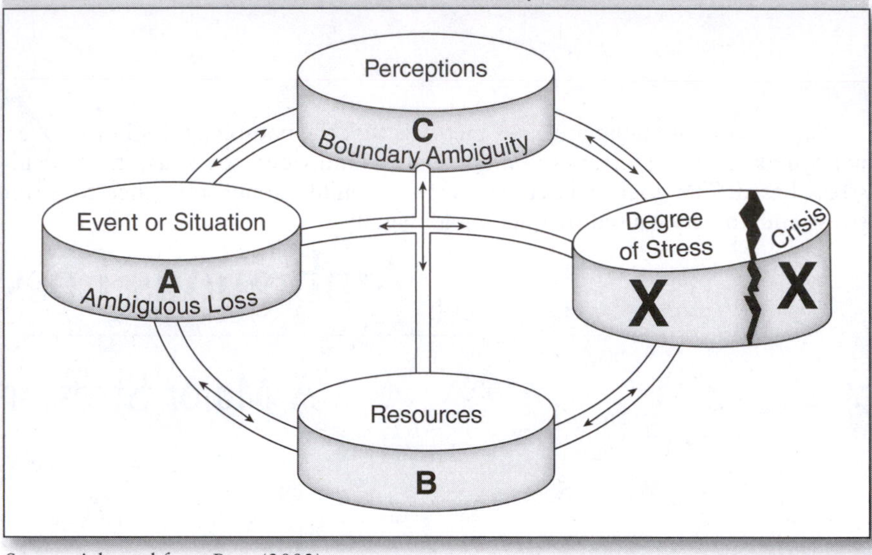

Source: Adapted from Boss (2002).

Ambiguous Loss Theory

Here are two stories: The first illustrates physical ambiguous loss, and the second illustrates psychological ambiguous loss.

Computer scientist and Turing Award winner Jim Gray sailed out of San Francisco Bay on January 28, 2007 and has not been seen since. No debris from the red sailboat was ever found nor is there any proof of death. His family and colleagues in the computer industry still do not know what happened to him. (Silberman, 2007)

Country singer legend Glen Campbell continued singing on tour with his family despite growing dementia from Alzheimer's disease. In 2015, he sang his final words to the world: "I'm still here but yet I'm gone." He recognized his own ambiguous loss. His family and fans learned from his public acknowledgment and gained strength from his ability to keep singing as long as he did. (Silverman, 2007; Albert & Keach, 2014)

Ambiguous loss is a loss that remains unclear and thus without closure. Unlike verifiable death, there is no official validation that any loss has occurred. The family is left in a limbo of confusion and unanswered questions. Ambiguous loss is a complicated loss, with reactions similar to those of complicated grief (Shear et al., 2011). This means that the frozen grief of ambiguous loss (Boss, 1999) may be easily misconstrued as a personal disorder. With ambiguous loss, however, the loss itself remains unresolved, sometimes for years. The family's grief continues not because of psychiatric weakness but rather because of the ambiguity of loss. The pathology lies in the persisting ambiguity, not the family.

Ambiguous loss is a relational phenomenon. That is, one cannot experience ambiguous loss unless previously attached to the missing person. Because attachment is a prerequisite, ambiguous loss is an inherent part of family relationships.

Premise

The premise of ambiguous loss theory is that the pathology lies in the external context of ambiguity, not in individual or family deficits. Thus, the model is stress based. The goal of interventions is to build enough resilience to lower stress and anxiety caused by ongoing ambiguity.

With ambiguous loss, family members have few options: to hold out for the truth or to develop a new narrative they can live with. In the absence of truth, we hope for the latter. To do this requires increasing the tolerance for living with unanswered questions. Without definitive information to clarify the loss, many learn to live well within the paradox of absence and presence (Boss, 2006).

To repeat, ambiguous loss centers on meaning, while boundary ambiguity centers on structure. There are thus essential differences in assessment or measurement. Here we briefly discuss the general aspects of assessment regarding ambiguous loss.

Because ambiguity is difficult to quantify, ambiguous loss has been assessed primarily with phenomenology or with qualitative methods. Yet some researchers have quantified some aspects of ambiguous loss—for example, outcome or length of time missing (Robins, 2010, 2014). Family gerontologists Blieszner, Roberto, Wilcox, Barham, and Winston (2007) found that using a combination of qualitative and quantitative measures provided a more accurate assessment of the meaning and outcome of ambiguous loss experiences. Although their study was of older families with mild cognitive impairment, studying people of any age or type of ambiguous loss may benefit from multiple methods. However, this requires a team that has competence in both quantitative and qualitative methods as well as in clinical practice. For recent examples of researchers who tested the theory of ambiguous loss with various populations and situations, and with various methodologies, see the special issue of *Journal of Family Theory and Review* (Blume, in press). For more examples, see Additional Readings, this chapter.

Types of Ambiguous Loss

There are two types of ambiguous loss. The first type is *physical ambiguous loss (Type I),* which occurs when a loved one is physically absent but kept psychologically present because there is no assurance of death or permanent loss; that is, "Gone but not for sure." Catastrophic examples include missing persons due to war; terrorism; ethnic cleansing; genocide; disappearances (sea, air, land); or natural disasters such as tsunamis, earthquakes, mudslides, and floods. More common examples of physical absence with psychological presence are military deployments, giving up a child for adoption, not knowing who your birth parents are, being placed in foster care, divorce, desertion, or leaving family behind after immigration. More recently, researchers have added gender transitioning to this list as some families feel they lost the loved one they thought they had; at the same time, the transitioning person may feel as if *they* have lost their family (Norwood, 2012, 2013a, 2013b; Wahlig, 2015). You may think of other examples.

The second type is *psychological ambiguous loss (Type II)*. This stressor situation occurs when a person to whom you are attached is physically present but psychologically absent; that is, "Here but not here." Catastrophic examples are Alzheimer's disease and other dementias, traumatic brain injury, autism, serious chronic mental illness, and addictions. More common examples are serious preoccupations with computer games, the Internet, or work. The person is physically present but psychologically unavailable to others at that time.

Both types of ambiguous loss can occur simultaneously to one person or family. For example, after 9/11 in New York City, a woman had a missing husband at the same time she was caring for her mother who had Alzheimer's disease. Some children who had a missing parent said that they lost *both* of their parents on 9/11 (Boss, Beaulieu, Wieling, Turner, & LaCruz, 2003). What they meant was that their remaining parent was so depressed that they also seemed "gone" even though they were physically present at home with them (Boss et al., 2003).

With both types of ambiguous loss, the ambiguity continues as long as there is no definitive information about the whereabouts or fate of the absent person. The sailor is never found; the dementia deepens. A child is autistic; a soldier disappears. Ambiguous losses often remain mysteries that enable families to keep a sliver of hope that the missing person may reappear. To add to the confusion, sometimes they do.

Effects of Ambiguous Loss

Regardless of the type of ambiguous loss, it is the ambiguity that immobilizes family processes. With no rituals of support for losses other than death, families are left on their own to cope. Isolation increases as friends and neighbors don't know what to do or say to the families of the missing. For these reasons, ambiguous loss is viewed as a systemic relational rupture and not a psychiatric condition (Boss, 2006, 2012a). Processes of decision making, coping, and grieving are frozen (Boss, 1999). People are stuck because they are in the dark about what is happening. While ambiguous loss is a family variable, it is systemic at multiple levels, and we must pay attention to each level.

Individual Level

For individuals, ambiguity freezes the grief process (Boss, 1999) and prevents cognition, thus blocking processes of coping and decision making. In not having definitive information, people are immobilized with feelings of helplessness, hopelessness, and confusion that may continue for years, even across the generations. The lack of information and "not knowing" can create a chronic hyper vigilance, anxiety, anxious attachment, chronic sorrow, or depressive symptoms (Boss, Roos, & Harris, 2011).

What to do? If this occurs, the individual should find someone to talk with—a professional, a peer, or another family member. Also, others in the family should take notice and talk with that person, offer help, and if needed, go with him or her to a professional therapist or counselor. Negative thoughts and feelings about a missing person are normal but wanting to act on them is not. Seeking retribution, for example, only compounds the pain of kidnapping.

Family Level

On the family level, ambiguous loss ruptures relationships and freezes or blocks coping, decision making, and grief processes (Boss, 1999, 2006, 2011). In the absence of facts, family members typically disagree on how they see the situation of loss so conflict tends to increase; the incongruence among perceptions becomes a trigger for dissent. Some see the loss as temporary; others see it as final. Still others want to wait and see. Without intervention, permanent family alienations and cutoffs may result. In addition, the family often cancels holiday rituals, gatherings, and celebrations, thinking that this is the proper thing to do. The family then becomes even more isolated and is without the human connection so essential to their resilience.

What to do? We highly recommend that families continue their usual celebrations and rituals, albeit with modifications. A wedding may take place at a nursing home chapel so as to include a frail grandparent; birthday celebrations may be moved in time and place to accommodate the loss situation. Flexibility is the key to continuing the rituals and celebrations that are the core of family life, even in times of adversity.

Community Level

Because of the ambiguity surrounding the loss, there may be little or no community support. Friends and neighbors are uncomfortable with lingering sadness and grief and instead may seek closure. Well-meaning people may do this in either of two extremes: They may treat the ambiguous loss like a death in the family, or they may ignore or deny it as if nothing has happened. Neither of these extremes is helpful to families of the missing.

What to do? Community members must acknowledge the stress that families of the missing are experiencing. They can best do this with memorialization (Robins, 2014) or a gathering of flowers or other symbols or a person-to-person acknowledgment of their ambiguous loss with a simple "I am so sorry." Neighbors, colleagues, and friends must provide support as they might for a death in the family (bringing food, driving, helping with chores) but should not push the family for closure. Telling them to get over it or to consider the lost person as dead is cruel. Rather, staying with a simple, "I am so sorry," while intentionally increasing their own tolerance for ambiguity is best.

Being a supportive community member means visiting a neighbor who is ill, helping a caregiver who is overwhelmed with work, or simply remembering those who went missing in war or other disappearances. What families need to know is that others in their community recognize their unique kind of loss and are patient with them, as the grief from ambiguous loss often has no end point.

Core Assumptions for Working With Ambiguous Loss

As we stated in Chapter 1, we need to know the assumptions embedded in any theory before we can determine if it will be useful in guiding our work or research. The following are the assumptions for working with ambiguous loss (Boss, 2004b, 2007b, in press).

1. The Myth of Closure

   When loss remains ambiguous, there is no possibility of closure (an end point). We assume, therefore, that sadness and grief continue for as long as the ambiguity continues, even for a lifetime or across the generations, as with slavery, the Holocaust, and more recently, events such as 9/11 or more personal ambiguous losses you know about. The void is never closed or resolved. This lack of closure is not pathology, as some would suggest. Rather, we assume it is the inevitable outcome of ambiguous loss. The window for change lies in shifting perceptions (Boss, 1992, 2006).

2. The Paradox of Meaning

   We assume that understanding that some losses are senseless, and always will be, can give people the permission and freedom to let go of searching for the perfect but illusive end point. In this way, families are more likely to accept the paradox of finding some new meaning even in meaninglessness. This often means working for a larger purpose or cause in honor of the missing or memorializing them so they are not forgotten (for more, see Betz & Thorngren, 2006; Boss & Carnes, 2012; Boss & Dahl, 2014; Boss & Ishii, 2015).

3. The Psychological Family

   We assume that family relationships are psychological as well as physical. The psychological family exists in people's minds and hearts (Boss, 1999, 2006; Fravel, McRoy, & Grotevant, 2000). This is akin to the idea of fictive kin[1] or families of choice[2] except that the family here can exist in one's mind. That is, the family can be comprised of loved ones now deceased or ancestors long gone but still remembered or called upon in times of trouble.

4. The Primacy of Perceptions—or Perceptions Matter, but They Are Not All That Matters

   Values and beliefs are culturally based; thus, we assume perceptions will vary about the same stressor event or situation of ambiguous loss. This could be true even within the same couple or family and is highly likely within a community or city.

5. Cultural Differences in Valuing Mastery

   We assume that suffering from ambiguity and not knowing is more problematic in Western cultures where the assumption is that people can avoid suffering and solve problems than in cultures that are more fatalistic or believe in destiny. We assume that the more mastery-oriented people are in their beliefs and values, the more difficulty they will have with ambiguous loss.

6. Cultural Differences in Tolerance for Ambiguity

   We assume that cultural beliefs and values will influence how a family tolerates ambiguous loss and how it is perceived. Sometimes those beliefs and values are rigidly closed to individual and family differences; this is why some families experience a great deal of upheaval or conflict when dealing with homosexuality or divorce. Family therapy researcher Hernandez and social work researcher Wilson (2007) found that religious values and beliefs that were intolerant of lesbian, gay, bisexual, and transgender (LGBT) persons and also of divorce, merged into an untenable situation of distress. One just needs to read the newspaper to see that many religious cultures and congregations today insist on homogeneity and will not tolerate the ambiguity that comes from accepting diversity.

7. With Ambiguous Loss, Truth Is Relative

   We assume that in situations of ambiguous loss, truth is, in reality, unattainable and thus becomes relative. That is, in the absence of facts, family members understandably will make up their own truth about the loss. Scholars, too, make unique assumptions. Instead of the usual epistemological question about truth, we ask, "How do people manage to live well despite not knowing?" Understanding ambiguous loss follows what sociologists Klein and White (1996) called the interpretive approach to knowing, with truth being subjective—meaning it is perceptual.

8. A Narrower Meaning of Resilience

   In situations of ambiguous loss, we assume resilience has a specific meaning—being able to live well despite unanswered questions. Said another way, resilience means having a high tolerance for ambiguity. The goal is to find meaning without the benefit of facts. (For differentiation from the concept of coping, see Chapter 7.)

9. Linear Stage Theory Is Incompatible With Ambiguous Loss Theory

   Theories or intervention models that involve stages or linear steps (e.g., Kübler-Ross's [1969] stages of grief) are not conceptually congruent with ambiguous loss theory. Rather than a linear stage model, we assume that the process of regaining resilience despite ambiguous loss is more compatible with postmodern dialectical systemic process models (e.g., see Hernandez & Wilson, 2007; Additional Readings, this chapter). More appropriate terms to use when working with ambiguous loss are themes, systems, processes, and dynamics (Boss, 2007b)—any terms that imply movement, paradoxical possibilities toward change, and diverse paths to resilience (Boss, 2006; see also Chapter 7).

These are core assumptions for working with people experiencing ambiguous loss. With more understanding of the underlying assumptions, we now move to a discussion of interventions that can be used to help families manage the stress of ambiguous loss.

Interventions: What Helps With Ambiguous Loss?

A new way of thinking is required for living well with ambiguous loss. We call this *both-and thinking*. This means we hold two opposing ideas at the same time: "My father is here but also gone" or "My missing sibling is probably dead but maybe not." Family members, individually and collectively, quickly learn to think in this practical way of coping with ambiguous loss. Some see this as the thesis and antithesis of dialectical thinking, but more simply, it is what poet John Keats called *negative capability*. (Keats loved mystery and wrote to his brother with a positive spin on ambiguity.) Keats believed people were "capable of being in uncertainties, mysteries, doubts, without any irritable reaching after fact or reason" (Forman, 1935, p. 72). He believed that we all have the ability to accept uncertainties, that not every question has to have an answer, and that not every problem has to be solved. Furthermore, he believed that ambiguity is the place where we more fully understand our existence and who we are. Negative capability is the ability to embrace life's mysteries. It allows us to let things go, without feeling guilty about not being able to solve a problem or find an answer to a question (Boss, 2011).

While more research is needed, this way of thinking helps people reduce their stress from an ambiguous loss (Boss, 2006, 2011, in press). Why? We propose that with ongoing ambiguous loss, holding two opposing ideas in one's mind at the same time is easier and more calming than absolute thinking ("He is gone for sure and dead to me" or "She is here and the same as she always was; nothing has changed") (Boss, 1999, 2004b, 2006, 2011).

As families apply both-and thinking, Boss (2006) proposes six guidelines for use by family therapists, social workers, educators, nurses, clergy, and families themselves. Although we refer you to Boss (2006), the guidelines are summarized briefly here:

1. Finding meaning: This means making some sense out of the situation.

   What Helps? Giving the problem a name: "ambiguous loss"; talking with peers; using both-and thinking; increasing one's tolerance for ambiguity; continuing but adapting family rituals and celebrations.

   What Hinders? Seeking revenge, retribution, or closure; family secrets; isolation.

2. Adjusting mastery, up or down: This involves increasing one's agency to live with the ambiguity or decreasing one's need for fixing or solving the problem.

   What Helps? Knowing that the world is not always fair; decreasing self-blame; externalizing blame; mastering one's internal self (meditation, prayer, mindfulness, yoga, exercise, music, etc.).

   What Hinders? Believing that you have failed if you are not "over it."

3. Reconstructing identity, seeing oneself in a new way now that someone is missing: "Am I a wife or widow if my husband is missing?"

   What Helps? Finding supportive family members or a "psychological" family; redefining family/marital boundaries: who's in, who's out, who plays what roles, who you are now.

   What Hinders? Not wanting to change who you are or what you do.

4. Normalizing ambivalence: This is tolerating the tension of mixed emotions and conflicted feelings.

What Helps? Normalizing feelings of love and hate; wishing for the ambiguity to be over with evidence of death and then feeling guilty for having that wish.

What Hinders? Not talking with anyone about these negative feelings.

5. Revising attachment: This means letting go while also holding on to someone you love.

    What Helps? Recognizing that your loved one is both here and gone (grieving what you have lost, acknowledging/celebrating what you still have); finding new human connections.

    What Hinders? Holding on without also developing new attachments.

6. Discovering new hope: This suggests imagining a new way of being with or without the missing person.

    What Helps? Becoming more comfortable with ambiguity (spirituality); laughing at absurdity; redefining justice; finding something you can control or master to balance the ambiguity.

    What Hinders? Isolation; insisting on always having the answer; seeking closure instead of meaning.

These intervention guidelines are now being tested in Eastern cultures by humanitarian researchers/practitioners in the field (Hollander, in press; Robins, 2010, 2013, in press). Thus far, the only change is that the guideline title "tempering mastery" is now changed to "adjusting mastery" because in some cultures, especially patriarchal cultures, wives of missing husbands have no status or agency because they are now neither wife nor widow. They need to be empowered, thus increasing their mastery and agency, not tempering it (Robins, 2010).

The most difficult step in managing and coping with ambiguous loss is to make sense of it—that is, to gain meaning from it. Gaining meaning from ambiguous loss, however, is even more difficult than doing so from a death in the family because the stressor situation is unclear. While it is difficult to find meaning in ambiguity, research findings and clinical observations (Boss, 1999) indicate that the following characteristics appear to influence how and whether families gain meaning despite having a family member with Alzheimer's disease (physically present but psychologically absent). These characteristics appear to emanate from (1) the family of origin and early social experiences, (2) spiritual beliefs and values, (3) habits of thinking optimistically versus pessimistically, and (4) beliefs about mastery and how the world works.

This list begins to identify the protective factors and resources that help keep families resilient in the difficult process of finding meaning in ambiguous loss. Further research is needed to identify both diversity and commonalities in how this occurs.

What Ambiguous Loss Is Not

To more precisely understand what ambiguous loss is, and to alleviate misunderstandings with similar terms, we now state what it is *not*.

Ambiguity Is Not Ambivalence

While ambivalence is a feeling or emotion, ambiguity is a cognitive state of having no answer. Ambivalence means having simultaneous positive and negative feelings about a person or object such as love and hate. In the case of an abusive father, a child may have conflicted feelings of love and hate for his father because it is confusing to have a parent who is not acting like a parent—protecting his child and not hurting him. Although there is much written about ambivalence in psychiatric manuals, it is important here to differentiate the type of ambivalence. Here, the ambivalence from ambiguous loss is not a psychiatric condition, but a "social rupture." We repeat: The ambiguity is the culprit. For more about the theoretical linkage of ambiguity to ambivalence, see Boss (2006), Boss and Kaplan (2004) regarding marital partners where one spouse has been institutionalized due to Alzheimer's disease, and Roper and Jackson (2007), family scientists who discovered themes of ambivalence (and guilt) in mothers of profoundly disabled children who were placed in out-of-home care. Such examples emphasize the need to normalize ambivalence by differentiating between psychiatric and social causes.

Ambiguity Is Not Uncertainty

Scholars sometimes use the term "uncertainty" as synonymous with "ambiguity." We discourage this because uncertainty has a literature and scale of its own in the field of nursing, where it focuses on illness diagnosis (Mishel, 1981, 1990). There is also the Uncertainty Reduction Theory used in communication studies (Berger & Calabrese, 1975). For precision and theoretical consistency, we strongly recommend using the terms "ambiguity" or "unclear" when discussing ambiguous loss.

Ambiguous Loss and Spirituality

Some clergy have said that having tolerance for ambiguity is having faith in the unknown. While there is indeed a connection between spirituality and ambiguous loss, Boss (2006) states that there is no pattern of prediction as she has also worked with religious people who have little tolerance for ambiguity and nonreligious persons who do. What then is the critical factor? It may be finding the meaning without having proof. It may be tolerating doubt. Marital and family resilience may emanate more from being able to find meaning in unanswered questions than from a particular dogma.

Ambiguous Gain Versus Ambiguous Loss

An idea Boss raised in 1980 but did not develop is ambiguous gain. As Carroll, Olson, & Buckmiller (2007) point out, ambiguous gain is an area ripe for study. While it is obvious that gain is different from loss, the terms are alike in that change in family boundaries (losses or gains) can lead to incongruent perceptions of who is in and who is out of the family—with subsequent conflict or alienation. Examples of ambiguous gains (Boss, 1980a) may be a new baby from birth or adoption, gaining in-laws, or in-home professional help such as nannies or professional caregivers who are in the home regularly to tend to an elder or disabled child. Today, there is both ambiguous gain and loss in families where someone is transitioning gender (Wahlig, 2015).While encouraging more study on ambiguous gain, Boss's focus has centered on ambiguous loss. Why? Because it is the stress of loss (more than gain) that lies at the core of human suffering. In the 1970s, when she began her work, few, if any, family scholars were studying loss. The lack of research on loss as a major family stressor was surprising. It may have been because loss was an unpopular idea. Back then, most people preferred to focus on gain.

What we hopefully understand now is that ambiguous loss is a unique construct that is not synonymous with ambivalence or uncertainty, nor is it a spiritual tolerance for the unknown. We hope the definition of ambiguous loss is made clearer and more precise by peeling away what it is not.

Conclusion

In reality, it is rare that loved ones are totally present or totally absent. This means that many of us have already had some experience in coping with ambiguous loss—a break up, a parent deployed by the military, a noncustodial parent moving away, a partner relocating for work, or unwanted separations from long-time friends. Once we see that absence and presence in human relationships are frequently unclear, then we begin to understand the possibilities of managing to live well despite the stress of ambiguous loss.

Summary

This chapter described ambiguous loss and explained the premises behind the theory. With ambiguous loss, there is no closure; the loss is unclear. This can leave individuals and families feeling confused and hopeless. Those feelings can last for years, even a lifetime, and may lead to depressive symptoms or anxiety. Given the relational nature of ambiguous loss, one must have been previously attached to the missing person in order to experience it. This stress-based theory posits that the pathology exists in the external context of the family, rather than the individual. Remember, making sense of the loss is the most challenging aspect of coping with ambiguous loss. Living with ambiguous loss is possible, but a new way of thinking is needed. Families must be able to engage in what is called "both-and" thinking.

Points to Remember

1. *Physical ambiguous loss (Type I)* occurs when a loved one is physically absent but kept psychologically present because there is no assurance of death or permanent loss.

2. *Psychological ambiguous loss (Type II)* occurs when a person to whom you are attached is physically present but psychologically absent.

3. Both types of ambiguous loss can occur simultaneously in one person or family.

4. Ambiguous loss is viewed as a systemic relational rupture and not a psychiatric problem.

5. With ambiguous loss, family members have few options: (1) either hold out for the truth or (2) in the absence of solid evidence of the loved one's death, develop a new narrative with which they can live.

6. When loss remains ambiguous, there is no possibility of closure (an end point) for sadness and grief. This lack of closure is not pathology.

7. Theories or intervention models that involve stages or linear steps are not conceptually congruent with ambiguous loss theory.

Notes

1. *Fictive kin* refers to family-type bonds that are not based on blood ties or marriage.

2. "The idea of 'families of choice' was framed as a form of political affirmation towards rights for homosexual ways of life, particularly in the USA" (Weston, 1991, as cited in McCarthy & Edwards, 2011, p. 56).

Discussion Questions

1. What events (current or past) have you heard or read about that reflect individuals or families experiencing ambiguous loss? (Try to identify an event that was not mentioned in this chapter.)

2. What would be more difficult for you to do: deal with a loved one who is physically absent but psychologically present or deal with a loved one who is physically present but psychologically absent? Why?

3. How are some people able to live well without knowing if a loved one is alive or dead? Why are some people able to live with ambiguity?

4. How does ambiguity freeze the grieving process?

5. How can an individual experience both types of ambiguous loss at the same time?

Additional Readings

Bentley, G. E., Zvonkovic, A., McCarty, M., & Springer, N. (2015). Down syndrome and fathering: An exploration of ambiguous loss. *Fathering, 13*(1), 1–17.

Chaffey, E., & Whyte, J. D. (2014). Dynamics and dimensions: Ambiguous loss and disenfranchised grief of partners following a miscarriage, stillbirth or TOPFA. *Grief Matters, 17*(2), 52–57.

Huebner, A. J., Mancini, J. A., Wilcox, R., Grass, S., & Grass, G. (2007). Parental deployment and youth in military families: Exploring uncertainty and ambiguous loss. *Family Relations: Interdisciplinary Journal of Applied Family Studies, 56*, 111–121.

Kreutzer, J. S., Mills, A., & Marwitz, J. H. (2016). Ambiguous loss and emotional recovery after traumatic brain injury. *Journal of Family Theory & Review, 8*(3).

McGuire, J. K., Catalpa, J. M., Lacey, V., & Kuvalanka, K. A. (in press). Relational rupture: Using ambiguous loss as a process for decentering cisnormativity. *Journal of Family Theory & Review, 8*(3).

Mitchell, M. (in press). The family dance: Ambiguous loss, meaning-making, and the psychological family in foster care. *Journal of Family Theory & Review, 8*(3).

Perez, R. (in press). Life-long ambiguous loss: The case of Cuban American exiles. *Journal of Family Theory & Review, 8*(3).

Robins, S. (2013). *Families of the missing: A test for contemporary approaches to transitional justice.* New York, NY/London, UK: Routledge Glasshouse.

Roos, S. (2013). Chronic sorrow and ambiguous loss: Gestalt methods for coping with grief. *Gestalt Review, 17*(3), 229–239.

Solheim, C. A., & Ballard, J. (in press). Ambiguous loss due to separation in voluntary transnational families. *Journal of Family Theory & Review, 8*(3).

Tóibín, C. (2009). *Brooklyn: A novel.* New York, NY: Scribner.

Wayland, S., Maple, M., McKay, K., & Glassock, G. (2015). Holding on to hope: A review of the literature exploring missing persons, hope and ambiguous loss. *Death Studies.* Advance online publication. doi: 10.1080/07481187.2015.1068245

Films

Bevan, T., Fellner, E., & Harrison, A., Hooper, T., & Mutrux, G. (Producers), & Hooper, T. (Director). (2015). *The Danish girl* [Motion picture]. London, UK: Universal Studios.

Iron, D., Urdel, S., & Weiss, J. (Producers), & Polley, S. (Director). (2006). *Away from her* [Motion picture]. Toronto, Ontario, Canada: Capri Releasing, Echo Lake Productions, Foundry Films, Hanway Films, The Film Farm.

Ambiguous Loss Research Using Primarily Qualitative Methods

Allen, K. R. (2007). Ambiguous loss after lesbian couples with children break up: A case for same-gender divorce. *Family Relations, 56*(2), 175–183.

Blieszner, R., Roberto, K. A., Wilcox, K. L., Barham, E. J., & Winston, B. L. (2007). Dimensions of ambiguous loss in couples coping with mild cognitive impairment. *Family Relations, 56*(2), 196–209.

Cacciatore, J., DeFrain, J., & Jones, K. L. C (2008). When a baby dies: Ambiguity and stillbirth.*Marriage & Family Review,44*(4),439–454.doi:10.1080/01494920802454017

Dziengel, L. (2012). Resilience, ambiguous loss, and older same-sex couples: The resilience constellation model. *Journal of Social Service Research, 38,* 74–88. doi: 10.1080/01488376.2011.626354

Faber, A. J., Willerton, E., Clymer, S. R., MacDermid, S. M., & Weiss, H. M. (2008). Ambiguous absence, ambiguous presence: A qualitative study of military reserve families in wartime. *Journal of Family Psychology, 22*(2), 222–230. doi: 10.1037/0893-3200.22.2.222

Giovannetti, A. M., Cerniauskait, M., Leonardi, M., Sattin, D., & Covelli, V. (2015). Informal caregivers of patients with disorders of consciousness: Experience of ambiguous loss. *Brain Injury, 29*(4), 473–480. doi: 10.3109/02699052.2014.990514

Hernandez, B. C., & Wilson, C. M. (2007). Another kind of ambiguous loss: Seventh-day Adventist women in mixed-orientation marriages. *Family Relations, 56*(2), 184–195.

Huebner, A. J., Mancini, J. A., Wilcox, R. M., Grass, S. R., & Grass, G. A. (2007). Parental deployment and youth in military families: Exploring uncertainty and ambiguous loss. *Family Relations, 56*(2), 112–122.

Kean, S. (2010). The experience of ambiguous loss in families of brain injured ICU patients. *Nursing in Critical Care, 15*(2), 66–75.

Keller, J. (2011). Experiences of public housing residents following relocation: Explorations of ambiguous loss, resiliency, and cross-generational perspectives. *Journal of Poverty, 15*, 141–163. doi: 10.1080/10875549.2011.563170

Landau, J., & Hissett, J. (2008). Mild traumatic brain injury: Impact on identity and ambiguous loss in the family. *Families, Systems, & Health, 26*(1), 69–85. doi: 10.1037/1091-7527.26.1.69

Lee, R. E., & Whiting, J. B. (2007). Foster children's expressions of ambiguous loss. *American Journal of Family Therapy, 35*, 417–428. doi: 10.1080/01926180601057499

Luster, T., Qin, D. B., Bates, L., Johnson, D. J., & Rana, M. (2008). The lost boys of Sudan: Ambiguous loss, search for family, and reestablishing relationships with family members. *Family Relations, 57*, 444–456.

Luster, T., Qin, D. B., Bates, L., Johnson, D. J., & Rana, M. (2009). The lost boys of Sudan: Coping with ambiguous loss and separation from parents. *American Journal of Orthopsychiatry, 79*(2), 203–211. doi: 10.1037/a0015559

Norwood, K. (2013). Grieving gender: Trans-identities, transition, and ambiguous loss. *Communication Monographs, 80*(1), 24–45. doi: 10.1080/03637751.2012.739705

O'Brien, M. (2007). Ambiguous loss in families of children with autism spectrum disorders. *Family Relations, 56*(2), 135–146.

Patrick-Ott, A., & Ladd, L. D. (2010). The blending of Boss's concept of ambiguous loss and Olshansky's concept of chronic sorrow: A case study of a family with a child who has significant disabilities. *Journal of Creativity in Mental Health, 5*, 74–86.

Perez, R. M. (2015). Cuba no; Miami Si: Cuban Americans coping with ambiguous loss. *Journal of Human Behavior in the Social Environment, 25*(1), 50–66. doi: 10.1080/10911359.2014.953433

Powell, K. A., & Afifi, T. D. (2005). Uncertainty management and adoptees' ambiguous loss of their birth parents. *Journal of Social and Personal Relationships, 22*(1), 129–151. doi: 10.1177/0265407505049325

Robins, S. (2010). Ambiguous loss in a non-western context: Families of the disappeared in postconflict Nepal. *Family Relations, 59*, 253–268. doi: 10.1111/j.1741-3729.2010.00600.x

Roper, S. O., & Jackson, J. B. (2007). The ambiguities of out-of-home care: Children with severe or profound disabilities. *Family Relations, 56*(2), 147–161.

Sampson, J. M., Yeats, J. R., & Harris, S. M. (2012). An evaluation of an ambiguous loss based psychoeducational support group for family members of persons who hoard: A pilot study. *Contemporary Family Therapy, 34*, 566–581. doi: 10.1007/s10591-012-9214-6

Samuels, G. M. (2009). Ambiguous loss of home: The experience of familial (im)permanence among adults with foster care backgrounds. *Children and Youth Services Review, 21*, 1229–1239. doi: 10.1016/j.childyouth.2009.05.008

Shalev, R., & Ben-Asher, S. (2011). Ambiguous loss: The long-term effects on the children of POWs. *Journal of Loss and Trauma, 16*, 511–528. doi: 10.1080/15325024.2011.576983

Solheim, C., Zaid, S., & Ballard, J. (2015). Ambiguous loss experienced by transnational Mexican immigrant families. *Family Process.* Advanced online publication. doi: 10.1111/famp.12130

Vargas, L. (2008). Ambiguous loss and the media practices of transnational Latina teens: A qualitative study. *Popular Communication, 6*, 37–52. doi: 10.1080/15405700701697587

5

Boundary Ambiguity

A Perceptual Risk in
Family Stress Management

*M**y dad was deployed for a long time in the Middle East so my mother was in charge at home. She made the decisions, took care of us, managed the money and the house, and kept up the car and our activities. We helped a lot, but we knew she was the boss. When Dad came home for good, things were confusing. Right away, he wanted to take over where he left off—being the head of the family, but Mom was now accustomed to that role and didn't want to give it up. It took some time before they worked out who was in charge of what and who did what. (Student story)*

* * *

My mother is a paranoid schizophrenic. She seemed okay at first. People thought she was a little weird but nothing serious. But when I was 12, she really started showing signs of mental illness. She was diagnosed after my parents divorced; the family was in crisis. We have struggled with not knowing whether she was going to get better and if she could still be part of our family. Currently, she is out of our family. She is still with us physically, but we don't see her as our mother anymore. Although my wish is for her to be better, my sisters and I have taken care of each other. We would have to rearrange our lives to let her back in. That would be tremendously stressful. (Student story)

These students' stories are examples of boundary ambiguity caused by ambiguous loss. In the first example, the father's return home after military service is cheered, but it also disturbs the equilibrium of a family system that has adapted to his absence. There were, therefore, some months of conflict as husband and wife realigned their roles and tasks. In time, and with negotiation, they moved from boundary ambiguity to an agreed upon view. In the second example, the mother is psychologically absent due to mental illness. The children now fill her roles, taking care of each other and the home. Recognizing that they no longer need help from their ill mother and having experienced the ambiguity of her "ins and outs" in the past, they now perceive her as "out," an either-or perception that can create permanent rifts in families. Here they did not realign.

Boundary ambiguity is defined as a lack of clarity about who is in or out of the family system (Boss, 2006; Boss & Greenberg, 1984; Boss, Greenberg, & Pearce-McCall, 1990). It is the incongruence among family members regarding their perceptions of family membership (structure) and who performs what roles and tasks (function).

While ambiguous loss is the stressor situation (located heuristically under the A factor in the Contextual Model of Family Stress [CMFS]), boundary ambiguity is the perceptual response to that stressor and is located heuristically under the C factor (Boss, 2002) (see Figure 4.1). That is, ambiguous loss is the situational stressor, and boundary ambiguity is the perceptual manifestation of that stressor. The terms *ambiguous loss* and *boundary ambiguity* are not interchangeable. Our choice of focus depends on our research question or the situation facing the families with whom we work.

Boundary ambiguity is a continuous variable; high levels are a risk factor that predicts negative outcomes (X factor), such as depression and family conflict, among others. The basic premise is that the higher the level of boundary ambiguity, the more the stressor of ambiguous loss can damage the family. When people are confused about who is in or out of their family, the systemic processes for functioning are blocked and frozen. The family is immobilized, not because of a particular illness or disaster, but because of the ambiguity that confuses their perceptions. In this context, mastery decreases and helplessness increases with subsequent negative outcomes (Berge & Holm, 2007; Boss, Caron, & Horbal, 1988; Boss, Caron, Horbal, & Mortimer, 1990; Caron, Boss, & Mortimer, 1999; Roper & Jackson, 2007).

Boundary ambiguity can be both an individual and family variable: On the family level, it is defined by the degree of congruence (or incongruence) among family members in their perceptions of how they perceive the family. A quick way to assess family boundary ambiguity qualitatively is to ask who will be included or excluded from the family's next traditional ritual or celebration. For quantitative measures, however, we recommend the *Measurement of Boundary Ambiguity in Families* (Boss, Greenberg, & Pearce-McCall, 1990, available on www.ambiguousloss.com). The almost predictable incongruence among individual scores is then calculated and used as a family variable.

Measurement of Boundary Ambiguity

Boundary ambiguity is typically assessed quantitatively because its indicators of roles, tasks, and family membership are relatively easy to quantify. Boss conceptualizes boundary ambiguity, however, from a neo-structure functional point of view (Kingsbury & Scanzoni, 1993). This means that Boss's more systemic view of the family goes beyond traditional structure functionalism toward flexible family roles not assigned by gender. Expanding this view even further, Boss sees family as a psychological construction in addition to the physical (Boss, 2006, in press). Since the 1970s, researchers who prefer quantification have studied boundary ambiguity because it is more easily operationalized than ambiguous loss. Researchers have consistently found boundary ambiguity to be a risk factor or barrier to the management of stress for families (Berge & Holm, 2007; Boss, 1977, 1980a, 2007a; Boss et al., 1988; Caron, Boss, & Mortimer, 1999; Leite, 2007). For a review of boundary ambiguity studies, findings, and future directions, see Carroll, Olson, & Buckmiller (2007). For more recent articles about boundary ambiguity with diverse situations of stress in diverse populations and cultures, see Additional Readings, provided at the end of this chapter.

History of Boundary Ambiguity

Although the construct, family boundary ambiguity, was first formulated and tested in the 1970s (Boss, 1977, 1980a), the underlying theme of incongruence between objective and subjective membership in a group was not new then. It had a rich history in the literature of social psychology, sociology, and family therapy (Boss, 2006, in press; Boss & Greenberg, 1984).

Sociological and Psychological Roots

In 1955, sociologist Georg Simmel wrote about affiliation and conflict and "uneasy combinations," meaning human groups that may sometimes be in disagreement—like adolescents and their parents. Simmel's more psychosocial perspective suggested that a significant aspect of individual development (like an adolescent's) was the process of clarifying boundaries between old and new group affiliations—like parents versus peers, for example. In 1984, Boss and Greenberg proposed that a family was an "uneasy group" (p. 540).

To add more nuances, psychologist Kurt Lewin, founder of social psychology, wrote about the "marginal man" (Lewin, 1951, as cited in Boss & Greenberg, 1984, p. 540), who stands on the boundary between two groups, not belonging to either of them (Boss & Greenberg, 1984). Marginal family members thus play into boundary ambiguity by being psychologically absent both at home and at work, never fully present in either place. Today, technical devices and gaming may be creating more marginal family members, as they are psychologically absent and preoccupied with their devices, both inside and outside the family.

Another historical root lies in the idea of misfit. George C. Homans (1950), founder of behavioral sociology, wrote about the temporary misfit between external and internal family systems when "the boundary at the interface of the two systems is at least temporarily ambiguous" (Boss & Greenberg, 1984, p. 540). Examples could be the boundary between the adolescent's family and his or her peer group (Boss & Greenberg, 1984). Here, the misfit may lie in disagreements of perceptions about the welfare and safety of the teenager. The family worries that he or she is in trouble, while the peer group thinks all is fine. The tension that lies at the interface (and misfit) of these groups is part of finding one's identity in the process of human development. It does, however, create family stress, which may be necessary for developmental change to occur.

Finally, in 1974, Erving Goffman wrote about ambiguity of frame in his book *Frame Analysis,* thus becoming one of the most influential sociologists for Boss's theory development.

What Goffman meant by *frame* was the ordering or framing of a person's experience (Boss, in press). Applying this idea to family stress meant that framing could help people find meaning in their adversity—and thus cope with it more effectively. In family therapy sessions with troubled families, Boss begins with this question to each person: "What does this situation mean to you?" The answers help to frame the stress and reveal who is in or out of that family (for a fuller discussion, see Boss, in press).

Family Therapy Roots

Historically, the family therapy literature influenced the conceptualization of boundary ambiguity. First came structural family therapy, which was developed by psychiatrist Salvador Minuchin (1974); second was the symbolic experiential family therapy of psychiatrist and pioneer family therapist Carl Whitaker (1982, 1989; Napier & Whitaker, 1978) (with whom Boss studied and worked); and finally came the work of Ivan Boszormenyi-Nagy, psychiatrist and founder of contextual family therapy (Boszormenyi-Nagy & Spark, 1973/1984). Minuchin addressed structure of the family, Whitaker addressed the symbolic aspects of who is family, and Boszormenyi-Nagy emphasized the importance of context. You will see influences of all three in the construct of boundary ambiguity as well as in the larger theory of ambiguous loss.

Structural Family Therapy

The underlying strategy of Minuchin's (1974) structural family therapy was to reorganize the system and clarify ambiguous boundaries by redefining who is in the family unit with associated roles and responsibilities. Said another way, Minuchin examined family dysfunction in relation to the lack of clarity or misalignment of internal family boundaries. The therapeutic task was to clarify systemic boundaries and realign the generational boundaries with parents in charge of the children. As was illustrated in our introductory vignette, the mother's inability to parent her children had reversed the generational roles. This would be of concern to a structural therapist.

A point of caution here—the structural therapy approach assumes that troubled families are characterized by ambiguous boundaries because family members occupy positions within the family that are inappropriate given normative developmental stages. In other words, the focus is on norms. Traditionally, this has meant that it is pathological for a child to take care of an ill mother or for a father to refuse the sole executive role in the family.

This bias in structure–function theory thus pathologizes family members who, through no fault of their own, must perform roles outside of the normative prescription. Common examples today (of what were considered anomalies in the past) are grandmothers and grandfathers who parent their grandchildren or even a child who cares for a frail elder, earns money for the family, or acts as a parent for younger siblings (Burton, Dilworth-Anderson, & Merriwether-de Vries, 1994). While these roles may not be acceptable or appropriate to some people, they exist in many regions. The generational crossovers may at times contribute to family survival. We keep an open mind about what is functional, for it is variation rather than prescription that creates family resilience.

Nevertheless, even when roles are reversed, a structural family therapist is useful to clarify ambiguous family boundaries by redefining "who is in" and "who is doing what." The clarification, even more than realignment to normative roles, allows many families to function well, even if they differ in structure and function (Boss & Greenberg, 1984).

Symbolic Experiential Family Therapy

In the 1970s and 1980s, Carl Whitaker broke the traditional rules of individual psychotherapy and became one of the founders of family therapy. As an early postmodernist, he was known for his "therapy of the absurd" (Whitaker, 1982, 1989; Napier & Whitaker, 1978). The absurdity was to work with multiple generations to heal an individual patient. He changed families, paradoxically, by not asking them to change. Instead, Whitaker increased the family's stress levels, and he did this symbolically—sometimes by falling asleep in the session. The family was startled but then joined together in their frustration. This was the change; they were now, at least momentarily, a cohesive group of family members, each targeting their frustration at a common foe. While we certainly do not recommend all of that absurdity, we do recommend family therapy and the use of symbolic experiential techniques. The idea is that there has to be some unity of meanings and actions before there is a family; the members have to pull together, like a team (Boss, 2006). With Whitaker as her professor, and she as his cotherapist, Boss learned about the symbolic in family interactions and processes. She proposed for her dissertation that families existed in the mind as well as in the census takers' notebook (Boss, 1975a). To some, her idea was absurd. But she persisted. Boss's original research on boundary ambiguity (1975b, 1977, 1980a) continued into the 1980s (Boss et al., 1988; Boss, Caron et al., 1990; Caron et al., 1999) and today is being conducted by many others (see Boss 2007a; Additional Readings, this chapter).

Contextual Family Therapy

Also a founder of family therapy, Boszormenyi-Nagy was a Hungarian psychiatrist who was the first to focus on the family's context (Boszormenyi-Nagy, 1987; Boszormenyi-Nagy & Spark, 1973/1984). He was referring to internal and external contexts, such as socioeconomic status, ethnic/cultural background, individual psychology, systemic transactions, and relational ethics.

Boszormenyi-Nagy (1973/1984, 1987) coined the term "invisible loyalty," which is illustrated, for example, by a child unconsciously trying to pay a debt to an abusive parent, even if she gets hurt doing so. That is, the child—even after becoming an adult—stays with an abusive father because she feels she owes it to him. Boszormenyi-Nagy's work expanded the thinking of psychotherapists beyond the individual and family system to include the broader context surrounding the family.

In sum, while it was Whitaker and Boszormenyi-Nagy who inspired Boss's inclusion of context in the conceptualization of boundary ambiguity, it was earlier scholars working at the intersection of sociology and psychology who inspired its inception.

Entries and Exits; Gains and Losses

For both individuals and families as a whole, tolerance for some ambiguity is a sign of maturity and good mental health and provides the resilience to navigate the inevitable life transitions. When a family member who has been in the system leaves, the family must reorganize to compensate for the void. This happens when someone leaves for more normative reasons (an adolescent goes to college or an aged grandparent dies) or it can occur unexpectedly (a family member is suddenly killed in a car crash or a child is kidnapped).

The family boundary is disturbed by the loss of a member and the roles they performed. The level of boundary ambiguity is likely high until a new equilibrium is reached in one of two ways: *physically*—the person returns or someone else is taken in as a replacement or *perceptually and ideally*—the family gradually reconciles themselves to the loss by being flexible and reassigning the vacated roles to others. Because family transitions throughout the life cycle are inevitable and desirable, some degree of boundary ambiguity is also inevitable; we cannot always have clarity in family relationships.

Normative Developmental Boundary Ambiguity Across the Family Life Cycle

Sometimes, family transitions are caused by a clear loss (death), but, at other times, they are the result of maturation; for example, a child grows up and leaves home or falls in love or becomes totally focused on work or education. The family loses a dependent child but hopefully gains a competent young adult. When an elderly parent grows frail, the family loses a person they leaned on and gains a serious and tender responsibility. When small children attend school for the first time, parents lose a tot who was exclusively dependent on them but gain an increasingly self-sufficient child. Whether such changes result in relief or sadness, families cannot go back to the way things were. Human development brings inevitable change; hence, family boundaries also change.

To illustrate the many developmental transitions in families with potential for boundary ambiguity, we present Table 5.1. To survive, couples and families must maintain their boundaries despite frequent developmental transitions that occur over time. The significant barrier is not the situation or event of ambiguous loss (or acquisition; A factor) but rather the doubt and ambiguity of not knowing if a particular person is in or out of the family circle. Throughout the life span, entries and exits of family members are inevitable, as births, adolescents leaving home and coming back again, marriages, retirements, illnesses, and deaths occur. All continuously create change and thus require that one constantly clarify "who is family."

Table 5.1   Developmental Transitions in Families With Potential for Boundary Ambiguity

Type of Boundary Change	Stressors Associated With Physical and Psychological Losses and Gains
Formation of the couple	Mate selection
	Acquisition of in-laws
	Realignment with family of orientation (or origin)
	Accepting or rejecting each other's social network members
Addition of a child (birth, adoption, stepchild)	Acquisition of new family member
	Possible separation from (or loss of time with) outside work world
	Loss of (or less time with) colleagues at work
	Gain of new social network members (associated with caring for a child)
Siblinghood/addition of more children (birth, adoption)	Loss of exclusive attention from parents
	Gain of playmate and companionship as well as for competition and conflict
Children entering school (school age)	Separation of children from family
	Acquisition of child's teachers, friends, and peers as part of child's world
Spouse or parent's job/career-related absence from home	Frequent fluctuations between absence and presence due to work roles outside the family (e.g., truck drivers, military service)
Spouse or parent's job/career-related return (planned or unplanned) home	Unemployment: layoff, fired
	Retirement
Accepting adolescence	Allowing child to participate in decision making
	Adjusting rules, loosening tie to family of orientation/origin

(Continued)

Table 5.1 (Continued)

Type of Boundary Change	Stressors Associated With Physical and Psychological Losses and Gains
Adolescents leaving home	Separation from family Increased peer, school, work influence (same and opposite sex)
Adolescents extended stay at home (not leaving home)	Pregnancies, illnesses, unemployment
Adult children returning home	Illness, unemployment, divorce
Taking children in who are not one's own; combining children from different dyads	Acquisition of another's offspring into the family system: grandchildren, foster care
Parents of adult child moving into adult child's home	Re-establishing, redefining boundaries
Loss of partner through death	Dissolution of relationship
Divorce or separation	Loss of some income and property; free access to home and usual time with children and pets Gain individual freedom (Note: In cases of divorce, dyad may continue to function as coparents.)
Death of aging parents	Loss of presence and support Gain inheritance of economic or sentimental objects, feelings of mortality (next to die), role as head of family now
Formation of a new dyad, remarriage	Acquisition of a new partner Acquisition of new in-laws Realignment with family of orientation (origin) and former in-laws, children Incorporating or rejecting former friendships, former spouses, children from each dyad
Singlehood (becoming single or remaining single)	Realignment with family of orientation (origin) If previously married, realignment with children, former in-laws, grandchildren Acquisition of new friends, intimates, colleagues

Source: Adapted from Boss (1980a) and Boss (2002).

As we see in Table 5.1, clarifying family boundaries after loss or acquisition is one of the most critical developmental tasks required of families (Boss, 1980a; Rodgers & White, 1993). The abilities to let go (e.g., death) and take in (e.g., birth) and adapt to the systemic changes that these processes of transition demand are necessary coping strategies for all families and individuals. Human beings change as they mature, so clarifying boundaries is a universal systemic task for family functioning, regardless of culture or class. Because of losses (primarily) as well as gains, it is a continual challenge. Boundary ambiguity is never perfectly fixed but hopefully managed through the family's resilience. More non-life threatening but still stressful incongruities between absence and presence will continue to occur in everyday life—a child grows up and leaves home, an elderly mate is moved to a nursing home, or a loved one transitions to another gender (Wahlig, 2015).

There is, however, a limit (in the degree and amount of time) to how much ambiguity a person or family can tolerate. A healthy family and mature parents should be able to endure the ambiguity during the years an adolescent is gaining independence. It is another matter, however, to say that individuals and families should be able to tolerate the decades of ambiguity in their family's boundary that is caused when a family member is kidnapped by terrorists or placed into foster care. Children of alcoholics report experiencing confusion and high stress because a parent is there physically but not psychologically. Were such absences more benign—such as when one is home but preoccupied with writing, studying, reading a book, or getting ready for a contest—the boundary ambiguity could be more easily tolerated.

Exceptions and Nuances

As with family stress, there are exceptions about what creates boundary ambiguity. We list some of those nuances and distinctions now.

Occurrence of Boundary Ambiguity

We have said that boundary ambiguity occurs when the facts surrounding a loss remain unclear. Boundary ambiguity, however, can also occur when the facts regarding the event are clear but, for some reason, the family denies or avoids the facts. We see this at times with denial of a family member's serious mental or physical illness, the avoidance of testing for genetic markers for amyotrophic lateral sclerosis (ALS) or cancer, or even for addiction. In the latter cases, the perception of a family member's presence may differ from that of an objective observer. That is, some in the family may perceive an addicted member as satisfactorily present even if they are psychologically gone. Or a family member who is dying may be perceived by some as ultimately recovering. These views may not be negative if the individuals go into recovery or remission. Over the long run, however, the family's functioning would be impaired.

Of critical importance to researchers, educators, and therapists who assess boundary ambiguity is that its effect (X factor) is not determined by whether the ambiguity results from unavailable facts regarding the event or from the family's distortion of those facts. It is instead the family's perception that provides the window for assessment and intervention. Professional standards are considered, but we must also assess the family's perception of who is in their family circle.

The Family Gamble

Sometimes, when family members cannot obtain the facts to know who is in or out of their family, they take it upon themselves to decide whether their missing person is in or out. This risk taking is called "the family gamble" (Boss, 1999, Cohen, 1993). The family as a whole or some parts of it takes a chance and gambles to "close out" their family member and proceed with family life as if he or she were permanently gone. This "closing out" may be because of severe and ongoing family conflict, so one could say, for example, "He's dead to me." Such absolute thinking could backfire. More typically, the family gamble occurs in situations of stress that have befallen the family (e.g., a missing person might be found; a dying person's cancer could go into remission). Depending on their rigidity, the family or couple may have difficulty reopening boundaries to let that person back in. (Note: We saw this in the two vignettes at the beginning of this chapter.) Such cases are not unusual: a soldier comes home, a child's illness goes into remission, a missing father is found, a young woman finds her birth mother, an addicted person becomes sober. Such changes may have surprising stress effects on families as they must readjust their boundaries to let the absent person back in. Although reunions may be positive, they can also be negative. If they painfully struggled with the loss, they may now find it too stressful to adjust to the gain and may be reluctant to take that person back in.

More painful are hints that a missing person has been sighted or that remains have been found—a tooth or a small bone fragment. When there are reports of missing persons being seen alive, of remains being found, or of hostages being sighted, the ambiguity increases as each report increases the prospect of another change. Whether positive or negative, change disturbs the family boundary. Once again, the family is unsure if the lost person is in or out of the system. Once again, the gamble has been made (Boss, 1999).

Effects of Boundary Ambiguity

To understand the effects of boundary ambiguity, it helps to consider multiple views. From a *sociological perspective*, the family's boundary is no longer maintained when roles are frozen and tasks remain undone. From a *psychological perspective*, cognition is blocked by the ambiguity, emotions are mixed, and grieving processes are frozen (Boss, 1993, 1999, 2006, 2007b; Boss, Beaulieu, Wieling, Turner, & LaCruz, 2003). From a *family science perspective*, both sociological and psychological views are relevant together; they allow us to address the family as a whole system as well as its individual members.

If people cannot clarify who is in and who is out of their family systems regarding roles, rules, rituals, and responsibilities, the process of systemic restructuring is blocked, and the system is held in limbo. Life is put on hold

(Boss & Greenberg, 1984). Systemic processes are immobilized, decisions are delayed, rituals and celebrations are canceled, and tasks remain undone. Outcomes are both individual and systemic. For individuals, boundary ambiguity predicts depressive symptoms, unresolved grief symptoms, high anxiety, and somatic symptoms. For couples and families as a whole, it leads to family conflict, rifts, alienation, and relational difficulties (Berge & Holm, 2007; Boss, Caron et al., 1990; Caron et al., 1999; Huebner, Mancini, Wilcox, Grass, & Grass, 2007). Researchers in nursing Campbell and Demi (2000) found that ruminations about pilots missing in action (MIA) continue for decades. Such persisting levels of boundary ambiguity erode individual and family well-being.

Assumptions About Boundary Ambiguity

The following are the assumptions that shape our ideas about boundary ambiguity:

1. Cultural diversity influences perceptions.

   Given the focus on perceptions, we acknowledge that there is vast diversity among genders, generations, races, ethnicities, and sexual orientations, which cause people to perceive family boundaries differently. Rather than seeking normative boundary ambiguity scores, we look for the degree of congruence (or incongruence) among a particular set of family members (Boss, Greenberg et al., 1990).

   The perception of who is in one's family is often unique to one's gender, culture, and beliefs. For example, in northeastern Japan, after the earthquake and tsunami of March 11, 2011 (3/11), thousands of families who have no evidence of death or body to bury are finding comfort in talking with their ancestors. At in-home altars, they ask deceased ancestors to look after their missing and dead family members (Boss & Ishii, 2015; Mockett, 2015). By keeping ancestors psychologically present inside their family, these families report receiving comfort and strength (Mockett, 2015). For many grieving families, ancestors are perceived as part of the family with the role of protecting the missing and dead.

2. Outsiders cannot maintain a family's boundaries; each family must maintain their perception of membership and roles from the inside.

   To do this, family members must know—and reasonably agree upon—who is in their family. As a family therapist, Boss asks: "Who do you see as inside your family? Who do you see as no longer in it?" Because family rituals and gatherings are core to family life, she also asks: "Who do you want to be at your graduation? Your birthday? Your wedding? Your special event? Who do you include—or exclude—at times of significant family rituals and celebrations?" The answers can give therapists and researchers an inside view of who is considered "family."

3. The variability of boundary ambiguity is not neutral; how it is perceived has valence.

   That is, it is a continuous variable with higher degrees that are more problematic than lower degrees. For example, the higher the degree of boundary ambiguity, the lower the sense of mastery with more negative outcomes (e.g., Boss et al., 1988; Boss, Caron, Horbal, & Mortimer, 1990; Caron et al., 1999; Mitchell, in press; O'Brien, 2007).

4. Boundary ambiguity is ubiquitous but not always a problem.

Family members are rarely fully present or fully absent. There is always some doubt about where a loved one is and when he or she will return. There are also some ambiguities about who will leave and who will enter as a new addition to the family system. From loss and acquisition, absence and presence, birth as well as death, changes in the family's boundary occur as a natural part of human development and the family's life cycle. Such transitions, involving both losses and gains—clear and ambiguous—are stressful because they represent change but do not necessarily lead to troublesome levels of boundary ambiguity.

Our assumptions about boundary ambiguity emphasize cultural influences, perception, and the uniqueness of each family's definitions of boundary. We also assume boundary ambiguity is a continuous variable. This means that unlike a discrete variable, boundary ambiguity can vary in degrees from high to low and anywhere in between. Finally, while a high degree of boundary ambiguity is considered a risk factor, we assume it is less problematic in cultures that have a high tolerance for ambiguity.

What Boundary Ambiguity Is Not

To aid in learning new concepts, it is helpful—and essential—to learn what they are not. Toward this end and to prevent confusion in research and application, we differentiate boundary ambiguity from similar—but not synonymous—constructs.

Boundary Ambiguity Is Not Boundary Maintenance

First, boundary ambiguity is not boundary maintenance. Boundary maintenance represents the opposite of boundary ambiguity. In the original general systems theory of sociologist Walter Buckley (1967), *boundary maintenance is defined as an intrinsic construct* that means the perimeters of a system are secure and well-defined. The assumption is that living systems cannot survive without clearly defined boundaries. Yet, for families, boundaries are rarely 100% clear.

In family sociology, Joan Aldous (1978) notes the paradoxical nature of the concept of family boundary. On one hand, families tend to establish distinct boundaries through daily interactions, rituals, and language. On the other hand, families are often called or forced to open their boundaries selectively to transact business with external social institutions, such as schools, clinics, banks, or workplaces. Such "ins" and "outs" across the family boundary may create some stress, but if the degree of ambiguity is tolerated and managed at lower levels, the family benefits more than if they were socially isolated with a perfectly clear boundary all the time.

The greatest number of boundary maintenance problems in families is likely to occur as young adults mature (Boss, 1980a). Whether teenagers are in or out of their families and what roles they are expected (or willing) to play often remains unclear. While development is key, an external context of war, poverty, job scarcity, or uprooting may also play a part. In immigrant families, for example, adolescents often learn the new language before their parents, thus exacerbating role ambiguity and the flipping of generational power. In such cases, boundary ambiguity may reach a problematic level if roles are permanently reversed and the young take charge in all areas of their family members' lives.

Boundary Ambiguity Is Not Boundary Permeability

Boundary ambiguity is not the same as boundary permeability. Boundary permeability means that a family's boundary is porous so that family members can come and go. Parents go to work and come home, children go to school and return, friends drop in, relatives visit, and service providers come and go as needed. Such boundary permeability is functional as opposed to a rigidity that doesn't allow any flow in and out. Examples of boundaries that are nonpermeable are families in which no one is allowed to leave, and no one is allowed to visit, for example, cults or families with heavily guarded secrets.

We hope this discussion of differences helps to understand boundary ambiguity more precisely. While boundary maintenance and boundary permeability are research variables, it is essential to know that boundary ambiguity is something else.

Intervention for Boundary Ambiguity

When there is incongruence among spouses or family members as to how they see systemic boundaries, the therapeutic goal is to help them restructure in a functional way for their circumstances. Importantly, flexible gender roles are essential for family resilience. With more interchange, the family is less fragile. Such roles as caring for children, cooking, cleaning, and earning money should be interchangeable between men and women. By resisting rigid gender role assignments, the family system becomes more agile to cope and remain resilient.

With the benefit of family meetings of peers or family therapy, family members often manage to make peace with their boundary ambiguity. The core of the intervention is learning to keep two opposing ideas in their minds at the same time (Boss, 2006). With this shift away from either-or thinking, family members gradually come to some agreement that the missing family member is symbolically both here and gone, both present and absent. They lower their stress and helplessness by shifting their perceptions of the situation. If only symbolically, they see the *physically absent* person as still inside their family boundary. We see this in divorced and remarried stepfamilies as well as in adoptive families. We also see this in families where work demands take parents physically far away from the family, for example, deployed military personnel, construction workers, oil riggers, fishermen, and, commonly, men and women who travel frequently for business. Many of these families are nevertheless functional because they lower their levels of boundary ambiguity with the technology of smartphones, FaceTime, Skype, instant messaging, and Twitter.

Examples of families where work requires parents or spouses to be *psychologically absent* while physically present are families of individuals who require deep concentration for long periods of time, such as composers, writers, and scientists. This also occurs in families where a member is addicted. For this, the peer group meetings of Alcoholics Anonymous (AA) or specialized therapy treatment are needed. Finally, there may also be obsessions with computer games or the Internet that keep a family member psychologically absent. For obsessive-compulsive disorder, individual treatment may be needed, but of importance for long-term recovery is family therapy involving the whole family system.

To begin the change process, we can bring the family's perceptions to the surface by asking them, individually and collectively: "Who is in your family? Who is out? Who performs what roles? Who carries out what tasks? Who is included in the family's rituals and celebrations (weddings, graduations, funerals, holidays, and religious events)? Who is excluded?" What we find out may not always be what we expect, but it does reveal resilience or the lack of it (Boss, Greenberg et al., 1990).

Through systems therapy and interventions, families can become sufficiently aware and resilient so that they increase their tolerance for not completely knowing who is in or out of the family. This process may involve psychoeducation, narrative or cognitive therapies, or peer support groups (see Boss, 2006, for details). While all family members may not view the family's boundary in the same way, the therapeutic goal is to reach some degree of agreement that allows the family to function well without conflict (for more, see Boss, 2006, 2011).

New Studies and Future Directions

Studies on boundary ambiguity are currently being tested with new populations and in new situations of ambiguous loss. To stimulate further study, we provide a list of articles categorized as quantitative or qualitative or both. See Additional Readings, this chapter.

Our goal in this chapter has been to define boundary ambiguity and its nuances, caveats, and theoretical underpinnings. Our goal in Chapters 4 and 5 has been to differentiate between ambiguous loss and boundary ambiguity. Indeed, approaches to research and interventions will vary. While perceptions are the key with both constructs, they are very different in theoretical roots, view point, and operationalization.

Summary

When family members are unclear about who is in or out of the family, they are experiencing boundary ambiguity. Perceptions are critical components of boundary ambiguity. When families rigidly decide that a loved one suffering from drug addiction, dementia, serious physical ailment, or so on, is out of the family (either-or perception), rifts may be created. Rifts may form when family members' perceptions regarding who is in or out of the family are incongruent. All families have to maintain their own perceptions of membership and roles; outsiders cannot do that for them.

Points to Remember

1. Boundary ambiguity can be caused by ambiguous loss.

2. Ambiguous loss is the situational stressor, and boundary ambiguity is the perceptual manifestation of that stressor.

3. Sometimes, family transitions are caused by a clear loss (death), but sometimes, they are caused by maturation (e.g., a child grows up and leaves home).

4. Sometimes, when families cannot obtain the facts needed to help them determine if a loved one is living or dead, they take it upon themselves to decide whether their missing person is in or out. This risk taking is called "the family gamble."

5. If family members cannot clarify who is in and who is out of their family systems (with regard to roles, rules, rituals, and responsibilities), the process of systemic restructuring is blocked, and the system is held in limbo.

6. Boundary ambiguity is not a neutral variable. It has valence. It is a continuous variable. Higher levels of boundary ambiguity are associated with lower levels of sense of mastery.

7. Family members are rarely fully present or fully absent.

Discussion Questions

1. Think about a time in your life when a family member left the system. Who left? Under what circumstances did the person leave? How did your family reorganize to compensate for the void? What did your family do?

2. Describe situations that you know of involving a family deciding to "close out" a loved one and proceed with family life as if that loved one was permanently gone. Under what circumstances was that decision made? Did everyone in the family agree with the decision? If they didn't agree, describe what happened.

3. Think about who you consider as being inside your family as you respond to the next set of questions. Who do you include when planning a family celebration? Why? Who do you exclude? Why? Who do (or did) you want to attend your high school (or college) graduation or your wedding? Who didn't you want there, and why?

4. Is it possible for a family's boundaries to be too permeable? Why, or why not? If you think that it is possible, describe the types of interactions that might occur in such a family.

Additional Readings

Dekel, R., Levinstein, Y., Siegel, A., Fridkin, S., & Svetlitzky, V. (2015). Secondary traumatization of partners of war veterans. *Journal of Family Psychology*. Advance online publication. doi.org/10.1037/fam0000163

Kavas, S., & Gündüz-Hoşgor, A. (2013). The parenting practice of single mothers in Turkey: Challenges and strategies. *Women's Studies International Forum, 40*, 56–67.

March, K. (2015). Finding my place: Birth mothers manage the boundary ambiguity of adoption reunion contact. *Qualitative Sociology Review, 11*(3), 106–122.

Suanet, B., van Tilburg, T. G, & van der Pas, S. (2012). Who is in and who is out? Implications of family structure for boundary ambiguity among older parents with regard to their stepchildren in 1992 and 2009. *Gerontologist, 52*, 715–715.

Film

Blumofe, R. (Producer). (1968). *Yours, mine and ours* [Motion Picture]. United States: Desilu Productions, Walden Productions.

Boundary Ambiguity Research Using Primarily Quantitative Methods

Bocknek, E. L., Brophy-Herb, H. E., Fitzgerald, H., Burns-Jager, K., & Carolan, M. T. (2012). Maternal psychological absence and toddlers' social-emotional development: Interpretations from the perspective of boundary ambiguity theory. *Family Processes, 51*(4), 527–541. doi: 10.1111/j.1545-5300.2012.01411.x

Brown, S. L., & Manning, W. D. (2009). Family boundary ambiguity and the measurement of family structure: The significance of cohabitation. *Demography, 46*(1), 85–101.

Mu, P. F., & Chang, K. P. (2010). The effectiveness of a programme of enhancing resiliency by reducing family boundary ambiguity among children with epilepsy. *Journal of Clinical Nursing, 19*, 1443–1453. doi: 10.1111/j.1365-2702.2009.03075.x

Mu, P. F., Kuo, H. C., & Chang, K. P. (2005). Boundary ambiguity, coping patterns and depression in mothers caring for children with epilepsy in Taiwan. *International Journal of Nursing Studies, 42*, 273–282. doi: 10.1016/j.ijnurstu.2004.07.002

Stewart, S. D. (2005). Boundary ambiguity in stepfamilies. *Journal of Family Issues, 26*(7), 1002–1029. doi: 10.1177/0192513X04273591

Suanet, B., van der Pas, S., & van Tilburg, T. G. (2013). Who is in the stepfamily? Change in stepparents' family boundaries between 1992 and 2009. *Journal of Marriage and Family, 75*, 1070–1083. doi: 10.1111/jomf.12053

Boundary Ambiguity Research Using Primarily Qualitative Methods

Jenkins, D. A. (2013). Boundary ambiguity in gay stepfamilies: Perspectives of gay biological fathers and their same-sex partners. *Journal of Divorce & Remarriage, 54*, 329–348. doi: 10.1080/10502556.2013.780501

Khaw, L., & Hardesty, J. L. (2015). Perceptions of boundary ambiguity in the process of leaving an abusive partner. *Family Process, 54*(2), 327–343. doi: 10.1111/famp.12104

Leite, R. (2007). An exploration of aspects of boundary ambiguity among young, unmarried fathers during the prenatal period. *Family Relations, 56*, 162–174.

Thomson, L., & McArthur, M. (2009). Who's in our family? An application of the theory of family boundary ambiguity to the experiences of former foster carers. *Adoption & Fostering, 33*(1), 68–79.

Boundary Ambiguity
Research Using Mixed Methods

Berge, J. M., & Holm, K. E. (2007). Boundary ambiguity in parents with chronically ill children: Integrating theory and research. *Family Relations, 56*, 123–134.

McWey, L. M., Bolen, M., Lehan, T., & Bojczyk, K. E. (2009). I thought I was the adult in this house: Boundary ambiguity for parents involved in the foster care system. *Journal of Social Service Research, 35*, 77–91. doi: 10.1080/01488370802477493

6

Family Coping, Adapting, and Managing

*O*n a Thursday evening in September 1998, a 24-year-old Minnesota woman, Khoua Her, strangled her six children, aged 11, 9, 8, 7, 6, and 5 and then unsuccessfully tried to kill herself. The year before, she had called 911 many times when her estranged husband attacked her and the children; she had filed two orders for protection against him. Because she belonged to a Hmong clan, however, the police deferred to the patriarchs, who said they would handle the problem. The troubled woman received no outside help or protection, however. Short on money and food, she fell into a downward spiral of depression and hopelessness. At the trial, she said that leaving this life was the only way she could think of to protect her children and herself from any further abuse. She received a 50-year prison sentence for her crime. (Gardner & Moore, 1998; Moore, 1999; Quinlivan, 1999; Suzukamo, 1998a, 1998b; Baker & Semple, 2015)

***

In the holiday season of 2015, a mother left her baby (swaddled in towels just purchased at a dollar store) in the crèche of a nativity scene inside a church in Queens. She knew about New York's "Safe Haven" Law, which allows a parent to leave a child at a designated safe location. This church was such a place. The Queens district attorney said he would not press charges because "it appears that the mother, in this case, felt her newborn child would be found safely in the church . . . [she] chose to place the baby in the manger because it was the warmest place in the church . . . she returned the following morning to make certain that the baby had been found." A parish maintenance worker found the baby boy and made sure he was safely cared for. (Baker & Semple, 2015)

Here we have two different stories about mothers who could not take care of their children. One coped in a positive way; the other in a destructive way. The theme of this chapter is coping, especially how we, as family scientists and practitioners, can foster more positive coping.

Defining Individual and Family Coping

It is important to understand both individual and family coping because the family is comprised of individuals, young and old, who make up the whole. The primary focus of this book is the family, but that does not mean we ignore the individual. They are linked.

Individual Coping

According to the classic and still accepted views of coping espoused by psychologist Lazarus (1966, 1976, 1993), individual coping is defined as both direct action behaviors (fight or flight) and palliative behaviors (actions or thoughts that make a person feel calmer) that occur in response to a stressor. Lazurus' view is that an individual's coping behaviors are organized not by emotions but by the cognitive process that leads to the emotional response. One may choose a particular coping behavior as a means of controlling or regulating emotions generated by a stressor.

Recently, neuroscientists have suggested a third stress response, especially to fear. It is called "freeze," a stress response that immobilizes people (see Koutsikou et al., 2014). Although this research is still emerging, we point out that stress responses may now include fight, flight, and freeze. That is, coping behaviors may include a neural response of freezing in addition to the original choices of fight or flight based on Lazarus's early work.

Although Lazarus's theoretical work is psychological in nature and directed toward individual stress, it is also relevant to family coping. He emphasized how cognition (thinking, learning, remembering) influences emotions and cognitions (values, beliefs, expectations, motivations). This means that indicators of cognitions and emotions are important in managing family stress. When Reuben Hill (1949/1971) emphasized the importance of the meaning (definition) that a stressor event had for families, the family's values, beliefs, expectations, and motivations implicitly came to the fore in the primary and secondary appraisals of threat. Like Lazarus, Hill also highlighted the need to understand both the sociological and psychological aspects of coping. Today, we continue this interdisciplinary view of coping.

Family Coping

Family coping is defined as the process of managing a stressful event or situation by using a relational system without detrimental effects on any individual in that system. Family coping is a cognitive, affective, and behavioral process by which individuals and families as a whole manage, rather than eradicate, their stressful events or situations. As a process, family coping is more than a set of attributes. Initially, one person or the family as a whole may accidentally discover what behaviors ease stress and tension, or, through processes of rational decision making, they may decide to repeat a course of action that proved effective in the past. In either case, once a family finds a coping strategy that works, that strategy is likely to become part of its coping repertoire and used repeatedly in future situations of stress.

To understand how families cope, researchers often focus on dyadic (or couple) coping (Bodenmann, 2005; Lavee, 2013). Swiss psychiatrist Bodenmann (2005) identified various types of couple coping: (1) common—the couple jointly solves problems or shares feelings, (2) supportive—one member of the couple helps the other in practical or emotional ways such as offering empathy, and (3) delegated— one member of the couple takes on more burden and responsibility so that there is less stress on the other partner. Couple researchers Coyne and Fiske (1992) found active engagement coping to be helpful when one member of a couple involved the other in problem solving as well as activities that showed that previously hidden feelings were now understood.

These findings about the need for better couple communication align with the findings of Israeli stress researcher Lavee (2013), who explained that the primary context for couple coping is the couple's relationship. While there are differing ways for couples to cope, more open communication and a strong relationship appears to help couples deal more effectively with their stressors and challenges.

The concept of family coping was introduced into family stress theory by family stress researcher McCubbin (1979) and elaborated by family scientists Dyk and Schvaneveldt (1987), who discussed family coping as a process, as well as functions, resources, and strategies. Upon reviewing the family science literature, Dyk and Schvaneveldt (1987) concluded that "family coping is the effort of the family system to master, resolve, tolerate, or reduce demands of stressors that tax or exceed" (p. 35) their collective resources and strategies. Family coping is a constantly changing process because individuals and the system as a whole shift in their cognitive appraisals and behavioral efforts to manage the family's stress.

Earlier, a more social-psychological definition of family coping was deductively based on a series of poststressor studies carried out in the 1970s at the Center for Prisoner of War Studies in San Diego (note that the process of deduction involves reasoning and logic and moves from the general to the specific; induction, on the other hand, infers and moves from the specific to the general). These studies focused on coping after the stressor event of family separation or father absence, in most cases due to military service in Vietnam or job responsibilities in a corporation (Boss, 1975a, 1975b, 1977, 1980b; Boss, McCubbin, & Lester, 1979; Hunter, 1984; McCubbin, 1979). Findings from these studies and those from McCubbin, Patterson, and Wilson (1981) and LaVee, McCubbin, and Patterson (1985) indicated that the following coping strategies were basically constant across all samples: (1) establishing independence and self-sufficiency by the remaining parent and (2) maintaining family integrity.

These two major coping strategies indicated the importance of both individual (psychological) and group (sociological) variables in the research and treatment of families under stress. In sociological models, individual psychological variables have often not been made explicit; in psychological research, family and contextual variables have not been apparent. Still today, we maintain that both are essential.

Research suggests that family coping and problem-solving strategies focus on both self-development and the integration of the family as a system (Boss, 1987, 2002). This finding is consistent with Buckley's (1967) systems theory and, most significant, with the work of early family stress researchers (Angell, 1936/1965; Hill, 1949/1971) who found that the families that coped best with stress were strong as a unit and as individual members.

Overall, from early to present research on couples and families coping with stress, it appears that a balance between individual and family variables provides the most valid theoretical base for a deeper understanding of their stress management processes.

Current Trends in Coping Research

Coping research is an interdisciplinary endeavor. Individual and family coping studies (e.g., couple, parent/child, caregiver/patient) are found in various social sciences and in the nursing and medical sciences. International research on coping is increasing, with participants and researchers from China, Ireland, Cameroon, Australia, and Africa (Caldwell & Boyd, 2009; Ní Raghallaigh & Gilligan, 2010; Tchombe et al., 2012; Wei, Liao, Heppner, Chao, & Ku, 2012; Yeh, Arora, & Wu, 2006). Such expansion in research provides even more nuance to help us clarify how coping leads to resilience in individuals and families, no matter where they are.

While much of the research on coping still focuses on individuals (e.g., infants, adolescents, elders), these studies are becoming more systemic and contextual. From the field of child development, there are studies on risk and protective factors regarding parenting practices for children and adolescents in contexts of chronic adversity and trauma from poverty, illness, or maltreatment (e.g., Kiser, Backer, Winkles, & Medoff, 2015).

Researchers have found that coping is context dependent (Ní Raghallaigh & Gilligan, 2010) and is a complex systemic process of seeing the forest *and* the trees (Keenan, 2010). Therefore, there has been an impressive increase in more systemic coping studies that assess couples, families, and even communities (such as Pinkerton & Dolan, 2007), suggesting community-based projects for marginalized youth.

Thus, what we see today is that although coping research with individual participants still predominates, coping studies are beginning to focus more heavily on couples and families (e.g., Fiese & Wambolt, 2000; Kiser, 2015; Kiser et al., 2015). In their review of life span theories as applied to major life change and loss, Boerner and Jopp (2007) highlight the "collective selection, optimization, and compensation (SOC)" model of Paul Baltes (1997) that focuses on how adaptive processes evolve in couples and families, as well as in groups and social systems. They point out that loss and other stressors rarely occur in a social and relational vacuum; consequently, the way people cope with change must include a relational or family component. This concurs with our contextual view of family stress management.

As coping research has become more contextual and systemic, differing types of coping are being discovered. Lazarus discovered two types of coping: (1) *emotion-focused coping*, which is used when there is little one can do to change the stressor, and (2) *problem-focused coping*, which is used to master or manage a stressor that can be altered (psychologists Folkman & Lazarus, 1980; Lazarus, 1993, 2012; and sociologists Pearlin & Schooler, 1978). Another nuance found by psychologists Folkman, Lazarus, Pimley, and Novacek (1987) was that older people used emotion-focused coping more than younger people. With our burgeoning aging population, more research is needed on types of coping, not only how elders cope but also how their families cope with aging parents. In order to be effective in lowering intergenerational stress, practitioners need to know who uses active versus passive coping behaviors as well as cognitive versus emotion-focused coping.

Today, researchers continue to build on the original definitions of coping, which include appraisal as well as actions. However, definitions and examples have become more varied. Using recent studies, we compiled a new list of coping types.

Denial Coping

Denial coping is defined as "the process by which the mind defends itself against painful or threatening information" (Siemerink, Jaspers, Plukker, Mulder, & Hospers, 2011, p. 69). It includes minimization, resisting knowing, and not acknowledging the truth. In the past, denial was considered a defense mechanism that could be used in the short term for coping (Boss, 2002), but it was viewed negatively in continuing situations in which individuals do not accept reality and repress it (Benkel, Wijk, & Molander, 2010).

For example, denial or delay as coping mechanisms may be useful when it comes to an individual's health, but it depends on the situation. Denial or delay is dangerous with a heart attack or stroke—times when immediate hospitalization is needed; however, it could be useful during hospitalization itself, because it may ward off the fear of dying. Denial and delay are useful in elective surgery (Cohen & Lazarus, 1973) but harmful with diseases such as asthma where one must be constantly vigilant (Staudenmayer, Kinsman, Dirks, Spector, & Wangaard, 1979; see Maes, Leventhal, & de Ridder, 1996, for review). We must be mindful of when denial is effective for coping with stress and when denial is not effective.

With increasing numbers of studies suggesting that denial can be effective, at least in the short term, we acknowledge that denial is a type of coping mechanism (Boss, 2002). Yet, it remains paradoxical (Macquarrie, 2005). That is, denial can be good or bad; helpful or dangerous. The assessment of denial as functional for coping requires our vigilance and careful consideration of nuance, time, and whether or not the stressor can be ameliorated or cured.

Approach/Avoidance Coping

Based on the original fight or flight model, behavioral scientist Rudolf Moos (1993) proposed two coping methods: approach and avoidance. Approach coping uses logic and reappraisal to deal directly with the stressor. Avoidance coping may include distractions to minimize negative emotions and feelings, ranging from using drugs or alcohol to reading, exercising, or simply diving into work.

Both approach and avoidance coping can be helpful if one uses less of a normative lens. Researchers Ng, Ang, and Ho (2012) found that with angry adolescents, approach coping (sometimes viewed as aggressive) was their first line of defense for maintaining their resilience. Dealing directly with a stressor, they used positive thinking, tenacity, and help seeking. Such approach coping apparently worked in two ways for the youth: It reduced their internalization of anger and aggression as well as their anxiety and depression (Ng et al., 2012). For researchers and practitioners who work with youth and their families, such findings "lay the ground work for resilience interventions in an increasingly troubled world" (Ng et al., 2012, p. 544).

On the other hand, with avoidance coping, all members of the family may retreat behind closed doors. The result is that families avoid talking or dealing with stressors, and instead, scapegoat or blame their troubles on one family member. The family as a whole then sees that one person as the problem. Often that person, the scapegoat, then acts out mischievously or violently to heat up a system that is artificially too rigid and silent. This means that the real stressors (e.g., mental illness, suicide, financial failure) are never talked about. In such noncommunicative families, stressors often become family secrets and immobilize systemic interactions.

Forbearance Coping

A coping strategy common among Chinese individuals and families is called forbearance coping; this "refers to the minimization or concealment of problems . . . in order to maintain social harmony" (Wei et al., 2012, p. 98) and also to avoid disturbing others (Moore & Constantine, 2005; Yeh et al., 2006 as cited in Wei et al., 2012). This raises the issue of cultural coping. In cultures that value the community over the individual, the concealment of problems is the preferred way to cope as it is in the best interest of the community. In cultures that focus on the individual, as in the United States, it may not be.

In a study of Native American families, stress researchers McCubbin, Thompson, Thompson, and Fromer (1998) found that these families place less value on individuality and self-sufficiency as coping strategies while more value was placed on continuity of the tribe or community. While further studies are needed, it is important to consider the cultural context of any distressed families before assessing or judging their coping strategies.

Preparedness Coping

Preparedness coping means taking action to be prepared for future catastrophes. For example, elderly people in England who were in danger of coastal flooding received training in order to know how to reorganize and live with uncertainty (Shaw, Scully, & Hart, 2014). However, Shaw et al. (2014) go on to show that "the perception of building resilience can be negative because individuals believe they can/have taken adequate resilient preparations (but have actually failed)" (p. 200). Because preparedness coping had not prevented the disaster for these elders, their realization of failure eroded their well-being.

Boss and Ishii (2015) found this same paradox in Fukushima, Japan, following their March 11, 2011 earthquake and tsunami. People in those coastal communities had been taught tsunami preparedness, but in 2011, the waters were so high that lives and villages were still destroyed. Feelings of failure followed. The lesson was that officials and professionals should not overstate learning coping strategies as the solution to future disasters because preparedness may actually decrease human resilience when it fails to prevent crises. This example illustrates the inevitable link between coping and resilience. For more on resilience, see Chapter 7.

Humor Coping

Often used to cope with extreme trauma, humor coping is the use of cynical or "gallows humor" to relieve tension in dangerous situations that involve war, emergency rooms, fire fighters, police, and so on. Humor coping is a distinctive and effective strategy among youth for managing stress, in particular, depression (Okafor, Lucier-Greer, & Mancini, 2015). Again there is paradox; humor coping can also be maladaptive if it involves "racial prejudice and social dominance" (Kuiper, 2012, p. 483).

Religious Coping

Religious coping means using religious beliefs and rituals to ease individual or family stress. In their study on asylum seeking and unaccompanied minors now living in Ireland, Irish child and family social work researchers Ní Raghallaigh and Gilligan (2010) found that "religious faith plays an important role in their efforts to cope" (p. 234). Performing religious rituals, especially with others, is viewed as active coping and thus effective. But paradoxically (again), using religion as a distraction to avoid companionship or to suppress emotions is less effective, especially if it isolates a newcomer from the larger community. There may also be racial or cultural differences. In a study of coping with caregiving, researchers found that African American caregivers reported greater rewards (assessed in terms of positive feelings and positive outcomes) than did White caregivers. Comfort from religion and prayer mediated the association between perceived caregiver rewards and race (Picot, Debanne, Namazi, & Wykle, 1997). Thus, for some individuals, religion played a role in how caregiving was viewed.

While the "faith factor" (Chang, Noonan, & Tennstedt, 1998, p. 469) needs to be considered in all coping research, belief systems vary immensely. It may be that the closeness and support of religious communities—or any similar "psycho-social intervention" (Chang et al., 1998, p. 469) are the elements that help individuals or families cope with stress. While further testing is needed, it may not be religion per se that helps people cope with stress but whether or not they are connected to a group with beliefs and values similar to their own (Boss, 2006).

Repressive Coping

Finally, the most surprising and important update in types of coping is repressive coping. Repressive coping refers to the tendency to direct attention *away* from the negative effect of an extreme stressor such as the death of a spouse or childhood sexual abuse. What this means is that individuals who use repressive coping will think about or talk about their experience or loss at times, but they do not do so constantly. Repressive coping is not a deliberate effort to avoid thinking or talking about one's extreme experience, but rather, it is a more automatic response. Social psychologists Coifman, Bonanno, Ray, and Gross (2007) suggest that repressive coping is a protective factor.

Repression has, historically, been considered pathological (Freud, 1915/1957; Lindemann, 1944), but today, a growing number of researchers are finding repression to be a positive type of coping (Bonanno, Keltner, Holen, & Horowitz, 1995; Bonanno, Papa, Lalande, Nanping, & Noll, 2005; Coifman et al., 2007). Future research will substantiate whether or not repression remains a positive type of coping, but for now, it is (Bonanno, 2009; Coifman et al., 2007).

Coping Ugly

We end the list with a new term born out of the research on repressive coping. It is called "coping ugly," a term coined by pioneering grief and trauma researcher, George Bonanno (Bonanno, 2004, 2009; Bonanno & Mancini, 2008; Stix, 2011). Coping ugly means coping in ways that differ from what has been considered correct and proper by society, for example, psychiatric diagnostic manuals, popular media, or your neighbors. When victims of disaster are unwilling to share their stories and yet are doing well, they may be labeled negatively as cold or repressive. Adding coping ugly to our contemporary list of coping types reminds us that there is a surprising range of functional coping.

While Bonanno's work remains somewhat controversial, time will tell where research leads: toward repression, or expression, or the idea that ways of coping with extreme stress (e.g., death and disaster) can be functional in many forms. We continue to call for more inclusion of diversity in what is now assessed as effective coping.

Coping and the Contextual Model of Family Stress

Although coping is a process, it belongs heuristically under the B factor in the Contextual Model of Family Stress (CMFS) (see Figure 2.1). It represents resources that the family can draw upon in times of stress and crisis. These resources emerge at various levels: (1) individual, (2) couple/family (including psychological family defined in Chapter 1), and (3) community/neighborhood (see Chapter 8). All levels must be assessed. Whether or not a family activates its coping resources depends on its perception of the event (the C factor). See Figure 2.1.

The process of coping reveals how the family as a whole and its individual members define and assign meaning to their situation of stress. For example, perceptions of shame or anger about the event may prevent coping by not asking friends or relatives for help, while stigma and discrimination or being in a life-threatening context may prevent families from asking for professional help. The use of resources is thus influenced by the family's context, which influences its resilience. This illustrates the recursive process of the CMFS. Simply having a list of resources does not tell us when and why a family uses the resources on that list—or why they do not use the resources. That belongs to the process of coping. Note that coping was a new dimension added to the CMFS by Boss in 1988 and 2002; coping was not part of Reuben Hill's original ABC-X model (1949/1971). He considered coping *only* under the list of a family's resources, but we see coping as much more—a process influenced heavily by the family's internal and external contexts (see Figure 2.1).

Family Coping Resources

The family's coping resources are its individual and collective strengths at the time the stressor event occurs. Examples of such resources include economic security, health, intelligence, job skills, proximity of support, spirit of cooperation in the family, relationship skills, and network and social supports. Therefore, the family's resources are the economic, psychological, and physical assets on which members can draw in response to a single stressor event or an accumulation of events. These are types of capital that they can spend, in order to do well, feel secure, and poised to confront challenges.

An intervention program for high-risk families, Strengthening Family Coping Resources (Kiser, Donohue, Hodgkinson, Medoff, & Black, 2010), teaches the following: deliberateness; structure and a sense of safety; connectedness; resource seeking; coregulation and crisis management; and positive affect, memories, and meaning. After completing this family-centered program, children in the family scored lower on depression and anxiety, as well as problem behavior and attention problems.

Individual Coping Resources

In 2010, a comprehensive measure of coping from a dialectical behavior therapy perspective was examined for its validity with five coping skill areas identified: emotion regulation, mindfulness, crisis survival, reality acceptance, and interpersonal effectiveness (Neacsiu, Rivzi, Vitaliano, Lynch, & Linehan, 2010). Several of the measure's items are presented here to provide a sense of what coping looks like. They include the following "Told myself how much I had already accomplished"; "Just took things one step at a time"; "Made a plan of action and followed it"; "Talked to someone about how I've been feeling"; "Stood my ground and fought for what I wanted"; "Bargained or compromised to get something positive from the situation"; "Kept feelings to myself"; "Blamed others"; "Compared myself to others who are less fortunate" (Neacsiu et al., 2010, p. 7–8). Coping behaviors and attitudes take various forms and moreover, are often dependent on the situation a person faces.

At an individual level, coping strategies develop fairly early in life, as discussed by applied psychologists Skinner and Zimmer-Gembeck (2007). Their assessment of many empirical studies of children and adolescents revealed that 12 coping strategies were consistently used. The four most often used strategies were support seeking/help seeking (this includes source of support, kind of support sought, and how the support was sought), problem solving (including planning and developing specific strategies), distraction (purposely keeping busy or playing games), and escape (actually leaving the distressing environment). All of these reflect a core element of coping, which is taking action/doing something.

However, research shows that families may also take a more passive approach to coping. A recent European study regarding how adolescents view their family coping strategies found that redefining the family's problems is a commonly used strategy, as is being passive about the problem (Zuković, Knezević-Florić, & Ninković, 2013). They also report that families are far more likely to use informal support rather than formal (institutional) support and conclude that families in their study have underdeveloped or insufficient functional coping strategies.

Community Resources for Family Coping

Communities can aid in family coping by providing social support, informational support, and perhaps most important, by creating a memorial to acknowledge and remember the family's loss or disaster. Families of the missing, for example, see they are not alone; they see that their neighbors and fellow citizens recognize the family's tragedy and are empathic, not judgmental (Robins, 2010, 2013; Saul, 2014). (See also Chapter 8.)

Intervention and Prevention

To begin treatment or prevention, we must first determine the real stressor event. For practical reasons, we tend to focus on the obvious—the stressor events at the moment. The complexity, however, goes deeper. The implication is that we may be focusing on an event that is, in fact, not the real stressor. For example, Boss counseled a young woman who was in crisis. She had just had an abortion, so

Boss assumed that this event was the cause of her crisis. When she resisted, Boss listened more carefully and heard her real story: She had been abandoned again. Her parents had not protected her from harm when she was a child, her boyfriend abandoned her now, and her therapist was out of town. She was indeed alone. The real stressor was her continuing experience of *abandonment*.

Mancini interviewed a homeless man who relayed his story as an adult looking to reconnect with his father, who had walked out on the family when this man was very young. (He still remembered seeing his father walk away from their home and down the street, never to return.) As an adult, he found his father, who still lived in the same town, contacted him, and arranged to meet at a certain place and time. Though the son showed up at their agreed upon meeting place, his father never did, and the son was unable to contact him again. What happened in the present replicated what had happened more than 20 years earlier. The stressor event of abandonment was replicated for him just as it was in the young woman's story. To support or intervene with either of them, we would have to listen to their full stories to determine the real sources of stress.

Not all distressed people can go to therapy, however. Beginning in the 1970s, family science professionals, including psychologists and sociologists, shifted from a focus on crisis and the need for therapy to one of prevention. The task was to stimulate, mediate, or facilitate the individual's or family's perception of reality regarding what was happening and how to cope. Today, while family therapists continue to treat many troubled families, psychoeducation is also offered in nonclinical settings so that people can help themselves to prevent maladaptation and learn new ways to cope more functionally. Informational peer groups, medical lectures on public television, self-help books, and reliable Internet resources may all educate and thus help to prevent further distress.

Psychoeducation as Effective Family Stress Intervention

Psychoeducation is based on the assumption that information empowers individuals and families to help themselves. From a cognitive-behavioral perspective, psychoeducation is defined as the therapeutic use of information about the stressor to help families increase their understanding of their particular stressor, how to cope more effectively, and how best to manage their emotional reactions to that stressor (Anderson, Hogarty, & Reiss, 1980; McFarlane et al., 1995). Once families know the facts (or lack thereof) about their stressor, then they are more empowered to cope and manage the stress as well as their emotional reactions (Boss, 2006; Goldenberg & Goldenberg, 2004/2008; Nichols & Schwartz, 2004).

How Did This Simple but Revolutionary Idea in Mental Health Treatment Come About?

In 1980, family therapist Carol Anderson worked with families who had a schizophrenic family member. She was the first to suggest psychoeducation as a method for easing family stress and emotional reactivity. She and research colleagues (Anderson, Reiss, & Hogarty, 1986) found that they were dealing with a biological disorder and that families—or mothers—should not be blamed for the schizophrenia. Based on their research, a method of intervention emerged whereby the entire family benefited from learning how to cope with this challenging disease (Goldenberg & Goldenberg, 2004/2008). Rather than viewing family members, especially mothers, as needing psychiatric treatment, they found it more effective to support and empower the entire family with information. With this, the family lowered their expectations about curing a disease that was incurable. Instead, they were taught to manage the stressor (Nichols & Schwartz, 2004).

Today, the psychoeducational approach is highly recommended as a best practice to help families with a host of incurable or unfixable stressors (Boss, 2006). It empowers families to cope with their own particular stressor and not be labeled as sick or dysfunctional. This implies that instead of using harmful historical terms, such as "schizophrenic mother," "schizophrenic family," or "alcoholic family," we recommend using the more respectful and accurate terms, for example, "families with the stress of mental illness" or "families with the stress of addiction."

The First Step: Where to Begin?

With treatment or prevention, the first step is to assess the congruence or incongruence of family members' perceptions about their situation. What does the stressor event mean to each of them? Often there is disagreement. Sometimes, just one person in the family breaks through the family belief system and begins the process toward resilience and change with more functional coping. When even one person's perception of reality shifts, the ripple effect causes the entire family system to shift. The process of change begins, and the system begins to recalibrate its processes, hopefully from dysfunctional coping to more functional coping.

Dysfunctional coping is often learned, perhaps from a family culture passed down across many generations. Due to such learned behaviors and implicit family rules or paradigms plus rigidity and resistance to change, coping strategies in dysfunctional families appear to be automatic and without thought or intention. For example, a parent may cope with job stress by coming home and yelling at the children or by reaching for a cigarette without even thinking (a palliative coping behavior).

Before people can begin to shift to more functional coping processes, family members must become cognitively aware of what they have been doing and what other options they now have. By taking in new information and accepting responsibility, the process of change toward more functional coping begins. The family's rigidity is penetrated. If the problem is one of physical, sexual, or verbal abuse, a primary goal is to help individuals within a denying family system to learn cognitive restructuring or cognitive coping (Boss, 1993, 2006). This is not an easy task for families, especially if the dysfunctional pattern of coping has been in place for several generations.

Yet, change is possible. In 2005, psychiatric nursing researchers Edward and Warelow found that "Coping in the face of adversity involves emotional intelligence and resilience, both of which can be developed through support and education" (p. 101). They continue to support the case for psychoeducation, which improves clinical outcomes in mental health. While information empowers functional coping, we must work harder where information is unavailable.

The immigrant woman in our earlier story who killed her children and tried to kill herself to escape an abusive husband did not know English and had no one to give her information about safe houses. She was a member of a clan in which the patriarchal elders in the old country controlled violence and conflict among married couples. In the United States, with new rules conflicting with the old, she found no help for the violence to her and her children. A lack of language skills also prevented her from finding other options, either seeking help or telling others.

On the other hand, the mother who left her child in the Queens church, a legal option in her state, likely had more language skills and thus information to identify and access safer options. Although her choice of action may have been as agonizing as that of the immigrant woman, this mother's way of coping by leaving her child in a designated safe place was adaptive—and legal. More public education is needed in a variety of languages to inform the public about these safer options to family and parental stress.

Complexities of the Coping Process

The coping process is complex so we explicitly address four of those complexities. They involve (1) the paradox of individual vs. family coping, (2) the paradox of functional vs. dysfunctional coping, (3) the use of dialectical thinking, and (4) the chain reaction of coping or what is more precisely called, the codetermination of events.

The Paradox of Individual Versus Family Coping

"It's weird not to be weird." John Lennon

"Religion. It's given people hope in a world torn apart by religion." Jon Stewart

"Procrastinate now, don't put it off." Ellen DeGeneres

A paradox is a statement that says two opposite things, both of which may be true, as seen in the quotes above. Paradoxical statements are also found in the definition of family coping. That is, family coping includes the contradictory but valid elements of two paradoxes—those involving *individual versus group* as well as *functional versus dysfunctional* adaptations. Being doubly paradoxical, family coping is a complex phenomenon.

In short, a dialectical process depends on reasoning and discussion that juxtaposes contradictory ideas and strives to resolve what appears to be in conflict. However, that resolution is never really attained, so our assessments and interventions must include a "both-and" perspective, and less often, a binary or "either-or" view (Boss, 2006).

What does this mean? Family stress theory is composed of many opposing elements: conflict versus solidarity; adaptation versus revolution; coping versus falling into crisis; independence versus family cohesion; and, the most basic of all, opposing elements in family research—the individual versus the family. Family researchers, therapists, and educators dealing with family stress must therefore incorporate dialectical (both-and) thinking into their work. Either-or thinking may be less useful due to the tension between individuals and the family as a whole.

When we talk about family and individual coping, the question arises as to whether the phenomenon of family coping exists or whether family coping is simply the coping of a collection of individuals; is it merely addition, or is there a gestalt that is more than the simple sum of individuals in a family? From a social-psychological and dialectical perspective, both individual and family coping are important, so the theoretical perspective becomes one of dialectics.

Sociologist Walter Buckley (1967) identified dialectics as one of three types of systems theory: mechanistic, organismic, and dialectical. Only a systems approach based on dialectical methods allows a researcher or therapist to incorporate the process dimensions of families coping with stress. Family therapists Carl Whitaker and Gus Napier (Napier & Whitaker, 1978) used dialectical methods to work with troubled families. Their approach avoided blaming and scapegoating and instead helped the family to change and thus live with the tension from opposing forces.

The cognitive appraisal of a stressful situation or event, the emotional reaction to it, and the behavioral responses to both the appraisal and the reaction all occur within an individual family member, albeit within a systems context. However, these individual family members ultimately influence whether the family as a whole is or is not able to deal with the stressor whether it comes from within or outside the family.

Although family coping has been defined as the group's management of a stressful event or situation, we maintain, from a dialectical systemic perspective, that a family as a group is not coping functionally if even one member manifests distress symptoms (depression, eating disorders, addiction, etc.). No matter how calm the family as a whole may seem (and even if they appear to be managing a particular stressor event), if on closer examination, we see that the mother is depressed, an adolescent has psychosomatic problems, or the father's blood pressure is dangerously high, then this family is not coping effectively.

The Paradox of Functional Versus Dysfunctional Coping

Although coping increases the ability to withstand stress, it can also increase vulnerability if adaptations have harmful side effects (Caldwell & Boyd, 2009). From any one strategy, there can be both positive and negative consequences. For example, the wife of an alcoholic who copes by becoming a workaholic may also have chosen a behavior that is maladaptive for her and the family. It causes her to be physically exhausted and distant from her children in a spiral that creates a family where *both* parents are now absent for the children. It becomes a family with nobody in it. Indeed, coping behaviors can simultaneously become stressors. Here, both parents have dysfunctional coping behaviors.

Events of family violence also require caution in terms of coping. As sociologist Richard Gelles (Gelles & Cornell, 1990; Strauss & Gelles, 1995) stated, hitting someone is often defended as a coping mechanism, albeit a dysfunctional one: "I had to hit her because she provoked me." "I had to hit him to defend myself." Violent behavior, however, often stems from an inadequate repertoire of behaviors with which to manage stress, meaning that the process of learning functional coping and stress management never even began. Family violence and other forms of dysfunction such as addiction, abuse, self-harm, or bullying can be analyzed more productively from a dialectical perspective, given that these coping behaviors may simultaneously seem like a way to cope with stress but one that also causes more stress.

In the face of so many opposing truths about functional vs. dysfunctional coping, we repeat that the complexity of family processes is best accommodated by the dialectical view. This approach avoids irrationality, an antonym for dialectical. For example, a man may get drunk and hit his wife to cope with a frustrating day on the job, or a woman may become an addict (e.g., by the abuse of food, tranquilizers, or work) to cope with marital frustrations, but in such cases, the coping mechanism selected stimulates the development of even more distress. Individual and family vulnerability increase when coping behaviors become stress producers instead of stress reducers. Work, food, alcohol, gambling, computers, television, shopping, medication, and even sex can all be both.

The point is this: Whether coping strategies are adaptive or maladaptive, both individuals and the family system are involved in the process. To assess family coping, we must consider the individual and the family as a group.

Dialectical Thinking: Definition and Early Roots

In the paradoxical situations just described, it is useful to use dialectical thinking for intervention and prevention. The dialectical worldview stems from the work of Aristotle, an early Greek philosopher, who said that opposition holds the elements of a universe together. Therefore, dialectics is a philosophy based on the process of movement, development, and interaction. (This implies change.) The process depends on elements in opposition, such as individual versus family and adaptation versus maladaptation; the process of resolution involves destruction, emergence, and alteration, which are the bases for change. In the early 1800s, this philosophy became the basis for German philosopher Georg Wilhelm Friedrich Hegel's premise of progressive development. He said that from every thesis there evolves an antithesis, and this results in the development of synthesis (unified whole), which in turn reacts on the original thesis. The process continues indefinitely (Boss, Dahl, & Kaplan, 1996).

Developmental psychologist Erik Erikson introduced Hegel's notion of thesis and antithesis to the field of psychology in 1950, and Erikson's influence continues as students learn about the nature of socio-emotional development. He described individuals and society or parents and children as contradictions to each other. Klaus Riegel (1979), a developmental psychologist, carried the case for the dialectical perspective even further into American psychological theory by noting the conflicting development of individuals in four areas: the biological, the psychological, the physical, and the cultural. For example, the psychological development of adolescents may not always be in harmony with their physical development; hence the psychological and physical components of their development are actually conflicting. If a family moves to a new culture during this time, the conflicting development for an adolescent will be compounded.

Conflicting development applies to families as a whole as well. For example, parents want their children to leave home, but they also want them to stay and remain loyal to them. Children want to leave home and be independent but at the same time want to be supported financially. Today, many return to live in the family home but declare their independence from any chores or family responsibilities. From this push and pull of dialectics, there ideally can be a synthesis for both parents and offspring. The adult children remain a part of the family but in a new and more mature way, helping and accepting responsibilities of the home and family.

In addition to the complexity of paradox and dialectics, there is one other complexity of coping, the codetermination of events.

The Chain Reaction of Coping or the Codetermination of Events

Families that appear to be coping with a traumatic event may not really have adapted and changed so that years later, when a similar event triggers past memories, this chain reaction causes them to fall into crisis again. Here, history is not so much in the past but ready to be reactivated and troublesome yet again. Like the straw that broke the camel's back, the more obvious current event may not be the real stressor.

Social work researcher Scherz first described the complexity of a chain reaction concept in 1966. It is, however, important to note that the more qualitative chain reaction phenomenon is not the same as the quantitative concept of stressor pileup as operationalized by child development researchers Vaughn, Egeland, Sroufe, and Waters (1979) and family stress researchers McCubbin and Patterson (1983). The difference is this: The chain reaction phenomenon is more psychologically based and is concerned with impact and relentless succession, whereas the pileup of stressor events is primarily the summation of the events that have happened to the family during a particular period of time.

In the end, chain reaction may be a confusing term. The more precise term may be what Riegel (1979) referred to as the "codetermination of events"— meaning events that occur in one dimension but precede, trigger, or cause events in another dimension. For example, a current loss or separation may reactivate an earlier family loss that was never fully grieved or resolved. This does not mean that the family failed to reach acceptance or closure, terms, which we submit, are inappropriate (Boss, 2006; Boss & Carnes, 2012), but simply, for some reason, they were never able to grieve their loss at the time it occurred. For example, Boss worked with a family who appeared to have coped with their child's death, but 10 years later, when President John F. Kennedy was shot, they fell into crisis again and returned to therapy. They had been watching the funeral on television. The massive public expression of grief triggered their own earlier feelings about the death of their child. For the first time, they began to grieve openly—and with each other.

Coping indeed has many nuances in how the process occurs and when. There are also some cautions to keep in mind as you work with or study families under duress who are trying to cope as best they can.

Cautions About Coping

While coping is meant to be a positive phenomenon, and with its complexities discussed, there remain several cautions about coping to consider as we work with stressed families.

1. **Assessing coping strategies is judgmental.**

   Assessing coping strategies can become judgmental when we use a normative baseline of what is proper or improper coping. This does not allow for cultural and ethnic differences in ways of coping. For example, being resilient, connected, confident, and flexible are usually assessed as qualities that are adaptive. Being depressed, a loner, anxious, insecure, and selfish are assessed as maladaptive (Clauss-Ehlers, 2008). Counseling psychologist Clauss-Ehlers (2008) conducted a study of 305 female university students from various ethnicities and found that sometimes researchers' judgments did not consider the culture of the people who are trying to cope in their own unique ways (Clauss-Ehlers, 2008). In another example, sitting without talking to others in the room was functional coping for the Lower Manhattan Chinese American garment workers after the 9/11 terrorist attack (Boss, 2006).

   In their 2012 study on coping strategies for street-involved youth, Kolar, Erickson, and Stewart also found a normative basis used for judging. Since youth often use unorthodox ways of coping, assessing the outcomes rather than the process of how the youth get there is essential. Like resilience, coping often occurs in surprising ways, which vary greatly between individuals. Also like resilience (Riley & Masten, 2005, cited in Kolar et al., 2012), assessing coping requires a contextual view, which moves us beyond observation that coping has occurred and to the study of *how* it is occurring. How do people get there? We study the process and not just outcomes, which are often normatively based and culturally biased. It is better to look at change over time to see how people change to the point of more functional coping. In this way, with less judgment, we gain more valid information and understanding about differences and similarities in how people manage stress and adversity.

2. **Cultural paradigms for coping differ regarding individualism and collectivism, but they may be changing.**

   Modern development in a society does not always improve coping. In cultures of collaboration that value community, and for people unaccustomed to coping alone, modernity can erode social supports and connections. For example, South

African psychologists, Tchombe et al. (2012) studied psychological undertones of family poverty in rural communities in Cameroon and found that families in poverty coped in such ways as collaborative problem solving, reflecting their Afrocentric philosophy. They also found that "African values of social support and solidarity are increasingly in crisis" (p. 240) because of a growing shift to modernism and its focus on the individual. We must be cautious about accepting absolutes or fixed ideas in cultural paradigms, which often judge individualism to be more functional than collaboration and teamwork. It is likely that both are needed in this more global age.

3. **Sometimes it may be better not to cope.**

   If the implicit value is family peace over family conflict at all costs, we are cautious about the use of the concepts of coping, adaptation, and managing. The expression of anger (not violence) and even rebellion can be functional in breaking the status quo and bringing about change in a dysfunctional couple or family (Boss, 2006; Gottman, 1999; Gottman, Carrere, Swanson, & Coan, 2000; Gottman, Coan, Carrere, & Swanson, 1998; Stanley, Bradbury, & Markman, 2000). Stress is not always bad, but it implies change. Anger is not always bad; it can provide the momentum for change.

4. **It is incorrect to think that coping strategies are inherited.**

   Although families may use similar coping patterns and strategies across generations, they are not inherited. Families' strategies of coping are, however, often learned and passed on through modeling. More precisely, this is called *the family's transmission of knowledge.* Family therapists, who often use this term, assume that individuals are highly influenced by their families of origin—the systems in which they grew up and were socialized. For example, newlyweds each bring to their marriage the rules of coping and managing that are learned (or not learned) in their families of origin. This includes decision making and problem-solving rules, which they bring to the marriage even when they would like to discontinue their use (Hardy & Laszloffy, 1995; McGoldrick, Gerson, & Shellenberger, 1999). Because each person brings his or her history to a new relationship, there are inevitable disagreements and thus some stress.

   Parent-child relationships can also be affected. Research shows that adverse parental experiences not only influence their own mental and physical health but that of their children as well. This attests to the importance of knowing that there is not an inheritance, but rather, a psychosocial transmission of family patterns of coping (O'Neal, Richardson, Mancini, & Grimsley, 2016). Change is possible.

Concluding Thoughts for Future Work

In the future, perhaps the most fruitful direction for coping researchers, educators, and practitioners lies in the intersection of human development and family science (Boss, in press). This is because coping strategies differ with age—a variable that cuts across all cultures and races. With maturation, there may be more similarities than differences in how people cope. We see this in cultures of youth as well as elders. We also see common features in new parents who use less risky coping strategies than when they were responsible for just themselves. Research development within the Contextual Model of Family Stress will yield useful information for practitioners and families themselves.

In Chapter 7 we differentiate between coping and resilience and explain their theoretical links. Both are processes, but which comes first is still being determined. In this book, to risk answering the chicken and egg question, we propose that coping precedes resilience—and thus have placed this chapter on coping ahead of the chapter on resilience.

Summary

The process of coping is complex and often composed of opposing elements. It is thus paradoxical. Today what is normal or proper or functional coping can take various forms. This means that binary thinking (such as categorizing families or individuals as either "normal" or "abnormal") is no longer a useful way of assessing family coping. Remember, stressful events are managed through cognitive, affective, and behavioral processes. We underscore the term *process* because family coping does not suddenly occur. It is, indeed, a process. It may occur through a series of trials and errors as families encounter behaviors that alleviate tension and stress. Sometimes the helpful behaviors are encountered accidentally. When a family identifies a coping strategy that works (for that family), the members use it again and again. A relational or family component must be incorporated into efforts aimed at helping individuals cope with change, because stressors do not occur within a relational vacuum. Coping strategies (e.g., support-seeking/help-seeking, problem solving, distraction, escape) tend to develop relatively early in life. If not, they can be learned.

Points to Remember

1. The concept of "family coping" was introduced into family stress theory by H. McCubbin (1979) and was later elaborated by Dyk and Schvaneveldt (1987).

2. Lazarus posits that an individual's coping behavior is organized not by emotions but by the cognitive process that leads to the emotional response. A coping behavior may be chosen (1) to deal with the problem generated by the stress emotion (fight or flight) or (2) to control the emotion by covering it up.

3. Officials and professionals should not overstate that preparedness coping is a solution to future disasters because that very thought will demoralize and shame people when preparedness fails to prevent the disaster.

4. The family's coping resources are its individual and collective strengths at the time the stressor event occurs.

5. Financially, not all distressed people can go to therapy. For cultural reasons, they may not want to use such services. They may prefer churches or neighborhood clinics or simply talking with elders or a friend.

6. Families coping with stress can be empowered to help themselves if given information about how to manage their particular stressor, their emotional reactions, and likely family conflicts that may occur. This is called psychoeducation. Whether a self-help book, peer group—online or face to face—or educational sessions for families in a hospital or nursing home, psychoeducation is one of the most effective interventions for family stress. While self-help is useful, families also need information so they know when professional help is necessary (see Boss, 2011, for example).

7. Coping strategies are not necessarily inherited; they are often learned.

Discussion Questions

1. Provide three examples of maladaptive coping and three examples of adaptive coping.

2. What is the difference between active and passive coping? Provide three examples of each.

3. Think about your family. What coping processes are typically used when your family is faced with a stressor event? What are the processes, and what are the typical outcomes?

4. Provide two specific examples of an adolescent using an unorthodox way of coping that might be functional. (You must first identify a stressor the adolescent might be facing.)

5. What must helping professionals be aware of when working with a family and that family's coping strategies?

Additional Readings

Folkman, S. (2012). Stress, coping, and hope. In B. I. Carr & J. Steel (Eds.), *Psychological aspects of cancer: A guide to emotional and psychological consequences of cancer, their causes and their management*. New York, NY: Springer Science & Business Media.

Konisberg, R. D. (2011, January). New ways to think about grief. *Time*. Retrieved from http://content.time.com/time/magazine/article/0,9171,2042372,00.html

Kuo, B. C. H. (2011). Culture's consequences on coping: Theories, evidences, and dimensionalities. *Cross-Cultural Psychology, 42*(6), 1084-1100.

Kuo, B. C. (2013). Collectivism and coping: Current theories, evidence, and measurements of collective coping. *International Journal of Psychology, 48*(3), 374–388.

Lee, H. S., & Mason, D. (2013). Optimism and coping strategies among Caucasian, Korean, and African American older women. *Health Care for Women International, 34*(12), 1084–1096.

McMahon, E. M., Corcoran, P., McAuliffe, C., Keeley, H., Perry, I. J., & Arensman, E. (2013). Mediating effects of coping style on associations between mental health factors and self-harm among adolescents. *Crisis, 34*(4), 242–250.

Mohammad, E. T., Shapiro, E. R., Wainwright, L. D., & Carter, A. S. (2015). Impacts of family and community violence exposure on child coping and mental health. *Journal of Abnormal Child Psychology, 43*, 203–215.

Nicholls, A. R., Levy, A. R., & Perry, J. L. (2015). Emotional maturity, dispositional coping, and coping effectiveness among adolescent athletes. *Psychology of Sport and Exercise, 17,* 32–39.

Park, M., Chang, E. R., & You, S. (2015). Protective role of coping flexibility in PTSD and depressive symptoms following trauma. *Personality and Individual Differences, 82,* 102–106.

Roh, S., Brown-Rice, K. A., Lee, K. H., Lee, Y-S., Lawler, M. J., & Martin, J. I. (2015). Stressors, coping resources, and depressive symptoms among rural American Indian older adults. *Social Work in Public Health, 30*(4), 345–359.

Rossetto, K. R. (2015). Developing conceptual definitions and theoretical models of coping in military families during deployment. *Journal of Family Communication, 15*(3), 249–268.

Zsolnai, A., Kasik, L., & Braunitzer G. (2015). Coping strategies at the ages 8, 10, and 12. *Educational Psychology, 35*(1), 73–92.

7

Resilience for Managing Stress

*T*he 2013 Boston Marathon was marred by tragedy, a bombing that killed three spectators and wounded more than 260 participants and bystanders. One year after the bombing, USA Today published an article titled "Seeing the World in a Different Way: Boston Survivor Copes With Physical Realities" (Whiteside, 2014). This story is a testament to human resilience at the individual, family, and community levels. Nicole Gross, one of the victims, is facing the physical reality of her wounds and says, "I'm going to be at the back of the line at races, and that's fine by me. I don't mind having that change, because the person I was before was very Type A, very focused, with blinders on. Now I'm opening my eyes to see the world in a different way. It's been good for me both emotionally and physically."

Nicole, her husband Michael, and her sister Erika (whose leg was amputated as a result of her injuries) were standing near the finish line waiting for the women's mother to finish the race when the bomb exploded. Since the tragedy, the sisters have become each other's coach, encouraging one another as they deal with serious injuries. To make sense of this tragedy and attach meaning to what happened, Nicole and Michael are planning to build a center that bridges physical therapy and exercise and helps people heal in a community of support. Reporter Kelly Whiteside noted that "Survivors thrust into the spotlight are more than just what happened April 15, 2013. Their stories also are about what they hope to be, in part because of the tragedy" (Whiteside, 2014, p. 3-C). The essence of resilience is captured in that phrase "about what they hope to be, in part because of the tragedy." (Whiteside, 2014)

Resilience highlights that aspect of the human condition that can build on despair and substantial challenge; in effect, something is mobilized inside a person that may not have happened without the tragedy. While we should not be overly optimistic about resilience by placing it on a pedestal and acting as though people have a "resilience gene," there are many instances where victims of tragedy shake off the victim mantle and replace it with a mix of recovery and growth. In the case of Nicole Gross, she asks, *Where do we go from here? What sense can we make from all this?,"* and reporter Whiteside concludes, *"Nicole Gross will cross a finish line Saturday, but in many ways it will also be a start"* (Whiteside, 2014, p. 3-C).

The focus of this chapter is *family* resilience—how to help families regain their resilience in the midst of stress, crisis, or trauma. To do this, we define resilience, illustrate how it fits into the Contextual Model of Family Stress (CMFS), discuss its various meanings, review relevant research that applies to family systems, provide necessary cautions, and summarize why resilience has become so important for those who work with families in stress.

The Difference Between Coping and Resilience

Resilience is theoretically linked to the construct of coping, which was previously discussed in Chapter 6. To understand one, you also need to understand the other. Which comes first remains a question, but as previously stated, we risked answering this chicken and egg question by proposing that coping comes before resilience. This means that effective coping is essential for an individual or family to be resilient.

In the previous chapter, we defined coping as the ability to adapt to adversity. This focus on overcoming adversity is shared with the construct, resilience, but there are critical differences. Coping means managing, surviving, and getting by—in many respects, keeping the status quo. Unlike resilience, coping does not imply change or growth, which is why maintenance of the status quo is an accurate understanding of the term. In contrast, as you will see unfold in this chapter, resilience implies flexibility and bouncing back from adversity with more vibrancy, thus exceeding previous levels of functioning. Unlike coping, resilience usually implies growth—for example, greater strength, increased health, or greater success. This highlights perhaps the main distinction between these two often-confused terms. That is, while coping centers on holding the status quo, resilience implies change and transformation.

Another area of confusion between coping and resilience concerns timing. That is, which process occurs first—coping or resilience? We are not able to empirically answer this question but agree with Rutter (2007) that coping "may turn out to be important in the genesis of resilience" (p. 207). It has been suggested (as we proposed at the end of Chapter 6) that coping precedes resilience, but it is also suggested that resilience is a bridge between coping and human development (Leipold & Greve, 2009). Leipold and Greve (2009) state, "This phenomenon of resilience, in turn, needs to be explained by coping processes, which lead to certain developmental trajectories" (p. 41). In this sense, resilience may spring from successful development as well as successful coping processes.

In this chapter, as well as the previous chapter, although we come down on the side of coping being a precursor to resilience, research may indicate that they co-occur, that is, one informs/contributes to the other. It is a question that carefully planned longitudinal research will likely answer. There is another open question: That is, must resilience always lead to or be about becoming "better than ever" or better than before? In a clinical sense, do our clients really have to be better than before the adversity occurred in order to live well and do well?

While considering these chapters on coping and resilience, also consider how knowing about both coping and resilience increases a researcher's or practitioner's capacity to more fully understand how individuals and families deal well or not so well with both usual and unusual challenges. With this introductory clarification, we will now focus exclusively on resilience.

Defining Resilience

The origin of resilience remains an open question, but our view is that some people may have qualities and characteristics that increase their odds of being resilient because they have gained it contextually from family, community, or culture. We also know there is great diversity in how individuals and families cope and how they demonstrate resilience. The Swedes use two interesting terms in describing children's processes of thriving when challenged. A "dandelion" child has the capacity to survive and perhaps thrive no matter the circumstance that is faced (we know that dandelions seemingly grow everywhere, in the harshest of conditions), whereas an "orchid" child requires nurturance in order to flourish (we also know that orchids require great care in order to have a reasonable chance of surviving and to produce blooms) (Ellis & Boyce, 2008).

Resilience is commonly understood as flexibility and buoyancy, but in the social and behavioral sciences there is an additional aspect of resilience— achieving a level of performance or functioning that may be higher than it was before. At the very least, there is the assumption that we learn something as a result of grappling with problems and adversity. This aspect implies that experiencing stress and adversity has made a person stronger.

A comprehensive definition of resilience is offered by Windle and Bennett (2012) (also see Windle, 2011):

> Resilience is the process of negotiating, managing and adapting to significant sources of stress or trauma. Assets and resources within the individual, their life and environment facilitate this capacity for adaptation and bouncing back in the face of adversity. Across the life course, the experience of resilience will vary. (p. 219)

Note that these authors do not assign extraordinary qualities to the idea of resilience but see it as the maintenance of normal functioning, especially considering the adversity.

From the perspective of the Contextual Model of Family Stress (CMFS), Boss (2002, 2006, 2012b) defines resilience as the ability to bend or flex (like a suspension bridge), creating the ability to withstand external pressures and strains without breaking down. The core characteristic of resilience is the capacity to bounce back to levels of functioning equal to or greater than before the pressures or stress occurred. Families as well as the individuals in them can survive and even grow stronger from adversity. However, our view of resilience does not require this "better than ever" dimension, though that may be the case for some families. It may be asking a lot for a person or a family to be better off after adversity. Boss states, "Resilience is therefore more than being able to manage stress and more than the absence of pathology" (2014, p. 2206). There are many elements involved in the process of dealing well with adversity and ultimately how well families fare.

Resilience and Family Stress

Any discussion of resilience must be accompanied by the topics of stressors and stress. To review, Boss (2014) defines family stress as a "disturbance in the steady state of the family system" (p. 2202). This is an important take on conceptualization, as well as having important implications for working with families to build resilience, because it underscores the notion that various sources can upset the family system and that families will respond in very different ways to the same disturbance source. Perceptions, making sense of, and assigning meaning as family processes are pivotal for understanding stress, including its antecedents, processes, and consequences (refer to Chapter 2; also Boss, 2006).

Individual, Family, and Community Resilience

Resilience is associated with individuals, families, and communities (Becvar, 2013; Hooper, 2009; Norris, Stevens, Pfefferbaum, Wyche, & Pfefferbaum, 2008; Southwick, Bonanno, Masten, Panter-Brick, & Yehuda, 2014). Adversity occurs and is handled effectively at these three levels. Generally, the idea of resilience is the same across these levels, though complexity is a key difference among them. For example, community resilience depends on multiple individuals and families working together to address issues and challenges that affect the larger community. While the effectiveness of communities taking on challenges can be dramatic and the only possible approach to a big problem, mobilizing various community members and community groups can be daunting.

While resilience is not easily understood when looking at how individuals deal with problems, the challenges are amplified when they concern multiple individuals in a family and multiple families in a community (see Chapter 8 for our discussion of the nature of resilient communities). Biological, psychological, social, and cultural factors interact in the process of how an individual deals with stressors (Southwick et al., 2014), which aligns with the CMFS (see Chapter 2). For example, in some cultures, the community itself takes on the responsibility for helping a community member deal with tragedy and sadness, whereas in other cultures, specialists, such as therapists, are viewed as responsible for such healing.

Whether considering individual, family, or community resilience, scholars have moved from a deficit model in which psychopathology was the focus, to a model centered on strengths (Hooper, 2009). We take this strengths perspective as well, while still accounting for deficits and risks that families will face. The strengths approach focuses on those factors in family life that allow families to do well in adversity. Examples include whether family members interact well to begin with, whether a family has previously handled adversity together, whether a family typically makes productive decisions together, and whether they view the adversity in reasonably similar ways (their perceptions as individuals and as a family group). Whether helping professionals work mainly with individuals, families, or communities, understanding how vulnerabilities and resilience intersect is a powerful approach in preventing problems and difficulties.

Ordinary Magic

When thinking about how resilience is understood and how it applies to life and the helping profession, consider an insightful discussion on the processes of resilience that are provided by University of Minnesota professor Ann Masten (2001, 2014). She uses the term "ordinary magic" when discussing individual resilience among children. She states, "The great surprise of resilience research is the ordinariness of the phenomena . . . that results in most cases from the operation of basic human adaptational systems" (Masten, 2001, p. 227). Her developmental perspective seeks to identify elements, patterns, and situations in children's lives that have a bearing on doing well, even when there are substantial challenges (Masten & Coatsworth, 1998).

A primary example of this is a family in which parents are positive, caring, and show other aspects of quality parenting, even when the family faces substantial adversity. An individual-level example of an element that helps children do well in the face of adversity is their positive views of self, sometimes called self-efficacy (Mancini, Bowen, O'Neal, & Arnold, 2015). According to Masten, "What began as a quest to understand the extraordinary has revealed the power of the ordinary" (2001, p. 235). This ordinary magic also applies to families. Families possess multiple assets in their lives, even in the face of adversity and problem situations. We, as family professionals, focus on supporting families as they navigate challenges and activate resilience elements in their lives.

Resilience and the Contextual Model of Family Stress

Our take on family stress places a high premium on contexts: those within families, those near families, and those farther from families but that nevertheless affect them. Psychologist Michael Ungar (2012) states, "the resilience of individuals growing up in challenging contexts or facing significant personal adversity is dependent on the quality of the social and physical ecologies that surround them as much, and likely far more, than personality traits, cognitions or talents" (p. 1). In that same volume, family therapist Froma Walsh (2012) adds, "resilience involves struggling well, effectively working through and learning from adversity, and attempting to integrate the experience into our individual and shared lives as we move ahead" (p. 173).

Social, *shared*, and *physical* are key terms that speak to multiple contexts and move the pivot point from individual traits to explaining how surroundings either support or undermine individuals and their families. For example, some very serious family problems, such as maltreated children and adolescents, can be addressed effectively by community-based relationships that include diverse and active social networks said to be "counterpoints to adversity" (Wekerle, Waechter, & Chung, 2012, p. 190).

The Family's External Context

Chapter 2 presented the CMFS, which includes the family's external context. To review, the external context has five dimensions: culture, history, economy, development, and heredity. Family life is permeable to varying degrees and subject to these external influences. Consequently, understanding how resilient a family and its individual members are, as well as their community, includes paying attention to these elements. We must determine if there are aspects of the culture (such as commonly recognized rules for behavior) that seem to help families manage stress or hinder how well they handle stress or if there are particular historical events that are important to consider.

We have said that dramatic events can affect families for generations. For many families, the economic context is a continual concern that affects their everyday life as well as how they view their future. It may even cause them to feel their chances of bouncing back from economic challenges are slight. The developmental context is founded in biology and the natural unfolding of how families change over time, whether that change involves children growing up or older family members needing care. The challenges to resilience vary over time and circumstance, as will the family's capacity to handle adversity.

As one example, health is a major factor to account for in understanding how to best promote family resilience, as it is a major gateway for being able to handle stressors and for taking advantage of opportunities that support families. A more commonly occurring case is for those individuals and families that are affected by Alzheimer's disease, which requires family members to experience a loved one gradually slip away as the person they always knew (Boss, 2011). We propose that insight into understanding family resilience, as well as becoming a force for prevention in the lives of families, is enhanced by accounting for external contexts.

The Family's Internal Context

Chapter 2 also presented three aspects of a family's internal context: structural, psychological, and philosophical. An important part of that discussion is that family members have more control over the dimensions within the internal context than dimensions within the external context.

Examining families' internal contexts provides many insights into understanding why families do well, why they are resilient. What particular individuals in a family do (how they function) is one example of the structural dimension, while the psychological dimension refers to how individuals and the family as a whole perceive their experiences and the meaning they attach to them. Both the structural and psychological dimensions are related to family resilience because they may represent the various resources a family brings when facing adversity. Philosophical aspects of a family's internal context involve the beliefs that guide their behaviors and how they deal with the world outside of the family. Their beliefs, for example, can pertain to childrearing and how decisions are made in the family. Of particular significance for exhibiting resilience is how families make decisions, because in those families where decision-making processes are lacking to begin with, charting a positive course for the family when the family is experiencing stress is more challenging. A family philosophy can be aligned well with the larger culture and society, or it may be quite different from how those larger social group values and beliefs are perceived. As educators, therapists, or other helping professionals work with families, accounting for their internal context provides clarity to problems they encounter, as well as to possible solutions.

Revisiting the ABC-X Approach

Our ABC-X heuristic model of contexts, stressors, resources, perceptions, and outcomes (Hill, 1949/1971; refer to Chapter Two) also provides a framework for understanding resilience. There are two places in the ABC-X model where there is a good fit with resilience: the B and X factors.

B factor elements are the various resources that individuals and families activate that enable them to deal well or not so well with stressor situations (that is, processes that are helpful to them). X factor elements are what ultimately result from stressors (A factor), individual and family resources (B factor), and making sense of/interpreting/appraising/perceiving circumstances and situations (C factor). This bouncing back and moving forward process can result from grappling with stressors and can also be part of the process of dealing well with stressors.

Including resilience processes as part of a contextual approach (CMFS) for understanding what families face, and how they do well nevertheless, provides a window into prevention and intervention possibilities beyond what can be understood by only focusing on negative elements. For example, understanding warmth in a couple relationship is just as important, if not more so, than understanding relationship conflict (Cutrona et al., 2003; Fincham & Linfield, 1997; Gottman, Coan, Carrere, & Swanson, 1998; O'Neal, Ross, Oed, Lucier-Greer, & Mancini, 2014).

Adversity and Resilience

An important question for understanding resilience is to ask, what is the adversity (the A factor in the ABC-X framework)? This is important because the idea of resilience is placed in light of adversity, rather than what it takes to deal with daily stressors or hassles. The phrase "resilience in the face of adversity" is often used. There are many synonyms of adversity, including misfortune, ill luck, bad luck, trouble, difficulty, hardship, distress, disaster, suffering, affliction, sorrow, misery, tribulation, woe, pain, and trauma. Typically, resilience is discussed because there has been an unfortunate event or incident that is not considered an everyday life experience for a family or individual.

Positive, Tolerable, and Toxic Stress

Our CMFS states that how individuals and families perceive their experiences (Boss, 2002) ultimately determines how they are affected, that is, what becomes positive, tolerable, or toxic stress (Middlebrooks & Audage, 2008). However, we must remember that individuals and families can evaluate and respond to similar stressors in very different ways. It is not enough to know about a stressor event or situation because how families perceive what happens to them ultimately determines what happens next and therefore is where we as family professionals can intervene.

Positive stress is what we experience in a normal, almost unnoticeable way; it is based on experiences that are adverse (harmful or unfavorable) but that do not last very long. Everyday life experiences make up the positive stress category and may include discomfort with meeting new people, competing in sports, making decisions about spending money, or worrying about visiting a doctor and receiving a shot. Positive stress experiences are considered normal and are readily managed, especially if a person has close relationships with others. They are also of low intensity and, in fact, may be beneficial when they motivate people.

Tolerable stress shares a characteristic with positive stress in that its duration is not so long; however, tolerable stress has a greater intensity (strength, power, or force). Any number of disruptions to a family system may qualify as tolerable stress, including a relationship breakup or loss of a job. These are not minor disruptions by any means, but the occurrence itself is relatively short-lived; the aftermath might be acute or persistent depending on other elements in people's lives, including how they perceive what they experience. Tolerable stress may be helpful developmentally if a person has ample support from others, although it has the potential to lead to toxic stress and very long-term negative consequences (Middlebrooks & Audage, 2008).

Toxic stress is dramatically different from positive and tolerable stress, as it is sustained over a long-lasting and drawn-out period of time (Middlebrooks & Audage, 2008). Some examples of this type of stress are child maltreatment, intimate partner violence, and a life of poverty; the former two examples are perpetrated directly by others and the third is an artifact of society and economic disadvantage. It is likely that toxic stress is not easily managed without the intervention of others, such as caring adults and friends and also including the helping professions, like therapists. Many other "formal system" elements (agencies and organizations) may also play an important role in intervention, including law enforcement, child or family protective services, the health department, and so on.

Intensity of Adversity

Understanding the intensity and complexity of the stress itself is required to understand resilience, especially regarding adversity. The nature of the stressor, the stress that is felt, and the responses individuals and families have to the stress are part of the context in which individuals and their families struggle or thrive. Moreover, the meaning families attach to what they experience is a significant element in what happens next.

Significant adversity is an important term because, according to Trzesniak, Liborio, and Koller (2012), it helps to distinguish a resilience process from processes of coping, adaptation, and adjustment. This is a key theoretical clarification because terms that describe stress such as challenges, problems, difficulties, and adversity, are often used interchangeably in the resilience literature.

Although Trzesniak et al. (2012) expect that resilience is a term used to describe a process connected with adversity but further that the adversity must be significant, rather than what an individual or family finds bothersome or challenging (daily hassles being one example), we do not fully agree because ultimately what a family does with challenges, including how they mobilize resources (B factor in the ABC-X Model) and how they perceive and attach meaning to those challenges (C factor) is what leads to either positive or negative results. For example, it might be quite resilient for a single parent to withstand the daily hassles and challenges of child care, plus provide the family income, cook meals, clean the house, and so on. For this reason, we use caution when saying that building resilience is evidenced only when there is extreme or significant adversity.

We caution therefore that researchers and practitioners pay attention to each family's perception because what one family sees as significant adversity may not be so for another family and vice versa. Perceptions about intensity and significance often vary because family contexts, external and internal, vary.

To begin this chapter on resilience we reported on the Boston Marathon bombing because it is an example of what is described as significant adversity. Certainly for the families of the murdered and wounded, the stress and pain were intense and are still continuing. How each individual and family perceives and attaches their meaning to the experience of adversity is an important aspect for understanding how significant such adversity may be to them and thus how they will fare.

The Era of Resilience

In 2004, family scientists Lawrence Ganong and Marilyn Coleman suggested we were entering the "age of resilience." They note that while resilience had been an object of study for multiple decades, beginning with pioneer Norman Garmezy (1987), there is now full focus on this process of recovery from adversity and tragedy. No doubt this focus on resilience was accelerated by the events of September 11, 2001. Since then, there has been no lack of dire events and circumstances that bring up matters of resilience. For example, in 2013 there was the bombing at the Boston Marathon that was mentioned at the beginning of this chapter. Other traumatic events that led to worldwide discussions of loss, grief, and recovery include the mysterious loss of Malaysia Airlines Flight 370 as well as the capsizing of a Korean ferry with mainly high school youth aboard. Today, millions of people fleeing from Syria are being separated as loved ones disappear at sea or are swallowed up in refugee camps. There was also the tsunami that swept across the Indian Ocean, devastating Southeast Asia (about 230,000 people died, and 1.7 million people were displaced), as well as the 2011 earthquake and tsunami that eventuated in the nuclear accident in Fukushima, Japan and causes family displacement and separation still today (Boss & Ishii, 2015).

Resilience Theorizing and Research Over the Years

Early resilience research originally emphasized the stress and crisis of children only and how well they were doing after negative early life experiences (see Nichols, 2013, for a review). Early approaches to family stress research included sociologist Ernest Burgess's (1937) typology of family disruptions according to change in family status, conflict about roles, and loss of family members by death or desertion. But it was sociologist E. L. Koos's (1946) research of the roller-coaster process of adjustment (crisis to disorganization to recovery to reorganization) that inspired Boss's adaptation of his model to show that some families might recover and reorganize to a higher level than before the crisis occurred (Boss 1988, 2002).

As with coping, a more contemporary view of resilience finds that an informed approach to stress, crisis, coping, and resilience requires a "both-and" approach (Boss, 2006; Nichols, 2013). That is, both the dire and negative aspects of family life and family contexts as well as the positive, productive, and capability aspects of family life and family contexts must be accounted for to understand and support families.

Individual Resilience

There are four waves of research and theory development that capture *individual* resilience as it pertains to children (Masten, 2007). The first wave of research was characterized by seeking to identify resilience behaviors and, in particular, their correlates (whether they are characteristics of a child, a family, or a community). The second wave of research involved identifying the processes behind the correlates of resilience (for example, attachment relationships in families and their contribution to individual resilience). The third wave was less descriptive and centered on examining prevention and intervention initiatives (such as the study of protective factors that lessened the effects of negative experiences). The fourth wave, where we are presently, is characterized most notably by identifying resilience as a systems concept. Our contextual approach to family stress places the understanding of why some families do well and others do not squarely in a systems framework, and our particular focus on resilience continues on this path, that all of these processes must be viewed through the systems lens.

Family Resilience

In family resilience research, there were three waves. The first wave focused on family stress theory and identified what resilient families did when dealing with stress (McCubbin & McCubbin, 1988); the second wave emphasized family resilience as a process and focused on protective factors, social systems that surround families, as well as the effects of specific risks (Patterson, 2002); and the third wave (Henry, Morris, & Harrist, 2015) presented thinking and research on resilience as multidisciplinary and the characteristics of family dynamics and significant risk, positive adaptation of families, available protective factors to families, and ecosystems that surround families (Huebner, Mancini, Wilcox, Grass, & Grass, 2007). In effect, current approaches are more likely to account for multiple levels of importance inside and outside of the family, which aligns well with our contextual approach to family stress management (Boss, 2012b, in press; Henry et al., 2015; Masten, 2007).

Family Science Conceptual Frameworks Focused on Resilience

We suggest family science scholars continue to focus on theory in order to determine how families deal with stress and with the multiple contexts that influence families (see Chapter 9). Family science has a rich history of theorizing about families, but although earlier studies were primarily problem driven, they now include context and resilience. The theories we discuss—life course, symbolic interaction, and family stress—are all still well-established in the family science discipline regarding family stress, coping, and adaptation, but now they also include resilience. These three theories have all been identified as not only commonly used in research on families but also particularly relevant for understanding families experiencing regular and challenging transitions, such as military families (Bowen, Martin, & Mancini, 2013).

All three theories—life course, symbolic interaction, and family stress—speak to the four dimensions related to family resilience: first, there are the external and internal contexts that influence and surround families; second, the developmental level of a family; third, the interaction of risk and protective factors that intersect in both individual and family life; and fourth, a "family's shared outlook" (or collective perception) as they face challenges (Hawley & DeHaan, 1996, p. 293). The life course theory especially highlights larger contexts as well as the family's developmental elements, while symbolic interactionism drills down to family meanings and how experiences are defined and perceived. Current family stress theories (Boss, 2006, in press; Bowen et al., 2013; McCubbin & McCubbin, 1993; see also this book) address resilience head on with both perceptual and contextual views.

Life Course Theory

Time is a principal consideration in the life course approach to human development and to family dynamics. More specifically, the approach focuses on issues and events that occur over time and may have bearing on family experiences and family well-being. Consequently, this approach accounts for major societal or world events that are broadly experienced by individuals and by families, while explaining family behaviors and the outcomes, for better or for worse, that families experience. Family change over time is also a consideration of life course theory, which includes developmental eras (for example, young families compared to established families, young people in the family compared to older family members) and changing situations and experiences that accompany those eras. In essence, life course theory is about transitions (see Elder & Shanahan, 2006).

Symbolic Interaction Theory

Meaning and the sense that individuals and families make of their experiences are important elements in the symbolic interaction perspective (also discussed in Chapter 1). This is an important part of the CMFS, with its focus on how families define and perceive their experiences. In effect, interpretation exists between what people think might be an objective event and what they actually experience. Individuals and families define situations, and that definition has consequences for what they think and what they do (Thomas & Znaniecki, 1918). Symbolic interaction is also focused on roles that people have and on their social environment of multiple interpersonal relationships. Discussions from a symbolic interaction approach also include the "self" and how our self develops through interactions with others, in particular, within families.

Family Stress Theory

Although the CMFS is grounded in Hill's (1949/1971) early family stress theorizing, the theory is updated to be recursive and expanded to include internal and external contexts (Boss, 1987, 1988, 2002, 2014). In our particular approach, first presented by Boss (1987, 1988, 2002), the important departure from other family stress theorizing was—and still is—a focus on prevention. That is, even with interventions, our focus is on what keeps families strong and resilient.

Over the years, family resilience has become more prominent in discussions of family stress. In 2002, for example, Patterson differentiated family resiliency as capacity and family resilience as process. There are several instructive parts of this framework, including the elevation of family competence and success as pivotal to understanding stress and coping. The model also discusses the importance of how families define their circumstances (in Patterson's words, "make meaning from their significant risk experiences" [2002, p. 357] regarding the situation itself, their identity as a family, and how they view the world). A family's worldview is informed by contextual factors that are likely related to cultural or religious influences, which are also elements of the CMFS. Patterson's Family Adjustment and Adaptation Response Model (FAAR; 2002) addressed many of the same questions we still address, including how a resilient family differs from or is similar to a resilient individual.

Today, from the perspective of family resilience (a process), we see that much of what happens when families navigate everyday life and extraordinary experiences is shaped by the meanings they attach to them. We see that perceptions are the window through which families gain strength and resilience to move forward despite everyday challenges and extreme adversity. Although early family stress theory did not directly address "resilience," many of the elements of theory about coping and adaptation have pushed toward resilience and away from vulnerabilities.

An Example: Application to Military Families

Resilience is often studied in relation to military families using defined family science theoretical approaches (Bowen et al., 2013; Wiens & Boss, 2006). Wiens and Boss (2006) discuss these families' separations within the CMFS and include a substantial focus on how families perceive what they experience, the sense they make of those perceptions, and how that affects them going forward. Of particular note is a focus on ambiguity and family boundaries, which is a significant issue in military families who regularly experience separation. The Wiens and Boss (2006) discussion is an example of surrounding a particular family situation with a broader theory of family process and stress management, a theory not designed to address military family issues per se but one that addresses the range of family situations and experiences. The CMFS is a practical theory that can be applied to helping and supporting families with diverse characteristics and situations.

A Third-Wave Family Resilience Framework

Earlier in this chapter, we referred to the three waves of family resilience research and theorizing. This third wave resilience scholarship is marked by being multidisciplinary and centered around the view that "when family risk significantly disrupts ongoing family dynamics, families have the potential for positive adaptation based upon protection available through multiple family levels and adaptive systems as well as the interface with ecosystems" (Henry et al., 2015, p. 29). The Family Resilience Model proposed by family scientists Henry et al. (2015) contains the following elements: presence of family risk, family protection that helps families to restore balance, family vulnerability that heightens the potential for significant risk, and adjustment in the short-term and adaptation in the long-term. As an example of third-wave research, Henry et al. (2015) cite research on adolescents, families, and ambiguous loss (Huebner et al., 2007). As coauthors of this book, we have embraced third-wave views— the multidisciplinary nature of resilience research and the need for more focus on positive adaptations. (See also Boss, 2006, in press).

The main point of the Family Resilience Model is that family adaptive systems involve four subsystems: emotion (focused on emotions in a family that influences connections with others), control (authority, power, roles, and rules that influence family members), meaning (a family's worldview and identity), and maintenance (ways of meeting family needs and protection of vulnerable members). These are consistent with Walsh's (2012) intervention framework developed from the perspective of a family therapist (which we discuss in a later section). A primary contribution of this framework is its location of family dynamics within contexts of the meaning families make of their situations and responses, the range of adaptive systems that make a difference for families, and the larger ecosystems that surround families. Of particular note is their discussion of family meaning-making, which is reflected in our contextual model of family stress, coping, and resilience (see Chapter 2).

Resilience Frameworks Focused on Particular Situations

In contrast to the contextual emphasis of the CMFS, the present resilience frameworks are often based on a particular problem or situation. For example, social work professor Lietz (2013) focuses on high-risk situations that families face (such as addictions). She discusses five phases for dealing with stressors and moving toward resilience: survival, adaptation, acceptance, growing stronger, and helping others. It is important to note that these phases are neither linear nor sequential but are where families find themselves as they struggle with one or more challenges. Within these phases are ten protective factors/family strengths: social support (both receiving and giving), spirituality, flexibility, boundary setting, initiative, humor, communication, insight, commitment, and appraisal. Lietz notes the significance of appraisal because it pertains to families finding meaning in the difficulties they are facing. This aligns with our discussion of how families deal with stress (see Chapter 2).

Another example of directing attention to resilience in particular family challenges is seen in the situation of caring for older frail family members (Windle & Bennett, 2012). An important part of psychologists Windle and Bennett's (2012) framework concerns the presence or absence of resources, which may include those related to society (health and social services and social policies), the community (social support for caregivers), or the individual (material resources and health behaviors). Ultimately, the presence or absence of these resources creates a range of consequences, such as caregiver well-being, how challenging providing care becomes, and whether there is a need for institutionalization. An interesting part of this framework is the role that perception plays in accessing social support; a person's perceptions outweigh the significance of actual support received from networks and affect caregiver burden.

In 2011, Boss applied her theory of ambiguous loss to ease the stress of family members who care for loved ones who are suffering from dementia, thus being physically present but psychologically absent. She identifies resources for families that help them make the best of a challenging situation but also to thrive (resilience) in the midst of challenges. The guidance provided to caregivers includes finding meaning, balancing control with acceptance, broadening one's identity, managing mixed emotions, holding on *and* letting go, imagining new hopes and dreams, and taking the time to mind oneself. This guidance reflects Boss's resilience model of stress and also shows the complexity of dealing with challenging situations.

We have cited various theoretical approaches for understanding resilience and its many elements. Some of these approaches are very broad, while others have been directed at specific situations that families face. Understanding the ways of thinking about resilience has great practical value because it helps us identify the many avenues used to help families. For example, if a strategy for dealing with adversity effectively involves finding meaning in what is being experienced (Boss, 2011), then working with individuals and their families must include exploring with them the meanings they attach to that experience, and more importantly, helping them to discover new meanings that are productive for them.

Resilience-Informed Professional Practice

Many challenges to individuals and their families do not garner worldwide attention, mainly because they involve everyday life adversity (daily stressors), including divorce, abuse and maltreatment, or community violence. These are no less potentially devastating than other events, because families are faced with a substantial challenge that may derail their quality of life. The question about resilience is straightforward: "What is the nature of doing well when adversity and tragedy strike?" And for family science and other helping professionals the question is, "What can professionals do to assist families in doing well despite stress and adversity?"

Navigation and *negotiation* are words used to describe resilience processes (Ungar, 2013), which suggest that what contributes to resilience partly results from the capacity that individuals and their families have to "navigate" pathways to needed resources, as well as individual and family capacity to "negotiate" with others for the support they need to handle adversity. Ungar (2013) believes that resilience is mainly about the quality of relationships that an individual has in times of trouble, a person's family being a primary locus of relationships but also those with friends and confidants as well as larger networks in the community (see Chapter 8).

Prevention and Resilience

Dimensions of resilience are congruent with our preventive contextual process model of searching for ways in which individuals and families recover from crises or high levels of stress caused by chronic illness, chronic pain, unexpected job loss, mental illness, the demands of job and family, and caring for an elder. By focusing more on prevention and practice, we can intervene before maladaptations set in. Our focus shifts from risk factors to protective factors; the outcome factor is resilience as opposed to rigidity, immobilization, and depression.

Protective factors can be (1) attribution style (externalizing the blame to explainable forces rather than internalizing it to unexplainable forces or oneself), (2) response style (distracting oneself vs. ruminating), (3) cognitive style (being an optimist vs. a pessimist), (4) social skills (connecting vs. isolating), and (5) problem-solving skills (seeking help from others vs. stoicism and going it alone). It is important to know that protective factors can be learned, optimism being one example (Seligman, 1991). Developing assets and protective factors through experience dealing with difficulties is a primary aspect of resilience.

There are clear implications for those who work with families because we can work with them for the purpose of enhancing protective factors, such as effective problem-solving skills. To some degree, being frozen and not able to deal with the aftermath of adversity is tied to ineffective ways to make decisions, which requires gathering relevant information, weighing options, and being confident in coming to a decision. Another example pertains to the protective factor of social skills and connections with others. Boss, Beaulieu, Wieling, Turner, and LaCruz (2003) discovered that their therapeutic work with helping families connect with other families who had lost loved ones in the Twin Towers became one of their more significant interventions as therapists.

Use of Family Resilience Frameworks

Walsh's (2013) family resilience framework has informed the work of many family scientists, in particular, family therapists. Walsh's approach to understanding resilience is multileveled, with elements that pertain to individuals, families, and communities and provides a framework that speaks to how stressful events impact families, the range of family adaptational strategies, as well as their strengths and other (external) resources that support resilience. Belief systems, organizational patterns, and ways of communication/problem solving comprise the overarching framework. *Belief systems* refer to how families assign meaning to adversity—a positive outlook, including hope and optimism, and transcendence, including spirituality and inspiration. *Organizational patterns* pertain to flexibility (for example, being open to change), connectedness (mutual support and respect of individual needs), and social/economic resources (kin and community networks, larger systems that surround families). Finally, ways of *communication/problem solving* involve creative brainstorming, shared decision making, and preparedness/prevention.

In the hands of prevention and intervention professionals, there are practical applications that stem from a focus on resilience. Our book on family stress management is one example. Walsh (2002) notes how a resilience framework promotes highlighting and maximizing the strengths that families possess, even while they face difficulties. She contends that a family resilience approach means strengthening family capacities to master adversity, that a focus on family strengths aids in reducing risk and vulnerability, and that the approach recognizes potentials to transform individuals and families. She cites particular community-based programs oriented to building resilience in the face of these challenges, among others: job loss and transitions; heterosexism for lesbian, gay, bisexual, and transgender families; refugee trauma; end-of life-challenges; and interventions focused on youth gang involvement (Walsh, 2013). Among her recommendations for professional practice to strengthen family resilience are viewing family members as partners in the healing process, helping family members realize the strengths (assets) they possess even though they may be struggling, and helping families think more about possibilities rather than solely focus on problems.

Of significance for understanding resilience processes is paying attention to diversity (see Chapter 3). For example, family scientists Bermudez and Mancini (2013) have based their clinical framework directed toward issues of Latino families on Walsh's approach, with attention to the issues that involve biculturalism and multiculturalism, ethnic identity, and traditional strategies to deal with family experiences and adversity. In effect, they have added a fourth dimension to the Walsh intervention framework, which they call Ethnic Identity. Among the strategies they suggest for therapists is supporting Latino families as they attach meaning to adversity, by understanding how fatalistic beliefs help Latinos normalize life experiences with "*dichos*" (sayings) about the normal course of life (one example being "*asi es la vida*," meaning such is life). Family professionals must also assist immigrant families to deal effectively with the influences and expectations of multiple cultures, which sometimes are in opposition. Being "on new shores" while at the same time affirming the value of what life has been previously, is a primary task that family professionals can help families with as they navigate and negotiate.

Family therapist Dale Hawley (2000) presents therapeutic strategies that spring from a family resilience framework. One suggestion is, "Rather than seeing [clients] as victims of their past, this perspective supports a view that recognizes clients as competent people who are in the process of adapting to a setback" (p. 107). This perspective is at the core of taking a resilience approach to families and their problems, as contrasted with taking a deficit approach. Hawley (2000) cautions us against taking a one-size-fits-all approach because there are multiple pathways of resilience, though there are some common general pathways that an interventionist should be aware of. Some of these pathways include families that start off well and stay well, families that start off well but develop a disorder, and families that cycle in and out of distress (Cowan, Cowan, & Schulz, 1996). Hawley also advises therapists to be intentional about helping families develop a family schema that is useful to them; that is, to help them make meaning of their experiences and challenges. A family's collective view can be exceptionally helpful to them as they navigate adversity.

Boss (2006, 2011, 2012b, 2014, in press) discusses several resilience-focused guidelines for helping families. For example, she proposes six therapeutic goals for treating ambiguous loss: finding meaning, adjusting mastery, reconstructing identity, normalizing ambivalence, revising attachment, and discovering hope. In the instance of how to help families find meaning within the context of loss, Boss says, "Without meaning, both grief and coping processes are frozen, and there is no hope to move forward with one's life" (Boss, 2012b, p. 290). She also cautions, as we do in this volume, about certain aspects of resilience, including the risks of always being expected to adapt, rather than change and transform. There is also a situational dimension of resilience, whether based in ethnicity or in a certain event an individual or family has experienced. For example, in the case of an ambiguous loss, resilience means increasing one's tolerance for ambiguity by holding two opposing ideas in one's mind at the same time; a "both-and" approach (Boss, 2012b).

There are a number of important implications from the resilience literature for professionals who work with families, either as educators or as therapists. We have discussed several of them, which demonstrate the leverage points for helping families deal well with adversity (a leverage point is a spot where applied effort and focus can lead to change). Experienced interventionists know that one-size-fits-all approaches do not work very well, mainly because "all" do not come in one size. Professional practice implications as we have described them place value on where individuals and families find themselves at the present time, on working with families to uncover and enhance resilience elements in their lives, on accounting for the many forces that surround families, and for assisting them as they make sense of their lives and attach meaning.

Cautions About Resilience

Those who study families should account for how resilience plays into the twists and turns of family experience, including their structures, patterns, challenges, successes, and failures. While we value resilience, we do not recommend embracing it without caution. We now discuss those cautions and considerations, which pertain to matters of research and theory, as well as to professional practice and working with individuals and families.

Troublesome Theorizing

Theorizing about resilience, as well as researching resilience, continues to have its difficulties. One analysis discusses a number of ongoing issues, including how resilience differs from other important concepts such as protective factors, vulnerability, hardiness, and stress resistance and whether resilience is a trait or a process (this is an ongoing debate in family science with most scholars falling on the process side) (Lipsitt & Demick, 2012). Psychologists Lipsitt and Demick (2012) also question whether resilience applies to only extraordinary individuals (we add families as well; remember our earlier discussion of Masten and ordinary magic); whether a risk factor must be of major proportion; whether resilience has singular or multiple elements, including educational resilience, emotional resilience, and behavioral resilience, the idea being that resilience may not be an across-the-board phenomenon; and how resilience occurs across cultural groups (see Bermudez & Mancini, 2013, for an elaboration of culture and resilience).

Lipsitt and Demick (2012) consider theory, specifically whether resilience science is really more effectively placed in a larger theoretical framework (for example, broader family theories such as symbolic interaction or life course theory, as investigated by Bowen et al., 2013). They also debate whether certain research designs are better aligned with studying resilience, for example, longitudinal studies (following families over time and collecting data at multiple points) that take the collective pulse of families who have experienced significant adversity and the meanings they attach (C factor) to that experience.

The Cost of Resilience

Another source of caution when considering resilience, especially in the matter of its indicators, was found in a study of allostatic load among adolescents (Brody et al., 2013). Allostatic load is the wear and tear on the body that accumulates over time as a person is exposed to chronic stress. Brody and colleagues (2013) ask the question, "Is resilience only skin deep?" In their study of African American youth that focused on physiological wear and tear, the researchers discovered there may be a cost to resilience. While these youth were performing well according to visible measures (teacher ratings of competence), their allostatic load was high, indicating internal physiological wear and tear. Externally defined successes take an internal toll, especially among youth growing up in socioeconomically disadvantaged situations.

The implications of this research are substantial because internal and undiagnosed stress potentially disrupts youth and young adults in families moving productively toward a healthy adulthood. Brody et al. (2013) conclude, "This suggests that resilience is multidimensional; hidden indicators of compromised physiological health, such as high allostatic load, may accompany observable competence and positive adjustment" (p. 1291). Using our CMFS, the question of what forces are acting on the lives of the African American youth in this study is raised. For example, what stressors are in their lives that may not affect school performance but have a potentially enduring and negative effect on health, including societal and culture-related prejudices?

Rebellion and Opposing the Status Quo

Ideas about family resilience and strengths must include more than just "taking it on the chin" (for example, adapting) or thriving despite pressure (resilience). To avoid promoting the status quo, we must also include options for rebellion and change. For example, we must consider the possibility that a runaway child may be the healthiest member of the family. In family situations of abuse or incest, resilience is about change and may be full of turmoil before there is justice and growth. The word *resilience* should always be used with caution because it must be considered within contexts, conditions, and situations. A newspaper article used resilience to describe the activities of a terrorist organization and how it was thriving in the face of opposition from legitimate governments and law-abiding citizens. Resilience can operate in very negative, oppressive contexts and not only in instances describing positive adaptation and growth among individuals and their families.

We do not advise using the word *resilience* to represent adaptability that reinforces a homeostatic, status quo model of family, however, rather than a family that embraces change and leads to a new level of family organization. Often, the construct *resilience* is used in conjunction with children or families living in poverty or with a mentally ill parent. Although it is important to know what helps children withstand deprived and difficult environments, we must simultaneously work to change such societal conditions. In fact, a major point made by Ungar (2012) and Boss (2006) suggests that the emphasis on resilience should be a focus on the environments and conditions that impede individuals, families, and communities from having every opportunity to thrive. Concentrating our energies on what makes children or families resilient may lull us into forgetting the larger task—prevention of poverty and racism, at a societal level, and treatment and therapy for mentally ill parents, in the case of families who are in need of professional interventions. We must not accept the status quo when change is possible.

We propose a theoretical model that incorporates and values the possibilities of change and revolution as much as, if not more than, stability and calm. This dialectic approach (Boss, 1987) requires a process view of family stress and resilience (rather than a stable mechanistic view) and outcomes that reflect healthy individuals and strong families. Events are always in flux in family systems; there is always some tension. If not, this is what therapists call a "dead" family or marriage. Therefore, stability and conflict avoidance may not always be of value to every member of a family. This caution requires us to take a critical look at how we use the term *resilience*.

Conclusion

Resilience is important for our understanding of family stress because individuals and families draw upon those elements of their lives as they face challenges, as they understand contexts that help or hinder their well-being, and as they continue to build individual and family capacities for dealing with future challenges. Research on and theorizing about resilience has become increasingly evident in the family science literature, and the term *resilience* is part of the language used today to describe what we call family stress management. As family therapists and educators incorporate perspectives about resilience into their work, they are more able to see the positive dimensions of families, including how they view the world and the unique ways they cope and remain strong.

We began this chapter on resilience with an example of how an individual moved on with her life in the aftermath of the 2013 Boston Marathon bombing; in her own words, "Now I am opening my eyes to see the world in a different way. It's been good for me both emotionally and physically" (Whiteside, 2014, p. 3-C). This captures the essence of resilience, coming back to what she and her family were before the adversity but perhaps now, even growing stronger.

Summary

Resilience is defined as bouncing back and achieving a level of functioning that is equal to (or perhaps even higher than) the level achieved before the stressor event. It is about determining what helps families recover from adversity. Resilience involves more than just getting through the adversity; it includes learning from it and weaving what was learned into one's life on both an individual and a relational level. Research about individual resilience has changed over time. Whether considering resilience at the individual level (Masten, 2007) or at the family level (Henry et al., 2015), theory and research has moved from identifying basic behaviors and correlates to examining resilience processes and focusing more on contexts and systems that affect both individual and family well-being. Specific prevention and intervention approaches have also been developed, focusing on both internal family dynamics and external forces that act upon families, which provide guidance for family science professionals.

Points to Remember

1. Families as well as the individuals in them can survive and even grow stronger as a result of experiencing adversity.

2. A family's ability to handle adversity may change over time, as circumstances change.

3. *Positive stress* is what one experiences in a normal, almost unnoticeable way.

4. *Tolerable stress* has a greater intensity (strength, power, or force) than positive stress.

5. *Toxic stress* is sustained over a long period of time.

6. A runaway child may be the healthiest member of the family.

7. In family situations of abuse or incest, family members may experience a great deal of turmoil before they experience growth and resilience.

8. Symbolic interaction, life course, and family stress theories provide ways of thinking about resilience that intersect with the Contextual Model of Family Stress.

Discussion Questions

1. What is positive stress? List four examples of positive stress that are not mentioned in the chapter.

2. What is tolerable stress? Describe examples of tolerable stress in your life. What is the difference between tolerable stress and toxic stress? What examples of toxic stress have appeared recently in the news?

3. Think about the last stressor event that your family faced. What protective factors did you have? Compare your protective factors to those listed by your classmates. What are the similarities and differences? If they differ, explain why.

4. What programs in your community facilitate building resilience? What is the purpose of these community-based programs?

Additional Readings

Charney, D. S. (2004). Psychobiological mechanisms of resilience and vulnerability: Implications for successful adaptation to extreme stress. *American Journal of Psychiatry, 161,* 195–216.

Fletcher, D., & Sarkar, M. (2013). Psychological resilience: A review and critique of definitions, concepts, and theory. *European Psychologist*, *18*(1), 12–23.

Masten, A. S., & Monn, A. R. (2015). The temporal elements of psychological resilience: An integrative framework for the study of individuals, families, and communities. *Family Relations*, *64*, 5–21.

Shmotkin, D., Shrira, A., Goldberg, S., & Palgi, Y. (2011). Resilience and vulnerability among aging Holocaust survivors and their families: An intergenerational overview. *Journal of Intergenerational Relationships*, *9*(1), 7–21.

Theron, L. C., & Liebenberg, L. (2015). Understanding cultural contexts and their relationship to resilience processes. In L. Theron, L. Liebenberg, & M. Ungar (Eds.), *Youth resilience and culture: Commonalities and complexities* (pp. 23–36). Dordrecht, Netherlands: Springer.

Thoits, P. A. (2006). Personal agency in the stress process. *Journal of Health and Social Behavior*, *47*(4), 309–323.

Walls, J. (2005). *The glass castle: A memoir*. New York, NY: Scribner.

Wanga-Odhiambo, G. (2014). *Resilience in South Sudanese women: Hope for the daughters of the Nile*. Plymouth, UK: Lexington Books.

Film

Cohen, R., Edelbaum, J. (Producers), & Tillman, G. (Director). (2013). *The inevitable defeat of Mister & Pete* [Motion Picture]. United States: United Pictures, iDeal Partners Film Fund, State Street Pictures, et al.

8

Families, Communities, and Neighborhoods

A local newspaper reporter wrote of a woman working in her garden while her young children played in the yard and of a neighbor sitting on his porch watching children return home from school (Johnson, 2012). These are examples of the "specialness of the mundane" and do not seem remarkable except that not so long ago the people in this neighborhood were afraid to leave their homes. Activities that seemed ordinary became significant because previously there were barriers to doing them. One resident said that he could not get a pizza delivered after dark because there were so many robberies of those delivering pizzas.

This neighborhood belongs to a community of duplexes, and in 2010, many of those duplexes were boarded up, and lawns were strewn with trash. Violence erupted at night, and burglary was common; one young couple said they lived in fear for themselves and their children. Gangs were a constant problem. Then, a company bought the dilapidated duplexes and spent over $1 million renovating them; now the neighborhood is under new ownership and has a new name. The company decided to not only invest money in the duplexes but also to invest in the residents in the neighborhood as well. The company owner said investing in that community to help families feel safe worked for the good of all. As an example, residents were hired to provide maintenance in the neighborhood, including painting, electrical work, and lawn care. Management believed that this was how to build a community—by partnering with residents.

These neighborhood and community changes did not come easily, as a culture of dilapidation had developed. Over 400 old tires were removed from yards. What had also developed was a culture of fear, though now the police have reported decreases in crime. A long-time resident said she finally enjoyed living there because the streets were now safe so that people could comfortably sit outside and watch children playing. (Johnson, 2012)

Families, neighborhoods, and communities intersect in particular ways and thus need to be studied systemically—how one supports or thwarts the other, the commitment it takes to enact change, and how community professionals support families in times of stress or crisis. Both the people who live in communities and the trained professionals who are skilled in supporting them have important roles in determining how well both families and the community will fare. The communities that surround families make a difference in their lives. Communities are important because they can provide support to individuals and families so they are not alone when they face challenges, need resources, and seek meaning in their adversity. In this chapter, we focus primarily on the construct of community due to its psychological and relational factors and encourage including this larger system (in its various forms) in research and practice about family stress, coping, and resilience.

Defining Community and Neighborhood

We define community as a group of like-minded people with similar interests who interact and are connected by a shared history and feeling close to one another on emotional and psychological bases. Although they may or may not live in geographic proximity, being in the same community implies that people can rely on one another.

The construct of *community*, however, has a variety of definitions and meanings so that the terms *neighborhood* and *community* are sometimes used interchangeably. To clarify, both are composed of individuals, couples, and families, but neighborhood is primarily geographical, and community is primarily psychological—with social and interpersonal connections. Individuals, couples, or families may, for example, see themselves as part of a religious community, a military community, a sports team community, or a community based on sexual orientation. Due to variations, we may consider viewing community more broadly—as being both geographical and psychological in nature. There is now a third possibility: a virtual community on the Internet or with social media. All three communities—geographic, psychological, and virtual—may be important for individuals, couples, and families today.

Sense of Community

Because community represents more than a geographic place where people live physically, there also exists a sense of community—an individual's or family's feelings of being connected to others who share their values and activities. In effect, it is a sense of belonging (Allison, Broce, & Houston, 2013; Bowen, Martin, Mancini, & Nelson, 2001). Observable indicators of a sense of community include strangers connecting because of shared beliefs or interests in, for example, a favorite sports team or gay, lesbian, bisexual, or transgender (GLBT) communities. The sense of community is also found in religious groups, on military bases, and in faith-based communities, all of which make one feel less isolated. As Reiss and Oliveri proposed to family scholars in 1991, the management of stress and crisis is aided by understanding the family's community. Today, family therapists are even more certain that resilience is enhanced by the sense of community that comes from being connected to like-minded others (Boss, 2006).

Virtual Sense of Community

Over the past few years, there has been an increase in the use of social networking on the Internet as a platform for communicating, connecting, and meeting. Researchers have examined college students' use of web-based social network services and sites and found that such services and sites generate a sense of community for college students as reflected by number of friends and perceptions of support (having people to count on) as well as life satisfaction (generally feeling that life is good) (Oh, Ozkaya, & LaRose, 2014).

Increasingly, social and behavioral scientists, including family scientists, are focusing on the importance of a range of virtual communities—communities that may or may not be viewed as having visible boundaries. This technicality may become less important as new ways of being connected develop. Overall, we need to understand that a sense of community may be essential for family and individual resilience—and often, survival.

Community and Neighborhood

Social, behavioral, and family scientists have explored the concept of community (e.g., Allison et al., 2013; Coulton, 1995; Chaskin, Brown, Venkatesh, & Vidal, 2001; Mancini & Bowen, 2013), particularly in relation to the geography of where people live and how this environment impacts families. They define this geographical context as the local community, where families experience much of everyday life, with others who live in close proximity, and where they interact with neighbors at varying intensities (Coulton, 1995). In short, community is where people commune, connect, and converse.

In local communities, various agencies provide a collection of family services, such as social, health, and educational services. Depending on the quality and quantity of services, the geography of a community can affect family members' sense of safety as well as determine the schools that children can attend (Coulton, 1995). Coulton (1995) also defines communities geographically by the statistical information based on the census and voting areas based on precincts. We propose, however, that census data and voting precincts define neighborhood more than community.

A phenomenological approach can also be taken to define communities (Coulton, 1995), which means allowing people themselves to identify the boundaries regarding where they live and with whom they interact. Whatever the definition, the various conceptualizations of community are interrelated and influence one another in complex ways (Norris, Stevens, Pfefferbaum, Wyche, & Pfefferbaum, 2008). For example, communities may have built elements (e.g., houses and roads) and natural characteristics (e.g., trees and creeks), plus social and economic characteristics (e.g., employment rates and home ownership rates), all of which affect families' comings and goings throughout daily life. Buildings and trees, however, cannot create a sense of community without human connections. Again, similarities or differences likely determine whether community members are well connected or isolated. For example, a Jewish family living in a Scandinavian Lutheran community may feel isolated until they join others in a school community; a military family may feel connected living on or near the base because they want to be in a community with other military families.

A point to remember is that individuals and families are the raw materials used to build communities; they are the primary and integral units of change (Landau & Saul, 2004). This process can be positive or negative. Families contribute to and change communities, while being influenced by them in return. This means that families and communities interact together in a systemic process.

Communities and the Contextual Model of Family Stress

Dimensions of community occupy several parts of the Contextual Model of Family Stress (CMFS; see Chapter 2). First, a stressor event (A factor) can occur at the community level, such as an act of violence. Community members can serve as resources (B factor), with medical aid, with knowledge about safe houses, anger management groups, Alcoholic Anonymous (AA) groups, or other peer support groups. How the community perceives the violence (C factor) may reveal differences among genders and ages, even within the same campus, fraternity or sorority, or place of worship. To be sure, battering a family member is not a show of love; it is a misuse of power and is dangerous and life threatening. Family practitioners often provide support as communities make that point clear. The message coming from a group of community members—as opposed to the abuser's spouse or child—has more power to promote change for the better. Today, many communities are doing this but not all.

Focusing on the *internal* dimension of the CMFS (see Chapter 2), where families do have some control and influence, we see that its component parts—structure, psychology, and philosophy—can either lead to eroding or strengthening families. This speaks again to the systemic nature of family and community interaction. Each can influence the other.

Regarding the *external* context of the CMFS (see Chapter 2), recall that it contains dimensions that primarily are not under a family's control or influence, for example, culture, history, global economy, developmental maturation, and heredity. A community, however, may provide opportunities for more agency and influence by individuals and families, for example, which ball team to support, which stores to patronize, where to go to school, whom to spend time with. Said another way, the community provides a nearer environment over which families may have more control, less than within their own home but more than in the CMFS's more fixed dimensions.

Research Findings
on Families and Communities

Theories about families have little to say about community contexts except for Mogey (1964), Burton and Jarrett (2000), and Mancini and Bowen (2013). Their discussions, which span about 50 years, raise the significance of context for individual and family well-being. Research suggests that individuals' and families' informal networks as well as formal systems (agencies, organizations, and their programs for families) are critical to understanding why some families do well and others do not.

Community resources are what people turn to when they need help. The studies cited previously (Burton & Jarrett, 2000; Mancini & Bowen, 2013; Mogey, 1964) also show the existence of negative aspects of community contexts, including violence, which endangers the psychological well-being of family members.

Informal Connections and Relationships

Being more engaged in the community has positive effects on children. For instance, strong parental neighborhood social ties are associated with less depression among their children, greater school success, as well as greater social competence (Marshall, Noonan, McCartney, Marx, & Keefe, 2001). Research shows that the closeness that develops from ties within the community is related to reduced teen births, indicating positive aspects of neighbors being less isolated from each other (Houseknecht & Lewis, 2005). Closeness between neighbors is beneficial and reinforces the tendency to embrace the community. When residents report that neighbors are also friends, their view of the community as a friendly place increases (Swisher, Sweet, & Moen, 2004).

However, community engagement is not necessarily easy (McBride, Sherraden, & Pritzker, 2006). Even though low-income families want to engage with their community, they face impediments to being connected, including lack of transportation, lack of formalized community groups, and their own isolation from others due to frequent change of residences. This points to the important role of formal systems of agencies and organizations, and the programs they provide, for families who are economically disadvantaged, because these agencies and organizations can provide the support families need to more readily connect with others while at the same time providing families with needed resources.

Formal System Programs for Families

In addition to informal networks within communities, there are *agencies and organizations*, known as formal systems, which are helpful to families. Formal systems can bring individuals and families together in multiple ways. They are varied and can have a profound effect on the quality of community life. For example, opening schools at night for youth activities, including sports and performances, not only demonstrates a caring and flexible community but also addresses a practical need to provide activities outside of the usual school day.

Formal systems can also have other positive effects on communities. For instance, it has been found that the positive well-being of adolescents was related to their involvement in a neighborhood youth center (Anderson, Sabatelli, & Kosutic, 2007). Family scientists Bowen, Martin, Mancini, and Swick (2015) found that agency support helped reduce depression among military members by enhancing their sense of community support. And family therapy researchers Doherty, Jacob, & Cutting (2009) found community engagement to be an effective way to teach parent education within a community by connecting formal systems with informal networks. An especially interesting finding suggests that when helping professionals provide marriage revitalization programs within the community, divorce rates seem to decline at a faster pace than from programs provided outside of the community (Birch, Weed, & Olsen, 2004). These studies support the notion that formal networks within one's community can contribute to positive outcomes for various family members.

Neighborhood Risk

How people perceive their own safety and that of their family is influenced by how they perceive their community. People's perception of neighborhood risk (or safety) is a topic often studied due to its importance in understanding individual and family everyday behaviors. For example, perceptions of safety in the neighborhood had a positive influence on students' grades as well as their tendency to intentionally avoid trouble (Bowen, Rose, Powers, & Glennie, 2008). Another study examined how neighborhood risk affected grades, and researchers found that high school students' negative perceptions of their neighborhood environment were associated with their lower grades. Surprisingly, however, school performance and success were related more to their perceptions of the neighborhood environment as negative than the actual risk as indicated by poverty levels (Henry, Merten, Plunkett, & Sands, 2008). Although more study is needed, these findings appear to support the CMFS's emphasis on both context and perceptions (C factor) in assessing risk and in managing its stress.

Exposure to Violence

A related dimension to neighborhood risk is exposure to violence. One such study found that greater psychological distress occurs among mothers exposed to neighborhood problems, which is related to less engagement with their children (Kotchick, Dorsey, & Heller, 2005). The influence that parents have on their children is also demonstrated by the finding that when mothers perceive neighborhoods as high risk, children report more stress (Roosa et al., 2005). The effects of exposure to violence or feeling threatened can be coped with in dangerous ways. For example, youth who frequently heard gunshots, saw neighborhood violence, and viewed their surroundings as dangerous were more likely to carry handguns (Luster & Oh, 2001).

Living in risky neighborhoods can affect parenting. In studies of how adults parent in higher risk neighborhoods, fathers demonstrated more responsibility for the welfare of their children (Hofferth, 2003) and carefully monitored their daily activities, including stricter control of children's involvement with neighborhood life and activities outside of their home (Letiecq & Koblinsky, 2004). These fathers were also likely to directly confront troublemakers in the neighborhood. Neighborhoods rife with such disturbances caused parents to be more fearful, experience greater family conflict, and use harsher parenting (Barajas-Gonzalez & Brooks-Gunn, 2014).

Greater childhood adversity contributes to greater biological risk (comprised of multiple markers, including blood pressure) in adulthood, but if people live in neighborhoods with less adversity, some health markers improve (Slopen, Non, Williams, Roberts, & Albert, 2014). Research shows there are some negative health effects such as asthma and diabetes that community environments may impose on individuals and families.

Other Dimensions of Communities

There are many other elements that come into play when discussing families in community contexts, including culture and ethnicity, as well as gender. For example, the psychological adjustment of Mexican immigrant mothers is substantially related to their reliance on social networks and community resources, which are supports in the face of separation from extended family, social isolation due to being in new surroundings, as well as discrimination due to their ethnicity (Ornelas, Perreira, Beeber, & Maxwell, 2009). Of particular interest is how relying on female friends and relatives positively impacted their mental health. Among Mexican-American families, perceptions of living in an unsafe neighborhood led to more depression and less positive parenting for fathers but not for mothers (White, Roosa, Weaver, & Nair, 2009). The well-being of mothers in that study was affected relatively more by acculturative stress (as evidenced in proficiency with the English language). Ethnographer Reibolt (2001) viewed community in a very different way, with a focus on youth gangs as a subculture; results show youth gangs provided family-like ties to male adolescent immigrants.

These and other studies in family science and its related disciplines of psychology, sociology, and social work show the complexity surrounding families and their individual members, which is significant for understanding (1) stressors, (2) the stress that potentially results, (3) family resources and perceptions, (4) the internal context of the family, and the (5) coping and resilience practices that families activate.

The Social Organization Framework

In the later 1990s, the social organization framework was developed to help us understand how communities influence families, using the term *social organization* to describe a family's immediate and proximal environment and the many relationships and interactions that are part of it (see Figure 8.1; Mancini & Bowen, 2013). Social organization is "the collection of values, norms, processes, and behavior patterns within a community that organize, facilitate, and constrain the interactions among community members" (Mancini, Martin, & Bowen, 2003, p. 319). Of significance in this community context are informal networks and formal systems, which we described earlier. To review, informal networks include extended family, friends, work associates, and neighbors, and formal systems include agencies and organizations, such as those associated with mental health, physical health, public safety, and education.

The social organization model in Figure 8.1 has four major elements: community antecedents, social organizational processes, intermediate results, and

Figure 8.1   Social Organization Theory of Action and Change

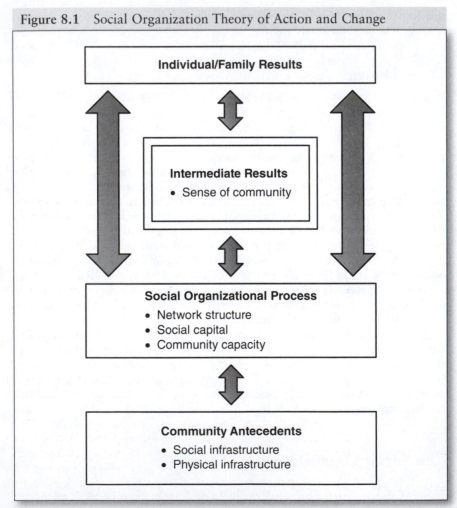

Source: Families and Communities: A Social Organization Theory of Action and Change (2013). Mancini, J. A. With permission of Springer.

individual and family results. Families are viewed as located in and surrounded by larger community networks that impact how everyday life is experienced. In turn, families have an impact on these community networks depending on how much they are involved in community life. Consistent with symbolic interaction perspectives on contexts and families, we suggest that families both act on and are acted upon by aspects of their surroundings. Most families are not insulated from social life; as we said earlier, the networks they are a part of become forces for making a difference in their community, which then affects their own experiences as families (see Bowen, Martin, & Mancini, 2013; Mancini, Bowen, & Martin, 2005). Like the CMFS's internal context, the families have some say in such community contexts. They have the option to use various agencies and can choose to connect with other families to promote positive change.

Although there has been some research into how social organization affects military families, there is a need for further work about stressed families in other community contexts (Bowen et al., 2013). The merits of doing this are evident in Boss and colleagues' community-based interventions after 9/11 (Boss, Beaulieu, Wieling, Turner, & LaCruz, 2003). These family therapists helped labor union families with "a family intervention that promoted community connections" (p. 455). Boss et al. (2003) report that not only did the community prefer meeting with others who also lost their loved ones on 9/11, but that it was these community connections that moved their healing process along in visible ways (Boss, 2006).

Informal Networks

An important aspect of the social organizational approach is an understanding of exactly what it is about relationships within informal networks that is important to people and that makes a difference in their lives. Psychologists and sociologists have been examining how relationships function in our lives for a number of years (Cutrona & Russell, 1987; Mancini & Blieszner, 1992; Mancini, Bowen, O'Neal, & Arnold, 2015; Weiss, 1974).

Individuals and families spend most of their time within informal networks and rely on them for practical and emotional help. These informal networks may be geographically close or distant. In researching ambiguous loss related to Nepal's decade-long Maoist insurgency, humanitarian practitioner Robins (2010, 2014) notes that family support after terrorism requires professional intervention (formal systems), but it is only effective when this support is located within the community context, that is, accounting for informal networks that surround people's lives. The core idea of building community capacity, which implies families coming together, depends on the informal networks of people committed to enacting community change.

Informal networks have six functions (Cutrona & Russell, 1987). *Attachment* involves feelings of intimacy, peace, and security as found in relationships with a partner or close friends. *Social integration* is the sense of belonging to a group that shares common interests and social activities. *Reliable alliance* involves knowing that one can count on receiving assistance in times of need, a function that can be provided by any number of network members, including kin. *Guidance* means having relationships with persons who can provide knowledge, advice, and expertise. *Reassurance of worth* is being given a sense of competence and esteem, for example, from work colleagues. Finally, *opportunity for nurturance* is being responsible for the care of others, including one's children, an older relative, or a neighbor (see Cutrona & Russell, 1987). These six aspects of relationships are more likely to be found in communities where there are stronger and more vibrant informal networks.

The Physical Environment

The social organizational approach also accounts for the physical environment. It is the built community (buildings, roads, and parks) and the demography of where people live that have some influence on how informal networks and formal systems work and how they are helpful to families. Individuals and families may be separated by distances that require extra effort for connections to occur. Some years ago, while conducting a study of the psychological well-being of older adults, Jay Mancini learned that new highways had been built that cut off easy access to other people and to other parts of the town (Mancini, Quinn, Gavigan, & Franklin, 1980). As a result, these older adults, who were mainly low-income and did not own their own cars, were almost always challenged to get to services they needed, whether it was access to physicians or to buy groceries. They were also challenged when they wanted to visit friends who lived in other parts of the city. Although physical aspects of communities such as parks can bring people together, other physical aspects such as new highways can separate them.

Community Capacity

Community capacity is the linchpin concept in the social organizational approach, and it is defined as a sense of shared responsibility (the obligation to be concerned with others) that individuals and families have in a community, as well as their collective competence (coming together to make something positive happen in a community) in accomplishing agreed-upon goals (Bowen, Martin, Mancini, & Nelson, 2000). More vibrant communities are populated by people who will look out for others, in addition to themselves, both philosophically and pragmatically.

Though families may not be entirely aware of how these community context processes affect them, an important dimension, sense of community, provides insight into this (Mancini & Bowen, 2013). *Sense of community* is the extent to which families and their members identify with and feel attachment to their community, therefore having positive outcomes for families who perceive a greater and meaningful connection with the community. Well-being is enhanced when individuals and families determine they are part of their surrounding community and identify with others in the community.

This sense of shared responsibility is part of the overall idea of sense of community previously discussed in this chapter. Both families and communities benefit from meaningful connections (sense of community) as well as from the sense of shared responsibility (Bowen, Mancini, Martin, Ware, & Nelson, 2003; Mancini & Bowen, 2013).

Results for Families

A final dimension in the social organization model is the result or outcome that occurs when families in communities come together. Results can take many forms, including (1) overcoming serious and devastating adversities, such as rebuilding after a tornado; (2) calming tensions in the face of community disagreement; or (3) more everyday life results, such as convincing motorists to slow down while driving through the community (Mancini, Arnold, Martin, & Bowen, 2014). Viewed systematically, however, we recognize that the results of such interactions are not static, they continue across time as reoccurring. Tensions among community groups often call for change.

The Value of Social Connections for Families

We place high value on social connections developed between families and their communities. Helping professionals, however, become concerned when people live in a "social hollow," where there is little social support, few connections with the surrounding community, or only connections with others at a distance (Rojano, 2004). Mancini and Bowen (2013) propose that, "In neighborhoods where there is more fluidity than stability, more uncertainty than predictability, and more ambiguity than clarity, the odds of chaos increase . . . and knowing who to go to for assistance is difficult" (p. 806).

As community interventionists Landau and Saul (2004) note, where there is a lack of structure in a community, there is an increased vulnerability to the impact of a trauma. Where there is a disruption in the routines, rituals, and structure in the family and the community, destructive behaviors also increase, for example, violence and abuse. Landau and Saul also contend that when families are faced with overwhelming challenges, their competence is less available. Consequently, traumatized people need ways to retain or regain connections to their natural support systems—family, friends, neighbors, and others in their community.

Resilient Communities

Even as resilience has been applied to individuals and to families (see Chapter 7), Landau and Saul (2004) have defined community resilience as "a community's capacity, hope, and faith to withstand major trauma and loss, overcome adversity, and to prevail, usually with increased resources, competence and connectedness" (p. 286). An interesting aspect of resilience, whether applied to individuals, families, or communities, is how recovery prepares for future adversity. Saul (2014) notes that the individuals and families of Plaza North in New York, who were affected by 9/11, were better prepared several years later to handle a different kind of threat, namely rents raised to market value, which would have devastated many families and destroyed the community as it had existed for many years. In the aftermath of 9/11, the residents learned how to make a collective response to adversity, rather than individuals and families feeling disconnected, disoriented, and alone. Consequently, they were better prepared to protect their collective community against economic hardships brought on by rent destabilization. Note once again that context matters—in this case, the context of community.

Four Types of Communities

Based on the community capacity elements of *shared responsibility* and *collective competence,* we propose four types of communities that have a bearing on family well-being: *synergetic, relational, able,* and *disengaged* (Mancini & Bowen, 2009; Figure 8.2). A community high in shared responsibility and collective competence is labeled as *synergetic* and is more likely to demonstrate resilience as a collection of individuals and families. Quite the opposite are communities low in both shared responsibility and collective competence, labeled as *disengaged.* Communities may also be high in one dimension and low in the other. A *relational* community is high in shared responsibility but low in collective competence; they have good intentions but have difficulties in making things actually happen, meaning they have the will but have not found the way. An *able* community is low in shared responsibility and high in collective competence; they have the ability and resources to pull together and enact positive changes but lack a sense of common identity, shared experiences, and relationships necessary to motivate them.

Figure 8.2   Community Capacity Typology

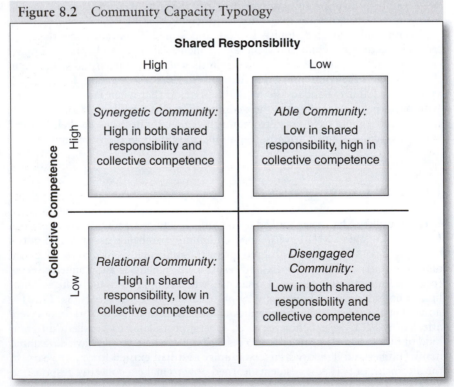

Source: Republished with permission of Lexington Books, from Community Resilience: A Social Organization Theory of Action and Change (2009). Mancini, J., and Bowen, G. L.; permission conveyed through Copyright Clearance Center, Inc.

Although the descriptions of these four community types may seemed fixed, in reality, communities are dynamic and their relative alignment with any one of these four types (see Figure 8.2) may change over time. Community capacity, therefore, can both increase and decrease as demands and availability of resources change over time.

Fluid and Dynamic Communities

Although we provided a community typology of resilience, communities should not be seen as static and unchanging; in fact, communities are better described as fluid and dynamic. Communities have rhythms, which involve patterns, activities, changes, and fluctuation and movement (The Harwood Group, 1999). Communities are malleable and, over time, may be havens for families or challenges to their well-being. Moreover, the fit between families and their surrounding communities can vary, often depending on what families need at a point in time (Bowen, Richman, & Bowen, 2000). For example, families with young children require communities that have provisions to support young and inexperienced parents. Those with adolescents want choices for positive and safe activities for their youth, and families with older members may mostly desire communities that have high-quality health care.

Communities need agility, the ability to change rapidly when needed. Whether it's banding together to build a safer playground or rallying because flood waters have damaged the community, or any problem that requires immediate action, the collective abilities of multiple families together position a community to be more effective immediately and for future challenges. Disasters that affect many people are especially in need of a fluid and dynamic response (see Boss et al., 2003; Norris et al., 2008).

Social Cohesion

A community's resilience, in part, depends on whether social cohesion (in effect, high community capacity) was in place prior to challenges within the community (Takazawa & Williams, 2011). Saul (2014) refers to how people deal with adversity, stating that "knowing who lived in their community, where they lived, and what needs and what resources they possessed was an invaluable asset" (p. 109). As stated earlier, many of the issues that individual families face that are often outside of their control (e.g., natural disasters) are more effectively addressed when families act together. This is evidence of social cohesion.

Communities as Place and Force for Prevention and Intervention With Distressed Families

A community can be a place and force for prevention and intervention or one that is destructive to human development and family well-being (Mancini & Bowen, 2009; Mancini, Nelson, Bowen, & Martin, 2006). Communities have the potential to enhance or complicate families' lives. Families can gain strength from their community surroundings or feel drained by them.

Though we have largely portrayed a positive view of community contexts, we caution that contexts are not inherently good or bad; it depends on how well a family fits within its community, and this may change over time (Bowen, Richman et al., 2000). Psychologist Anne Brodsky (1998) studied a sample of single-parent mothers who developed a negative psychological sense of community, a necessary strategy these mothers used to cope with their negative surroundings and to protect their children. In such cases, distancing from the community becomes functional because getting close to the surrounding community has too many risks for adults and children alike. This example shows again that a glowing "Pollyanna" approach or a "doomsayer" approach to viewing families or communities are both misleading (Mancini & Orthner, 1988).

Communities as Place

We view communities as *places* for prevention and family support. The word *place* suggests location in a geographical or physical sense, including physical boundaries. Like an aerial, satellite, or drone image, these physical boundaries may expand (city or county) or contract (block or neighborhood or Internet) depending on the particular scope of the intervention.

Prevention efforts require physical boundaries because they reflect specific resources (e.g., agencies, organizations, and close-knit groups that are available to families) as well as problems families may face. Once we consider a community or neighborhood in the context of boundaries and how people are in contact with each other (geographically and/or socially/emotionally), we open up possibilities for prevention and intervention with educational support, peer group support, program developers, and others, including community members committed to community improvement. Unlike therapeutic interventions, the *place* perspective directs attention to pathways into communities to help preventionists explore the various ways community members and families are organized within physical boundaries of their interactions.

Communities as Force

A second way to view intervention and prevention is to see communities as *forces* for change and support for families. Communities can be mobilized to shift the culture and conditions that affect families. Thinking of communities as forces for prevention transforms them from passive and impersonal locations to organic sets of families who want to enact change. Such a transformation occurred in a Texas community, when community members jumped into action to help their neighbors deal effectively with Type 2 diabetes (Mancini et al., 2014). Whereas outside health professionals, doctors and nurses, were stymied with regard to getting patients to stick to their diets and to take medication as prescribed to lower blood sugar levels, the trained community people were able to monitor and interact effectively with those with diabetes. This use of local persons to do this proved effective for compliance (Mancini et al., 2014).

Another example occurred in the aftermath of Hurricane Katrina when New Orleans became a force for change (Chamlee-Wright & Storr, 2011). These researchers gathered "collective narratives"[1] from community residents. The researchers found that when individuals and families identified their community as close-knit and family-oriented and made up of hard workers, they adopted a recovery strategy built on self-reliance—a critical strategy that furthered recovery. They also suggested that a collective narrative focused on waiting for help from outside the community impedes recovery. This finding supports other research that has examined how communities participate in healing themselves (Boss et al., 2003; Boss & Ishii, 2015; Saul, 2014).

Communities are not passive but rather vibrant and capable forces for reversing hardship and demonstrating resilience. If family professionals begin to see beyond a single family to surroundings and context, we will see that community is indeed the force for change—a place where prevention and intervention have collective energy.

Community Family Therapy

Over the past 15 to 20 years, more professionals who focus on prevention and intervention have incorporated a community lens into their work with families, in effect viewing the community as a place and as a force for supporting families. One approach that applies this lens to family stress and intervention is Community Family Therapy (CFT; Rojano, 2004), which is designed to meet the needs of low-income urban families. CFT is a systemic approach to working with families; its core premise is that families with low economic means are also influenced by other environmental factors, including individual and family underdevelopment, relatively few positive experiences, and not being involved in civic life. Low-income families may face a number of negative external community-related problems, including drug dealing and gangs, street violence, abandoned buildings, visual pollution, segregation, discrimination, and high unemployment (Rojano, 2004). These external community problems influence issues inside the household and within families, as well as individual well-being.

The approach that CFT takes regarding the connections between families and communities supports the research of Boss and colleagues (2003), Landau (2013), and Saul (2014), who also take a more therapeutic approach. CFT is also consistent with our social organization framework, discussed earlier in the chapter, as well as the CMFS that underlies this book. Though CFT was developed for use with clinical samples of families who are in need of treatment, its essential principles have wider application, for example, after community disasters or tragedies. *Engagement* is a key term in CFT, as it intentionally works against social isolation and exclusion and marginalization—a B factor in the ABC-X Model.

Of particular relevance to this chapter is a primary solution for supporting families: civic engagement. According to family therapist Rojano (2004), "CFT requires the commitment of both therapists and clients in becoming civically engaged and working actively on finding solutions to key issues in the community where the therapy takes place" (p. 63). A specific treatment goal of CFT is to construct a community network of personal supportive resources, including creating ties to family, friends, and coworkers, as well as community groups such as health care or religious institutions (note that formal systems and informal networks align with CFT). Rojano also describes third-level engagement that involves the connections of both therapists and clients with the neighborhood and the broader community. Rojano speaks to the "social hollows" that a person may find herself or himself in, where there is little social support, minimal social network connections, and where she or he has no leadership role (an important part of this CFT framework is acting on the environment). Helping others (positioning to provide leadership) becomes an important element in moving from social exclusion to social inclusion. Also important in the CFT approach is building and maintaining the "personalized community," that is, a mix of family and close friends (i.e., others defined as important by an individual, regardless of blood or legal relationship).

Family therapist Hollingsworth (2011) has applied CFT to issues that are experienced by military families, particularly those undergoing deployment. Hollingsworth's discussion, based on the social organization framework, maintains that taking a community-oriented approach will have positive effects on military family well-being. Such a community-oriented approach elevates the significance of informal networks and the interpersonal relationships that develop within them, and moreover, views these results from networks as building the capacity of a community to be supportive to members who face various challenges. In this application of CFT, Hollingsworth discusses how interventionists can work with clients on identifying sources of social support available to the family and how to become connected with that support.

CFT and its focus on civic engagement align with reports from those who have worked with communities in the aftermath of massive disruptions and violence. Family therapists and psychologists who provided support to New Yorkers in the aftermath of 9/11 discuss how their work was often directed toward bringing families in communities together so that they could share in their grief and healing (Boss et al., 2003; Saul, 2014).

Conclusion

Perhaps the clearest example of the intersections between families and communities can be seen in the recovery process post-9/11. Boss (2004b) was asked to reflect on what she had learned from working with families in New York City. She stated, "Most helpful is the grouping of multiple families together in their own familiar community setting, sitting in circles, so that they can hear each other's stories and form connections through common experience" (p. 558). She concluded that meaning emanates through interactions with others, giving meaning for ordinary everyday life, as well as for those instances when families face substantial challenges and hardships. Of significance for this chapter is Boss's observation that families' abilities to bounce back and grow from horrific experiences is enhanced by their community connections, principally because they are not isolated from each other.

In the aftermath of 9/11, there is ample evidence regarding how community relationships function, particularly reliable alliance and opportunity for nurturance. Families affected by 9/11 were resources to one another and helped each other to survive on a daily basis. Boss (2004b) and Mancini and Bowen (2013) agree that individual and family well-being is substantially related to social connections provided by the community. It is hard to know who to turn to if you don't know who is there, and having one or more people to rely on goes hand in hand with resilience. These connections act as potential buffers as adversity advances on families and should ideally be established prior to the full force of an adversity (Aldrich & Meyer, 2015; Landau & Saul, 2004). By the same token, vital families are pivotal for communities to move forward after adversity. Through coming together and interacting with one another, families can move communities forward even in troubled times.

Saul's (2004) suggestions based on the aftermath of 9/11 in his own neighborhood are now found useful for other community disasters (tornados, hurricanes, floods, etc.). His community-based intervention helps family members connect with friends and neighbors, plus develop new connections with other families in their community they do not yet know, thus recognizing that they are all in this together. The adversity affects them all, so all of their stories are valued, regardless of community standing, ethnicity, religious beliefs, or any other differences. Being heard by people you know validates one's trauma and allows healing to begin; coming together with others in the neighborhood to re-establish routines, holidays, annual events, and festivals are all immensely healing for individuals, families, and communities as a whole—especially after disaster or serious adversity.

In her comprehensive treatment of loss, trauma, and resilience, Boss (2006) says, "I remain optimistic about the community's being a major resource for building resilience in individuals and families" (p. 57). In discussing what determines whether families are "brittle" (easily broken) or resilient, she emphasizes connections with family members, friends, and others in the community and encourages helping professionals to be intentional about supporting families to connect or reconnect.

When visiting the National Hurricane Center in Miami, Jay Mancini asked one of the professionals who administers the center what he thought was the major issue in citizens doing well during and after a major event (Kiefer, Mancini, Morrow, Gladwin, & Stewart, 2008). His immediate reply focused on this: being connected with others and collectively dealing with adversity. Our concluding point is summed up by the mantra of this chapter: "It's hard to know who to turn to if you don't know who is there."

Summary

Understanding why some families do well whereas others do not requires understanding the degree to which families have access to and are able to use informal and formal systems of network support. Strong, positive ties to one's community are associated with positive outcomes for the family as a whole as well as for individuals in the family. For example, when parents have strong ties to their community, their children are more likely to do well in school and exhibit greater social competence. These social ties also reduce families' feelings of isolation. The notion of resilience is not limited to families. It can also be applied to communities.

Points to Remember

1. Neighborhoods have geographical boundaries, whereas communities are not necessarily bound by place or geography. Community represents more than where people physically live.

2. Communities vary in their level of resilience, and they vary in their capacity to support families (shared responsibility and collective competence).

3. When mothers perceive neighborhoods as high risk, children experience more stress.

4. Well-being is enhanced when individuals and families feel that they are a part of their surrounding community and identify with others in the community.

5. Lack of structure in a community is associated with increased vulnerability to stress.

6. For the majority of people after a large-scale disaster, community-based interventions can be more effective than individual therapies.

Note

1. Collective narratives are the shared beliefs, explanations, and meanings attached to events that are used not only to explain what has happened but also to reflect on how the future is viewed.

Discussion Questions

1. Recall the story at the beginning of the chapter about a company that invested money to repair a community's housing and hired residents to provide maintenance for the duplexes. Do you think this is the best way to build a community? Why, or why not?

2. What is collective competence? Provide a specific example of a challenge that a community might face that reflects high shared responsibility but low collective competence. Provide a specific way that a community can overcome low collective competence.

3. What are the characteristics of neighborhoods that are high in social cohesion? What might you see in such neighborhoods? What might be absent in such neighborhoods?

4. What is Community Family Therapy? Why is it a systemic approach?

5. What are the differences between formal systems and informal networks of support? How is each beneficial to families, and why?

Additional Readings

Boberiene, L. V., & Hornback, B. J. (2014). How can policy strengthen community support for children in military families? *American Journal of Orthopsychiatry*, *84*(5), 439–446.

Bonanno, G. A., Romero, S. A., & Klein, S. I. (2015). The temporal elements of psychological resilience: An integrative framework for the study of individuals, families, and communities. *Psychological Inquiry*, *26*(2), 139–169.

Bryant, C. M., & Wickrama, K. A. S. (2005). Marital relationships of African Americans: A contextual approach. In V. McLoyd, N. Hill, & K. A. Dodge (Eds.), *African American family life: Ecological and cultural diversity* (pp. 111–134). New York, NY: Guilford Press.

Colic-Peisker, V., & Robertson, S. (2015). Social change and community cohesion: An ethnographic study of two Melbourne suburbs. *Ethnic and Racial Studies*, *38*(1), 75–91.

Frey, J. J., Collins, K. S., Pastoor, J., & Linde, L. (2014). Social workers' observations of the needs to the total military community. *Journal of Social Work Education*, *50*(4), 712–729.

Lee, Y. S. C., Suchday, S., & Wylie-Rosett, J. (2015). Social support and networks: Cardiovascular responses following recall on immigration stress among Chinese Americans. *Journal of Immigrant and Minority Health*, *17*(2), 543–552.

Lofters, A., Virani, T., Grewal, G., & Lobb, R. (2015). Using knowledge exchange to build and sustain community support to reduce cancer screening inequities. *Progress in Community Health Partnerships*, *9*(3), 379–387.

Shen, Y., & Yeats, D. E. (2013). Social support and life satisfaction among older adults in China: Family-based support versus community-based support. *International Journal of Aging and Human Development*, *77*(3), 189–209.

Smith, L. E., Bernal, D. R., Schwartz, B. S., Whitt, C. L., Christman, S. T., Donnelly, S., . . . Kobetz, E. (2014). Coping with vicarious trauma in the aftermath of a natural disaster. *Journal of Multicultural Counseling and Development*, *42*, 1–12.

Wright, P. M., Shea, D. M., & Gallagher, R. (2014). From seed to tree: Developing community support for perinataly bereaved mothers. *Journal of Perinatal Education*, *23*(3), 151–154.

Future Challenges to Family Stress Management

It is the tradition of this book to end with a nod to what may be future challenges to family well-being. The following are several stressors that we think are impacting families now and may increase their stress in the future. You may or may not agree. Feel free to add to our list.

Health Disparities

Data suggest that there are significant inequalities in many health conditions worldwide such as cardiovascular disease, cancers, diabetes, and chronic respiratory diseases (Di Cesare et al., 2013). Risk factors, such as smoking, alcohol abuse, use of coal for cooking and heating, and obesity, tend to be prevalent among low-income groups of families. If those risk factors lead to poor health (asthma, diabetes), families are likely to experience stress. When children or parents experience poor health, their quality of life and mortality are affected. Moreover, there are equally significant inequalities in healthcare. Families with fewer resources have less access to adequate medical care and medicines, which decreases their ability to prevent and fight diseases.

Climate Change

Though politically controversial, there is increasing evidence that climate change is occurring and that immediate action is needed (Berry, Bowen, Kjellstrom, 2010; Davenport, 2015; DeSalvo et al., 2007; Swim et al., 2009).

Increasingly severe weather—floods, hurricanes, extreme heat, and droughts—all contribute to family stress through water shortages, starvation, and illness. The most vulnerable are poor families and frail family members, the very old and the very young, who are more likely to experience higher levels of negative outcomes. For example, in 2005, when Hurricane Katrina devastated New Orleans and the Gulf coast, the already economically disadvantaged families became even worse off. Homes were destroyed, belongings were lost, and family members were uprooted.

Widening Economic Gulf Between Low and High Income Families

Wealth inequality in the United States has been on the rise for decades and shows no sign of abating (Saez & Zucman, 2014). The decline of wealth among middle-class families in the United States has been occurring since about 1985 (Saez & Zucman, 2014). Economic stress experienced at the family and community level can make it difficult for families to function in their usual ways, communicate as clearly, or be as understanding of each other.

Increasing Work Pressures and Economic Conditions

A related economic issue involves the conditions under which family members work, particularly the length of their work career. People are working longer and sometimes well beyond typical retirement years because of financial necessity. From 1960 through the 1990s, age at retirement was declining; however, data suggest that after the late 1990s, people began retiring later (Caplinger, 2015). There are various reasons for these later trends. Social Security payments are higher the longer retirement is delayed. Inadequate retirement savings and generally poor economic circumstances, including debt, are also reasons (Coile, 2015).

On a more positive note, more Americans are in better health and consequently are able to work longer if they prefer to do so. If delaying retirement is a lifestyle choice, then it is not a cause for concern. However, if older family members must work out of necessity, even past age 65, this necessity can become a family stressor with major relational as well as health consequences. An elderly spouse is left alone because the partner needs to bring in income; an elderly worker ignores serious health issues to continue being paid.

Terrorism

The first decade of this century was marked by global instability and large-scale, violent attacks on civilians. The attacks have continued. Terrorism has growing implications not just for world affairs and politics but for families as well. Mass violence causes distress and loss. Those cases that require treatment tend to involve posttraumatic stress (PTS) and anxiety (Baingana, Bannon, & Thomas, 2005; cited in Wadsworth, 2010). PTS can disrupt families by generating an environment of anger and hostility in families.

On Friday, November 13, 2015, Paris was attacked; people were shocked and traumatized. For safety, families stayed in their homes behind locked doors. Sites where numerous residents and tourists gathered (a stadium where a soccer match was taking place, a popular music hall) were strategically targeted in what is believed to have been a coordinated effort (Almasy, Meilhan, & Bittermann, 2015; Nossiter & Gladstone, 2015). Hostages were taken, and many lives were lost. France's president called the attack on his homeland unprecedented (Nossiter & Gladstone, 2015). People in France and around the world were horror stricken. Today, many people, not just Parisians, are traumatized. For them and their families, the view of the world as a safe and just place is shattered.

Conflict Driven by Religious Differences

Domestic and global conflicts often involve elements of religion. As we complete this book, the popular press carries news reports of Muslims in America being fearful about congregating for worship. This is not the first time a religious group has feared gathering together to worship; Jewish families, for a very long time, have had this fear and not unfounded. In the United States, it is rare that a temple or synagogue does not have police presence during High Holiday celebrations. In many parts of the world, Christians lament being persecuted.

Research suggests that religious persecution is widespread, with rising rates of persecution against Jewish and Muslim individuals and families, and with Christians experiencing persecution in over 100 countries (Pew Research Center, 2014). Potential negative effects on families are substantial. For example, the religious socialization of children is disrupted by the family's fear of persecution; family participation in social networks with others who share their beliefs becomes dangerous. In effect, dimensions of community connections are under threat.

Family Caregiving Challenges and Dilemmas

With 76.4 million baby boomers (born between 1946 and 1964) living in 2012, the aging population is swelling (Pollard & Scommenga, 2014). Many will face debilitating illnesses that require aid, and for many that aid will take the form of in-home care. To provide this care, family members, male and female, will need training and support. Family caregivers will need informal and formal social network support that will provide assistance and especially respite care (that is, time off for caregivers) so that caregivers are able to maintain their emotional and physical well-being. Helping family caregivers stay healthy is a critical goal; it is just as important as caregiving. While there are cultural and racial differences in the effects of caregiving (Boss, 2011, Dilworth-Anderson, Goodwin, & Williams, 2004), many have suffered from this stress-inducing role (Schulz & Beach, 1999). In the future, more families will be faced with stressful choices when their elders need around-the-clock care. This may lead to family disagreements and even guilt, as some families will eventually need to turn to nursing homes or other facilities (Stevenson, 2015). For them, out-of-home care may be the most effective coping strategy.

According to the Alzheimer's Association (2015), there are in the United States almost 16 million unpaid caregivers for those with Alzheimer's disease or other dementias. This means that 85% of caregiving is provided by family members who save taxpapers $217.7 billion by taking care of their own (Alzheimer's Association, 2015) and not using government support. In the near future, the demands of caregiving will only increase as the population ages (Kane, 2011), so it is our responsibility as family scholars to find ways to ease this stress. For the benefit of future family caregivers as well as for larger society, it is urgent to find ways to improve the health and well-being of family caregivers as they now die at a rate 66% higher than people in their same age group who do not function as caregivers (Schulz & Beach, 1999; see also Boss, 2011; Kane, 2011; Kriseman, 2014).

Transgender Trends and Challenges

An internal family matter with large societal implications involves a growing transgender community that, according to Gates (2011), consists of about 700,000 people. A particular aspect of special significance for families involves youth and children who are transgender at fairly young ages. There are implications for parents but also for all other family members, including siblings and grandparents. For many it is a kind of ambiguous loss (Norwood, 2012, 2013a, 2013b).

Psychological stress is experienced by family members of transgender youth and by the communities in which they live. For example, an Illinois school district was found to have violated antidiscrimination laws because a transgender student who identifies as a girl was not allowed to use the girl's locker room, even though she played on girls' sports teams (Smith & Davey, 2015). This has created a great deal of stress for some parents (both those with transgender offspring and those with nontransgender offspring). On the surface, this looks as though it was simply a restroom issue, but the distress experienced by both sides was about much more (de Vries et al., 2014; Russell, McGuire, & Laub, 2008).

In other cases of transitioning, there is growing use of ambiguous loss theory. This theory can be used to explain the family experience of (1) the transitioning person who may be rejected by parents and/or siblings and (2) the parents themselves who may feel that they no longer have the child they thought they had (McGuire, Catalpa, Lacey, & Kuvalanka, in press; Norwood, 2012, 2013a, 2013b). Embedded in such views are socially constructed views of gender, but, as of now, the ambiguous loss theory provides a more systemic approach to understand the stress of transitioning at both the individual and family level.

Increasing Focus on Community

Chapter 8 provided a discussion of communities and their relevance for individual and family well-being. Increasingly, professionals as well as ordinary people are recognizing the importance of communities and the networks of relationships that occur within them as potential supports for families. Boss, Beaulieu, Wieling, Turner, and LaCruz (2003) show the significance of community meetings in the aftermath of 9/11 by their work with labor union families whose loved ones were missing in the rubble (Boss et al., 2003; Boss, 2006). Coming together in a large room at union headquarters was healing for them. Barrio (2000) also reports a preference for community mental health clinics or church-based support for mental illness with minority families as opposed to individual psychotherapy.

Barrio (2000) found, however, that despite the presence of supports, some communities remain distressed, either because of vast economic problems, troubles between residents and authorities, or mistrust of others. We recommend the development of neighborhood-centered clinics; such clinics, given their proximity and connections to neighborhood residents, can help lower tensions for many families.

Violence in Communities

Community violence currently has put everyone on edge. Between January and July 2015 there were over 200 mass shooting events in which victims were killed or wounded (Healy, 2015). It is hard to know when the next movie theatre shooting will occur or which office holiday party will be attacked. Neighborhood residents do not know when they will be caught in the crossfire.

Trust has eroded among families in many communities. Increasingly, we are asked to be vigilant when out and about, whether traveling abroad or across the street. We are not sure who is out there, who will be helpful, or who will inflict harm. There is collective anxiety that typifies the community as a whole, as well as individuals within the community. Violence does not have to occur in one's own community to cause concern and wariness.

Community violence has clear effects on family well-being. School children who are exposed to violence in their community have significantly more somatic complaints, such as headaches, stomachaches, and muscle pain (Hart, Hodgkinson, Belcher, Hyman, & Cooley-Strickland, 2013). Even as natural disasters affect many families in a community in significant ways, so, too, does community violence in its various forms. Individuals and their families feel less secure, are less accepting of people they do not know, and are not sure who will protect them against being harmed.

Families on New Shores

The physical comings and goings of families is not only a worldwide phenomenon, but controversies surrounding immigrants and refugees have been, and now especially, are widespread (Ambrosini, 2013; CBS This Morning, 2015; Chuang & Moreno, 2008; Chuang & Uwe, 2009). These controversies have become central in political debates and have found their way into discussions of national security. Matters of immigrants and refugees are viewed as political issues, rather than family issues. We believe this controversy over families on new shores will continue if not increase into the next decade and that much of our family work will be about uprooted and traumatized families seeking communities and seeking homes in those communities. That, of course, puts new pressure on existing communities, so our challenge, as family scientists and professionals, will be both at the family and community levels.

The arrival of immigrants and refugees has always been an important part of U.S. history, and these immigrant groups have changed the American landscape in positive ways. However, these changes are not without struggle because often the ways and practices of new immigrant and refugee groups are different. Skin complexion has historically been a major barrier to acceptance, as has language differences. *Diaspora* describes this process of families settling far from their homeland. Historically, this applied to the uprooting of Native Americans, African slaves, the diasporas of Jewish refugees, and the great migration from Europe and Ireland in the 1900s. Today, there are 20 million unsettled refugees around the world; one in four is Syrian (Griswold, 2016). What will happen to these families? The situation today has remarkable similarity to earlier forced migrations in that families experience great peril and persecution in their homeland; do whatever it takes to protect their children and themselves; move forward in the face of danger; experience resistance from countries not receptive to migrants and refugees; and feel the pain of sorrow and loss throughout the process. There are, however, stories of triumph in the face of such severe adversity. This is the wonder of human resilience.

This concludes our list of what we consider to be future challenges in family stress management, but the list is by no means exhaustive. Moreover, some of the issues listed may impact some families more than others. Just as responses to stressor events are likely to vary, so too are the events that evoke stress. Remember, families differ. Perceptions differ.

Additional Factors to Consider About the Study of Family Stress

In addition to the family challenges we have presented here, there are additional factors to consider in the future (as well as the present) for family stress research or interventions.

Acknowledge the family's "pre-loss" internal environment. Take into account the quality of family relationships before the loss (death, disappearance) of a loved one. Perhaps the essence of the problem lies not only with the unknown (not knowing if the person is alive or dead) but also with *knowing* that certain words had not yet been spoken or certain feelings had not yet been shared. Perhaps it is easier to be at peace with the stress of loss (be it ambiguous or confirmed) if the relationship itself had not been ambiguous. Helping individuals and families better pinpoint their actual source of stress may allow them to identify more appropriate coping strategies.

Intentionally examine the intersections of vulnerability and resilience because it is impossible to understand one without understanding the other. The Contextual Model of Family Stress (CMFS) encourages us to acknowledge that a collection of positive and negative elements and processes coexist in families' lives. Research then needs to account for these elements and processes when answering core questions about how well families are doing and how prevention or intervention may be helpful to families. The same can be said when studying communities and their influences on families because in all communities there are assets, some active and others ready to be mobilized, while at the same time there are deficits (Kretzmann & McKnight, 1993).

From a practice perspective, our advice is very similar. That is, since vulnerability and resilience coexist, therapeutic approaches must account for both, so that concurrently families are understanding and grappling with vulnerabilities at the same time they are uncovering elements of resilience.

Recognize that not only do individual perceptions of stress and coping contribute to well-being, but how families and communities perceive stress and coping also contribute to well-being. How situations are defined or perceived influence how individuals, families, and communities act or react. Therefore, in our contextual model, the C factor can be applied broadly. In the research world this presents a challenge because empirically assessing what a group perceives, whether at the family level or the community level, is complex. A primary advantage in accounting for perceptions (often called definition of the situation) at multiple levels is that ultimately we learn more about why families behave as they do and why they hold certain beliefs about their situation or about who they are as a family unit. At a practice level, there are similar advantages for pursuing "how situations are defined" in broader ways because we then understand more about the surroundings that families contend with in their everyday lives.

Continue to study family stress, including constructs such as community, ambiguous loss, boundary ambiguity, resilience, multiculturalism, and diversity (with regard to race, gender, sexual orientation, and religion) as a means of maintaining a focus on how families function rather than focusing just on the structure of the family. It seems that the matter of who is in and who is out of the family is fluid, as indicated by trends in legal marriage, patterns of cohabitation, and the multiple ways families are physically and psychologically defined. We think this will continue, if not increase, in the future. Increasingly, the notions of what a family should look like are being challenged and are now often based on how individuals identify or define their family. This is important for researchers because the study of familial influences can be out of sync with contemporary ways families are structured if families are defined in narrow ways.

Shift to ipsative assessment approaches. We are more able to understand the ability of a family or a family member to manage stress when we shift to a more ipsative (as opposed to normative) way of thinking. That is, we assess a particular family against its own ways of function or dysfunction (regarding care, nurturance, economic stability, etc.) rather than against national norms or random samples. After education, therapy, or other interventions, we assess the family's change from what it was, hopefully in the direction of more optimal functioning.

Approach the study of families with methodological rigor. This includes incorporating assessments from multiple sources and exploring change over time. We note that although perceptions are important, we must also consider assessments of professionals, such as teachers, physicians, or clinicians. While such assessments are often considered the gold standard, we must pay attention to perceptions in order to help families whose worldviews, beliefs, and values differ from our own or differ from what has been called "the norm." Determining how and to what extent stressors change families requires methodological rigor. Perceptions families hold or the meanings they attribute to stressors can change over time. They may naturally change over the life course or as a result of unexpected experiences of trauma or stress. Thus, in the future, more longitudinal study designs are necessary.

Incorporate theories and theorizing into examinations of family vulnerability and resilience, but push for clear connections between theory, research, and practice. Family science as a discipline should make more use of existing theories that have clear connections with professional practice and research or that are viewed as amenable to theorizing in order to make those connections. Might it be that family science scholars have tended to be more interested in quantitative findings about families than exploring theories that provide explanation for those findings? We encourage practitioners to apply and test theories about families under stress in order to develop prevention and intervention initiatives. Boss's (2006) work on trauma, loss, and resilience serves as just one model of moving from research to theory to clinical application and back again (Boss, in press). We need more useful theories that can be easily applied by professionals working with troubled families wherever they are.

These are our thoughts about family stress challenges in the near future, in addition to our encouragement for future research. We call for more focus on the "why" of family stress as well as more research aimed at application. Both researchers and practitioners are needed and can, if they work together, contribute to the accumulation of knowledge about family stress management. But most important, that knowledge has to help a diversity of families.

Every community, city, or region now has a mix of families, thus calling for more inclusive theories and interventions. Throughout our book, we have highlighted and discussed the many complexities and variations that surround stressed families and that are found within families themselves. The comings and goings of individuals and their families affect those who are seeking new beginnings, as well as those who either open their arms to the newcomers or those who resist them.

Conclusion

In the end, we encourage your own thoughts and discussions about current and future directions for understanding family stress management and for what you may do going forward to study or help families—however they may look and wherever they are found. To understand family stress is to give attention to the real obstacles families face while at the same time honoring their natural resilience and assisting them when necessary along the road to stress management.

As we continue to expand the Contextual Model of Family Stress originally developed by Boss (1987, 1988, 2002, 2014), we continue the process of theory development in this third edition with increased attention to multiculturalism, diversity, and community. This allows us to think more broadly and inclusively about (1) context and (2) perceptions in determining how and why families respond as they do. Perhaps because Boss was also a family therapist, she always preferred studying the C factor that reflects meanings and perceptions (Boss, 2015, in press), but we continue that emphasis today for researchers as well as practitioners. There are, however, new topics in this edition, not just on multiculturalism but on family resilience and the community, all critical elements in the study of family stress today.

We have approached this new edition of *Family Stress Management: A Contextual Approach* as family science scholars and also as members of our own families and communities with concerns about the challenges families face now and in the future. While we recognize the quicksand in which many families find themselves, we have strong beliefs about the capacity of families to cope and do well. Many surprise us with their resilience. We also recognize that life's complexities often require family members to band together in communities or families of choice in order to survive. For such reasons, our focus has been less on how families look structurally and more on what they do to not only survive but live well. Toward this end, the time has never been more important for us as family scientists and professionals—educators, policy makers, researchers, theorists, and clinicians—to help families cope with and manage their stress.

We began our book by quoting novelist Tolstoy's idea about differences in unhappy families. We end this book by saying that it is because families view the world through different lenses (lenses shaped by their experiences and background) that distressed families are distressed in their own ways. This is what makes the study of family stress challenging—and interesting.

Summary

Stressors are viewed through many lenses. Those lenses are shaped by our individual, familial, and sociohistorical backgrounds—all of which are intricately intertwined within a cultural context. The external factors of culture, time in history, the economy, human development, and heredity—plus the internal structural, psychological, and philosophical factors—all influence how families and the individuals in those families perceive and manage their stressor events. It is these factors that answer the questions: Given the same stressor, why are some families instantly and forever debilitated whereas others are not—and may even become stronger as a result of the adversity? Why do families differ in this way? We have in this book provided some answers, but the question of why some families stay strong and others fall apart continues to hold our curiosity—and we hope yours, as well.

Points to Remember

1. Intentionally examine the intersections of vulnerability and resilience.

2. Perceptions of stress and coping at the individual, family, and community levels shape well-being.

3. Since vulnerability and resilience coexist, therapeutic approaches must account for them both, so that families are simultaneously understanding and grappling with vulnerabilities at the same time they are uncovering elements of resilience.

4. Who is in and who is out of the family is fluid, especially when family members change and are no longer who they used to be.

5. Incorporate theories and theorizing into examinations of family vulnerability and resilience, but push for clear connections between theory, research, and practice.

Discussion Questions

1. What stressors do you think families are likely to face in the future?

2. What stressors have your loved ones faced in the past that are still stressors today?

3. What potential stressors have political implications? Why? How might the politics of the situation add a layer of stress to the situation?

4. In the future, how can we develop an environment in which stress management is encouraged? What would need to happen at home or at work? Is this possible?

Additional Readings

Canetti, D., Russ, E., Luborsky, J., Gerhart, J. I., & Hobfoll, S. E. (2014). Inflamed by the flames? The impact of terrorism and war on immunity. *Journal of Traumatic Stress*, 27(3), 345–352.

Collazo, A., Austin, A., & Craig, S. L. (2013). Facilitating transition among transgender clients: Components of effective clinical practice. *Journal of Clinical Social Work*, 41(3), 228-237.

Compton, M. T., & Shim, R. S. (Eds.). (2015). *The social determinants of mental health*. Arlington, VA: American Psychiatric Publishing.

Hill, R. (1949/1971). *Families under stress*. Westport, CT: Greenwood. (Original work published 1949)

Hill, R. (1958). Generic features of families under stress. *Social Casework*, 39, 139–150.

Kawachi, I., Daniels, N., & Robinson, D. E. (2005). Health disparities by race and class: Why both matter. *Health Disparities*, 24(2), 343–352.

Rote, S., Angel, J. L., & Markides, K. (2015). Health of elderly Mexican American adults and family caregiver distress. *Research on Aging*, 37(3), 306–331.

Russo, F. (2010). *They're your parents, too!: How siblings can survive their parents' aging without driving each other crazy*. New York, NY: Bantam.

Scott, S. B., Poulin, M. J., & Silver, R. C. (2013). A lifespan perspective on terrorism: Age differences in trajectories of response to 9/11. *Developmental Psychology, 49*(5), 986–998.

Thoresen, S., Jensen, T. K., Wentzel–Larsen, T., & Dyb, G. (2014). Social support barriers and mental health in terrorist attack survivors. *Journal of Affective Disorders, 156,* 187–193.

Film

Grant, C., Kavanaugh, R., & Spinks, L. (Executive Producers), & Grant, S. (Director, Writer). (2006). *Catch and release* [Motion Picture]. United States: Columbia Pictures Corporation, Relativity Media, & Tall Trees Productions.

References

Ahrons, C. R. (1994). *The good divorce: Keeping your family together when your marriage comes apart*. New York, NY: HarperCollins.

Ahrons, C. R., & Rodgers, R. H. (1994). The remarriage transition. In A. S. Skolnick & J. H. Skolnick (Eds.), *Family in transition* (pp. 257–268). New York, NY: HarperCollins.

Al-Adawi, S., Burjorjee, R., & Al-Issa, I. (1997). Mu-Ghayeb: A culture-specific response to bereavement in Oman. *International Journal of Social Psychiatry, 43*, 144–151.

Alamilla, S. G., Kim, B. S. K., & Lam, N. A. (2010). Acculturation, enculturation, perceived racism, minority status stressor, and psychological symptomatology among Latino/as. *Hispanic Journal of Behavioral Sciences, 32*(1), 55–76.

Albert, T. (Producer), & Keach, J. (Director). (2014). *Glen Campbell: I'll be me* [Motion picture]. Los Angeles, CA: PCH Films.

Aldous, J. (1978). *Family careers: Developmental change in family*. New York, NY: John Wiley.

Aldrich, D. P., & Meyer, M. A. (2015). Social capital and community resilience. *American Behavioral Scientist, 59*(2), 254–269.

Alexander, E., & Regier, E. (2011). Speaking out on violence and social change: Transmedia storytelling with remotely situated women in Nepal and Canada. *Canadian Theatre Review, 148*, 38–42.

Al-Issa, I. (1982). Gender and adult psychopathology. In I. Al-Issa (Ed.), *Gender and psychopathology* (pp. 83–110). New York, NY: Academic Press.

Allen, C. J. (2002). *The hold life has: Coca and cultural identity in an Andean Community* (2nd ed.). Washington, DC: Smithsonian Books.

Allison, K. W., Broce, R. S., & Houston, A. J. (2013). The importance of housing, neighborhood and community contexts. In G. L. Creasey & P. A. Jarvis (Eds.), *Adolescent development and school achievement in urban communities: Resilience in the neighborhood* (pp. 27–37). New York, NY: Routledge.

Almasy, S., Meilhan, P., & Bittermann, J. (2015, November 14). *Paris massacre: At least 128 killed in gunfire and blasts, French officials say*. Retrieved from http://www.cnn .com/2015/11/13/world/paris-shooting

Alzheimer's Association (2015). *2015 Alzheimer's disease facts and figures*. Chicago, IL: Author.

Ambrosini, M. (2013). *Irregular migration and invisible welfare*. London, UK: Palgrave Macmillan.

Anderson, C. M., Hogarty, G. E., & Reiss, D. J. (1980). Family treatment of adult schizophrenic patients: A psycho-educational approach. *Schizophrenia Bulletin, 6*(3), 490–505.

Anderson, C. M., Reiss, D. J., & Hogarty, G. E. (1986). *Schizophrenia and the family*. New York, NY: Guilford Press.

Anderson, K. C., Burns, M., & Huckaby, G. (Producers), & Friedkin, W. (Director). (2006). *Bug* [Motion picture]. USA: Lions Gate Films.

Anderson, S. A., Sabatelli, R. M., & Kosutic, I. (2007). Families, urban neighborhood youth centers, and peers as contexts for development. *Family Relations, 56*, 346–357.

Angell, R. C. (1936/1965). *The family encounters the Depression.* New York, NY: Scribner. (Original work published 1936)

Antonovsky, A. (1979). *Health, stress and coping.* San Francisco, CA: Jossey-Bass.

Armour, S. (2008, May 16). Foreclosures take an emotional toll on many homeowners. *USA Today.* Retrieved from http://usatoday30.usatoday.com/money/economy/housing/2008-05-14-mortgage-foreclosures-mental-health_N.htm

Arnold, A. L., Lucier-Greer, M., Mancini, J. A., Ford, J. L., & Wickrama, K. A. S. (2015). How family structures and processes interrelate the case of adolescent mental health and academic success in military families. *Journal of Family Issues.* Advance online publication. doi: 10.1177/0192513X15616849

Axinn, W. G. (1992). Family organization and fertility limitation in Nepal. *Demography, 29*(4), 503–521.

Babcock, J. C., Jacobson, N. S., Gottman, J. M., & Yerington, T. P. (2000). Attachment, emotional regulation, and the function of marital violence: Differences between secure, preoccupied, and dismissing violent and nonviolent husbands. *Journal of Family Violence, 15*(4), 391–409.

Backhouse, J., & Graham, A. (2013). Grandparents raising their grandchildren: Acknowledging the experience of grief. *Australian Social Work, 66*(3), 440–454.

Baingana, F., Bannon, I., & Thomas, R. (2005). *Mental health and conflicts: Conceptual framework and approaches.* Washington, DC: World Bank.

Baker, A., & Semple, K. (2015, November 25). Mother who left baby at Queens church is found; No charges will be filed. *The New York Times.* Retrieved from http://www.nytimes.com/2015/11/26/nyregion/police-search-for-answers-about-newborn-who-was-left-at-queens-church.html?_r=0

Baltes, P. B. (1997). On the incomplete architecture of human ontology: Selection, optimization, and compensation as foundation of developmental theory. *American Psychologist, 23,* 366–380.

Barajas-Gonzalez, R. G., & Brooks-Gunn, J. (2014). Income, neighborhood stressors, and harsh parenting: Test of moderation by ethnicity, age, and gender. *Journal of Family Psychology, 28,* 855–866.

Barnett, R. C. (2004). Women and multiple roles: Myths and reality. *Harvard Review of Psychiatry, 12*(3), 158–164.

Barnett, R. C., & Hyde, J. S. (2001). Women, men, work, and family. *American Psychologist, 56*(10), 781–796.

Barnett, R. C., & Rivers, C. (1996). *He works, she works.* New York, NY: HarperCollins.

Barrio, C. (2000). The cultural relevance of community support programs. *Psychiatric Services, 51,* 879–884.

Becvar, D. S. (2013). *Handbook of family resilience.* New York, NY: Springer.

Benet-Martinez, V., & Haritatos, J. (2005). Bicultural identity integration (BII). Components and psychosocial antecedents. *Journal of Personality, 73,* 1015–1050.

Bengtson, V. L., & Allen, K. R. (1993). The life course perspective applied to families over time. In P. G. Boss, W. J. Doherty, R. LaRossa, W. R. Schumm, & S. K. Steinmetz (Eds.), *Sourcebook of family theories and methods* (pp. 469–504). New York, NY: Plenum.

Benkel, I., Wijk, H., & Molander, U. (2010). Using coping strategies is not denial: Helping loved ones adjust to living with a patient with a palliative diagnosis. *Journal of Palliative Medicine, 13*(9), 1119–1123.

Bennetts, L. (2007). *The feminine mistake: Are we giving up too much?* New York, NY: Hachette Books.

Bereavement. (1993). *New shorter Oxford English dictionary* (4th ed.). New York, NY: Oxford University Press.

Berge, J. M., & Holm, K. E. (2007). Boundary ambiguity in parents with chronically ill children: Integrating theory and research. *Family Relations, 56*(2), 123–134.

Berger, C. R., & Calabrese, R. J. (1975). Some explorations in initial interaction and beyond: Toward a developmental theory of interpersonal communication. *Human Communication Research, 1,* 99–112.

Berger, P., & Luckmann, T. (1966). *The social construction of reality.* New York, NY: Doubleday.

Bermudez, J. M., & Mancini, J. A. (2013). Familias fuertas: Family resilience among Latinos. In D. S. Becvar (Ed.), *Handbook of family resilience* (pp. 215–227). New York, NY: Springer.

Bernard, J. (1971). The paradox of a happy marriage. In V. Gornick & B. K. Moran (Eds.), *Women in sexist society: Studies in power and powerlessness* (pp. 145–162). New York, NY: Basic Books.

Bernard, J. (1972). *The future of marriage.* New York, NY: World Press.

Bernard, T. S. (2014, October 22). Years after the market collapse, sidelined borrowers return. *The New York Times.* Retrieved from http://www.nytimes.com/2014/10/23/your-money/a-second-try-at-home-buying-after-the-market-collapse.html

Berry, H. L., Bowen, K., & Kjellstrom, T. (2010). Climate changes and mental health: A causal pathways framework. *International Journal of Public Health, 55,* 123–132.

Berry, J. W. (1980). Acculturation as varieties of adaptation. In A. M. Padilla (Ed.), *Acculturation: Theories, models, and some new findings* (pp. 45–56). Boulder, CO: Westview.

Berry, J. W. (1997). Immigration, acculturation, and adaptation. *Applied Psychology: An International Review, 46,* 5–34.

Berry, J. W. (2003). Conceptual approaches to acculturation. In K. M. Chun, P. B. Organista, & G. Marin (Eds.), *Acculturation: Advances in theory, measurement and applied research* (pp. 17–37). Washington, DC: American Psychological Association.

Berry, J. W. (2005). Acculturation: Living successfully in two cultures. *International Journal of Intercultural Relations, 29,* 697–712.

Berry, J. W. (2006). Acculturative stress. In P. T. P. Wong & L. C. J. Wong (Eds.), *Handbook of multicultural perspectives on stress and coping* (pp. 287–298). Dallas, TX: Springer.

Betz, G., & Thorngren, J. M. (2006). Ambiguous loss and the family grieving process. *The Family Journal: Counseling and Therapy for Couples and Families, 14*(1), 359–365.

Biddle, B., & Thomas, E. (1966). *Role theory: Concepts and research.* New York, NY: John Wiley.

Birch, P. J., Weed, S. E., & Olsen, J. (2004). Assessing the impact of community marriage policies on county divorce rates. *Family Relations, 53,* 495–503.

Blieszner, R., Roberts, K. A., Wilcox, K. L., Barham, E. J., & Winston, B. L. (2007). Dimensions of ambiguous loss in couples coping with mild cognitive impairment. *Family Relations, 56*(2), 196–209.

Blume, L. B. (Ed.). (in press). Ambiguous loss [Special issue]. *Journal of Family Theory & Review, 8*(3).

Bodenmann, G. (2005). Dyadic coping and its significance for marital functioning. In T. A. Revenson, K. Kayser, & G. Bodenmann (Eds.), *Couples coping with stress: Emerging perspectives on dyadic coping* (pp. 33–49). Washington, DC: American Psychological Association.

Boerner, K., & Jopp, D. (2007). Improvement/maintenance and reorientation as central features of coping with major life change and loss: Contributions of three life-span theories. *Human Development, 50*(4), 171–195.

Bonanno, G. A. (2004). Loss, trauma, and human resilience: Have we underestimated the human capacity to thrive after extremely aversive events? *American Psychologist, 59,* 20–28.

Bonanno, G. A. (2009). *The other side of sadness: What the new science of bereavement tells us about life after loss.* New York, NY: Basic Books.

Bonanno, G. A., Keltner, D., Holen, A., & Horowitz, M. J. (1995). When avoiding unpleasant emotions might not be such a bad thing: Verbal autonomic response dissociation and midlife conjugal bereavement. *Journal of Personality and Social Psychology, 69,* 975–989.

Bonanno, G. A., & Mancini, A. D. (2008). The human capacity to thrive in the face of extreme adversity. *Pediatrics, 121,* 369–375.

Bonanno, G. A., Papa, A., Lalande, K., Nanping, Z., & Noll, J. G. (2005). Grief processing and deliberate grief avoidance: A prospective comparison of bereaved spouses and parents in the United States and China. *Journal of Consulting and Clinical Psychology, 73,* 86–98.

Boss, P. (1973, October). Psychological father absence in intact families. *In Research and Theory Section.* Presentation at the Annual Meeting of the National Council on Family Relations, Toronto, Canada.

Boss, P. (1975a). *Psychological father absence and presence: A theoretical formation for an investigation into family systems interactions.* Unpublished doctoral dissertation, University of Wisconsin-Madison.

Boss, P. (1975b). Psychological father presence in the missing-in-action (MIA) family: Its effects on family functioning. In *Proceedings: Third Annual Joint Medical Meeting Concerning POW/MIA Matters* (pp. 61–65). Naval Health Research Center, Center for Prisoner of War Studies, San Diego, CA.

Boss, P. (1977). A clarification of the concept of psychological father presence in families experiencing ambiguity of boundary. *Journal of Marriage and the Family, 39,* 141–151.

Boss, P. (1980a). Normative family stress: Family boundary changes across the lifespan. *Family Relations, 29*(4), 445–450.

Boss, P. (1980b). The relationship of psychological father presence, wife's personal qualities, and wife/family dysfunction in families of missing fathers. *Journal of Marriage and the Family, 42*(3), 541–549.

Boss, P. (1987). Family stress: Perception and context. In M. Sussman & S. Steinmetz (Eds.), *Handbook on marriage and family* (pp. 695–723). New York, NY: Plenum.

Boss, P. (1988). *Family stress management.* Newbury Park, CA: Sage.

Boss, P. (1991). Ambiguous loss. In F. Walsh & M. McGoldrick (Eds.), *Living beyond loss: Death in the family* (pp. 164–175). New York, NY: Norton.

Boss, P. (1992). Primacy of perception in family stress theory and measurement. *Journal of Family Psychology, 6*(2), 113–119.

Boss, P. (1993). Boundary ambiguity: A block to cognitive coping. In A. Turnbull, J. Patterson, S. Behr, D. Murphy, J. Marquis, & M. Blue-Banning (Eds.), *Cognitive coping, families, and disability* (pp. 257–270). Baltimore, MD: Brookes.

Boss, P. (1999). *Ambiguous loss.* Cambridge, MA: Harvard University Press.

Boss, P. (2002). *Family stress management: A contextual approach* (2nd ed.). Thousand Oaks, CA: Sage.

Boss, P. (2004a). Ambiguous loss. In F. Walsh & M. McGoldrick (Eds.), *Living beyond loss: Death in the family* (2nd ed., pp. 237–246). New York, NY: Norton.

Boss, P. (2004b). Ambiguous loss research, theory, and practice: Reflections after 9/11. *Journal of Marriage & Family, 66*(3), 551–566.

Boss, P. (2006). *Loss, trauma, and resilience: Therapeutic work with ambiguous loss.* New York, NY: Norton.

Boss, P. (Guest Ed.). (2007a). Ambiguous loss [Special issue]. *Family Relations, 56*(2).

Boss, P. (2007b). Ambiguous loss theory: Challenges for scholars and practitioners [Special issue]. *Family Relations, 56*(2), 105–111.

Boss, P. (2008). A tribute, not a memorial: Understanding ambiguous loss. *SIGMOD Record, 37*(2), 19–20.

Boss, P. (2010). The trauma and complicated grief of ambiguous loss. *Pastoral Psychology, 59*(2), 137–145.

Boss, P. (2011). *Loving someone who has dementia: How to find hope while coping with stress and grief.* San Francisco, CA: Jossey-Bass.

Boss, P. (2012a). The ambiguous loss of dementia: A relational view of complicated grief in caregivers. In M. O'Reilly-Landry (Ed.), *A psychodynamic understanding of modern medicine: Placing the person at the center of care* (pp. 183–193). London, UK: Radcliffe.

Boss, P. (2012b). Resilience as tolerance for ambiguity. In D. S. Becvar (Ed.), *Handbook of family resilience* (pp. 285–297). New York, NY: Springer.

Boss, P. (2014). Family stress. In A. C. Michalos (Ed.), *Encyclopedia of quality of life and well-being research* (pp. 2202–2208). Dordrecht, Netherlands: Springer.

Boss, P. (2015). On the usefulness of theory: Applying family therapy and family science to the relational developmental systems metamodel. *Journal of Family Theory & Review, 7*(2), 105–108.

Boss, P. (in press). The context and process of theory development: The story of ambiguous loss theory. *Journal of Family Theory & Review, 18*(3).

Boss, P., Beaulieu, L., Wieling, E., Turner, W., & LaCruz, S. (2003). Healing loss, ambiguity, and trauma: A community-based intervention with families of union workers missing after the 9/11 attack in New York City. *Journal of Marital & Family Therapy, 29*(4), 455–467.

Boss, P., & Carnes, D. (2012). The myth of closure. *Family Process, 51*(4), 456–460.

Boss, P., Caron, W., & Horbal, J. (1988). Alzheimer's disease and ambiguous loss. In C. Chilman, F. Cox, & A. Nunnally (Eds.), *Families in trouble* (pp. 123–140). Newbury Park, CA: Sage.

Boss, P., Caron, W., Horbal, J., & Mortimer, J. (1990). Predictors of depression in caregivers of dementia patients: Boundary ambiguity and mastery. *Family Process, 29*, 245–254.

Boss, P., & Dahl, C. M. (2014). Family therapy for the unresolved grief of ambiguous loss. In D. W. Kissane & F. Parnes (Eds.), *Bereavement care for families* (pp. 171–182). New York, NY: Routledge.

Boss, P., Dahl, C., & Kaplan, L. (1996). The meaning of family: The phenomenological perspective in family research. In S. Moon & D. Sprenkle (Eds.), *Research methods in family therapy* (pp. 83–106). New York, NY: Guilford.

Boss, P., & Greenberg, J. (1984). Family boundary ambiguity: A new variable in family stress theory. *Family Process, 23*(4), 535–546.

Boss, P., Greenberg, J., & Pearce-McCall, D. (1990). *Measurement of boundary ambiguity in families* (Minnesota Agricultural Experiment Station Bulletin No. 5931990; Item No. Ad-SB-3763). St. Paul, MN: University of Minnesota.

Boss, P., & Ishii, C. (2015). Trauma and ambiguous loss: The lingering presence of the physically absent. In K. E. Cherry, (Ed.), *Traumatic stress and long-term recovery: Coping with disasters and other negative life events* (pp. 271–289). New York, NY: Springer.

Boss, P., & Kaplan, L. (2004). Ambiguous loss and ambivalence when a parent has dementia. In K. Pillemer & K. Luescher (Eds.), *Intergenerational ambivalences: New perspectives on parent-child relations in later life* (pp. 207–224). Oxford, UK: Elsevier.

Boss, P., Kaplan, L., & Gordon, M. (1995, September). Accepting the circle of life. *Center for Urban and Regional Affairs Reporter, 25*(3), 7–11.

Boss, P., McCubbin, H. I., & Lester, G. (1979). The corporate executive wife's coping patterns in response to routine husband-father absence. *Family Process, 18*, 79–86.

Boss, P., Roos, S., & Harris, D. L. (2011). Grief in the midst of uncertainty and ambiguity. In R. A. Neimeyer, D. L. Harris, H. R. Winokuer, & G. F. Thornton (Eds.), *Grief and bereavement in contemporary society: Bridging research and practice* (pp. 163–175). New York, NY: Taylor and Francis.

Boss, P., & Yeats, J. R. (2014). Ambiguous loss: A complicated type of grief when loved ones disappear. *Bereavement Care, 33*(2), 63–69.

Boszormenyi-Nagy, I. (1987). *Foundations of contextual therapy: Collected papers of Ivan Boszormenyi-Nagy, MD.* New York, NY: Brunner/Mazel.

Boszormenyi-Nagy, I., & Spark, G. (1973/1984). *Invisible loyalties: Reciprocity in intergenerational family therapy.* New York, NY: Harper & Row. (2nd edition, New York, NY: Brunner/Mazel)

Boushey, H. (2009). The new breadwinners. *The Shriver Report.* Retrieved from http://shriver-report.org/the-new-breadwinners

Bowen, G. L., Mancini, J. A., Martin, J. A., Ware, W. B., & Nelson, J. P. (2003). Promoting the adaptation of military families: An empirical test of a community practice model. *Family Relations, 52*, 33–44.

Bowen, G. L., Martin, J. A., & Mancini, J. A. (2013). The resilience of military families: Theoretical perspectives. In M. A. Fine & F. D. Fincham (Eds.), *Handbook of family theories: A content-based approach* (pp. 417–436). New York, NY: Routledge.

Bowen, G. L., Martin, J. A., Mancini, J. A., & Nelson, J. P. (2000). Community capacity: Antecedents and consequences. *Journal of Community Practice, 8*, 1–21.

Bowen, G. L., Martin, J. A., Mancini, J. A., & Nelson, J. P. (2001). Civic engagement and sense of community in the military. *Journal of Community Practice, 9*, 71–93.

Bowen, G. L., Martin, J. A., Mancini, J. A., & Swick, D. (2015). Community capacity and the psychological well-being of married United States Air Force members. In R. Moelker, M. Andres, G. L. Bowen, & P. Manigart (Eds.), *Military families and war in the 21st century* (pp. 210–226). Abingdon, Oxon, UK: Routledge.

Bowen, G. L., Richman, J. M., & Bowen, N. K. (2000). Families in the context of communities across time. In S. J. Price, P. C. McKenry, & M. J. Murphy (Eds.), *Families across time: A life course perspective* (pp. 117–128). Los Angeles, CA: Roxbury.

Bowen, G. L., Rose, R. A., Powers, J. D., & Glennie, E. J. (2008). The joint effects of neighborhoods, schools, peers, and families on changes in the school success of middle school students. *Family Relations, 57*, 504–516.

Bravo, E. (2012). "Having it all?"—The wrong question for most women. *Women's Media Center.* Retrieved from http://www.womensmediacenter.com/feature/entry/having-it-allthe-wrong-question-for-most-women

Brodsky, A. E. (1998). Resilient single mothers in risky neighborhoods: Negative psychological sense of community. *Journal of Community Psychology, 24*, 347–363.

Brody, G. H., Chen, Y., Murry, V. M., Ge, X., Simons, R. L., Gibbons, F. X., . . . Cutrona, C. E. (2006). Perceived discrimination and the adjustment of African American youths: A five-year longitudinal analysis with contextual moderation effects. *Child Development, 77*(5), 1170–1189.

Brody, G. H., Yu, T., Chen, E., Miller, G. E., Kogan, S. M., & Beach, S. R. H. (2013). Is resilience only skin deep? Rural African Americans' socioeconomic status-related risk and competence in preadolescence and psychological adjustment and allostatic load at age 19. *Psychological Science, 24*(7), 1285–1293.

Brondolo, E., Libby, D. J., Dento, E., Thompson, M. A., Beatty, D. L., Schwartz, J., . . . Gerin, W. (2008). Racism and ambulatory blood pressure in a community sample. *Psychosomatic Medicine, 70*, 49–56.

Brooks, V. R. (1981). *Minority stress and lesbian women.* Lexington, MA: Lexington Books.

Bryant, C., Wickrama, K. A. S., Bolland, J., Bryant, B. M., Cutrona, C. E., & Stanik, C. E. (2010). Race matters, even in marriage: Identifying factors linked to marital outcomes for African Americans. *Journal of Family Theory and Review, 2*, 157–174.

Brymer, M. J., Steinberg, A. M., Watson, P. J., & Pynoos, R. S. (2012). Prevention and early intervention programs for children and adolescents. In J. G. Beck & D. M. Sloan (Eds.), *The Oxford handbook of traumatic stress disorders* (pp. 381–392). Oxford, UK: Oxford University Press.

Buckley, W. (1967). *Sociology and modern systems theory.* Englewood Cliffs, NJ: Prentice Hall.

Buehler, C., & O'Brian, M. (2011). Mothers' part-time employment: Associations with mother and family well-being. *Journal of Family Psychology, 25*(6), 895–906.

Bui, Q., & Miller, C. C. (2015, December 23). The typical American lives only 18 miles from Mom. *The New York Times.* Retrieved from http://www.nytimes.com/interactive/2015/12/24/upshot/24up-family.html?_r=0

Burgess, E. (1926). The family as a unity of interacting personalities. *Family, 7*, 3–9.

Burgess, E. W. (1937). The family and sociological research. *Social Forces, 26*, 1–6.

Burr, W., Leigh, G., Day, R., & Constantine, J. (1979). Symbolic interaction and the family. In W. Burr, R. Hill, F. I. Nye, & I. Reiss (Eds.), *Contemporary theories about the family* (Vol. 2, pp. 42–111). New York, NY: Free Press.

Burton, L. M., Dilworth-Anderson, P., & Merriwether-de Vries, C. (1994). Context and surrogate parenting among contemporary grandparents. *Marriage & Family Review, 20* (3–4), 349–366.

Burton, L. M., & Jarrett, R. L. (2000). In the mix, yet on the margins: The place of families in urban neighborhood and child development research. *Journal of Marriage and Family, 62*(4), 1114–1135.

Caldwell, K., & Boyd, C. P. (2009). Coping and resilience in farming families affected by drought. *Rural and Remote Health, 9*(2), 45–41.

Campbell, C. L., & Demi, A. S. (2000). Adult children of fathers missing in action (MIA): An examination of emotional distress, grief and family hardiness. *Family Relations, 49*(3), 267–276.

Caplinger, D. (2015, March 9). The average American retires at this age. Will you? *The Motley Fool*. Retrieved from http://www.fool.com/retirement/general/2015/03/09/the-average-american-retires-at-this-age-will-you.aspx

Caron, W., Boss, P., & Mortimer, J. (1999). Family boundary ambiguity predicts Alzheimer's outcomes. *Psychiatry, 62*, 347–356.

Carroll, J. S., Olson, C. D., & Buckmiller, N. (2007). Family boundary ambiguity: A 30-year review of theory, research, and measurement. *Family Relations, 56*, 210–230.

Carter, B., & McGoldrick, M. (Eds.). (1999). *The expanded family life cycle: Individual, family, and social perspectives*. Boston, MA: Allyn & Bacon.

CBS News. (2011, April 4). Raising a kid takes a village . . . of grandmas. Interview by S. Hartman. *CBS Evening News* [Television Broadcast]. New York, NY: Central Broadcasting Service. Retrieved from http://www.cbsnews.com/news/raising-a-kid-takes-a-villageof-grandmas

CBS This Morning. (2015, November 16). Critics slam Obama's migrant policy after Paris attacks. *CBS This Morning*. Retrieved from http://www.cbsnews.com/videos/critics-slam-obamas-migrant-policy-after-paris-attacks

Chakraborty, R., Schull, W. J., Harburg, E., Schork, M. A., & Roeper, P. (1977). Heredity, stress and blood pressure, a family set method—V: Heritability estimates. *Journal of Chronic Diseases, 30*(10), 683–699.

Chakravarti, U. (2006). *Gendering caste: Through a feminist lens*. Calcutta, India: Stree.

Chamlee-Wright, E., & Storr, V. H. (2011). Social capital as collective narratives and post-disaster community recovery. *The Sociological Review, 59*, 266–282.

Chang, B-H., Noonan, A. E., & Tennstedt. S. L. (1998). The role of religion/spirituality in coping with caregiving for disabled elders. *The Gerontologist, 38*(4), 463–470.

Chaskin, R. J., Brown, P., Venkatesh, S., & Vidal, A. (2001). *Building community capacity*. New York, NY: Aldine De Gruyter.

Chow, A. Y. M., & Chan, C. L. W. (2006). Introduction. In C. L. W. Chan & A. Y. M. Chow (Eds.), *Death, dying, and bereavement: A Hong Kong Chinese experience* (Vol. 1, pp. 1–14). Hong Kong, CHN: Hong Kong Press.

Chuang, S. S., & Moreno, R. P. (Eds.). (2008). *On new shores: Understanding immigrant fathers in North America*. Lanham, MD: Lexington Books.

Chuang, S. S., & Uwe, P. (2009). Understanding immigrant families from around the world: Introduction to the special issue. *Journal of Family Psychology, 23*, 275–278.

Clauss-Ehlers, C. S. (2008). Sociocultural factors, resilience, and coping: Support for a culturally sensitive measure of resilience. *Journal of Applied Developmental Psychology, 29*, 197–212.

Cleary, P., & Mechanic, D. (1983). Sex differences in psychological distress among married people. *Journal of Health and Social Behavior, 24*, 111–121.

Cochran, B. N., Stewart, A. J., Ginzler, J. A., & Cauce, A. M. (2002). Challenges faced by homeless sexual minorities: Comparison of gay, lesbian, bisexual, and transgender homeless adolescents with their heterosexual counterparts. *American Journal of Public Health, 92*(5), 773–777.

Cohen, F., & Lazarus, R. S. (1973). Active coping processes, coping dispositions, and recovery from surgery. *Psychosomatic Medicine, 35*(5), 375–389.

Cohen, M. H. (1993). The unknown and the unknowable—Managing sustained uncertainty. *Western Journal of Nursing Research, 15*(1), 77–96.

Coifman, K. G., Bonanno, G. A., Ray, R. D., & Gross, J. J. (2007). Does repressive coping promote resilience? Affective-autonomic response discrepancy during bereavement. *Journal of Personality and Social Psychology*, 92(4), 745–758.

Coile, C. C. (2015). Economic determinants of workers' retirement decisions. *Journal of Economic Surveys*, 29, 830–853.

Coley, R. L., Lohman, B. J., Votruba-Drzal, E., Pittman, L. D., & Chase-Lansdale, P. L. (2007). Maternal functioning, time, and money: The world of work and welfare. *Children and Youth Services Review*, 29(6), 721–741.

Conger, R. D., Rueter, M. A., & Elder, G. H., Jr. (1999). Couple resilience to economic pressure. *Journal of Personality and Social Psychology*, 76(1), 54–71.

Cooke, L. P. (2006). "Doing" gender in context: Household bargaining and risk of divorce in Germany and the United States. *American Journal of Sociology*, 112(2), 442–472.

Coontz, S. (1992). *The way we never were: American families and the nostalgia trap*. New York, NY: Basic Books.

Coontz, S. (1997). *The way we really are: Coming to terms with America's changing families*. New York, NY: Basic Books.

Coontz, S. (2006). *Marriage, a history: How love conquered marriage*. New York, NY: Penguin.

CoreLogic (June 29, 2012). CoreLogic reports 63,000 completed foreclosures in May. Retrieved from http://www.corelogic.com/about-us/news/corelogic-reports-63,000-completed-foreclosures-in-may.aspx

Coulton, C. J. (1995). Using community level indicators of children's well-being in comprehensive community initiatives. In J. P. Connell, A. C. Kubisch, L. B. Schorr, & C. H. Weiss (Eds.), *New approaches to evaluating community initiatives: Concepts, methods, and contexts* (pp. 173–199). Washington, DC: Aspen Institute.

Cowan, P. A., Cowan, C. P., & Schulz, M. S. (1996). Thinking about risk and resilience in families. In E. M. Hetherington & E. A. Blechman (Eds.), *Stress, coping and resiliency in children and families* (pp. 1–38). Mahwah, NJ: Lawrence Erlbaum.

Coyne, J. C., & Fiske, V. (1992). Couples coping with chronic and catastrophic illness. In T. J. Akamatsu, M. A. P. Stephens, S. E. Hobfoll, & J. H. Crowther (Eds.), *Family health psychology* (pp. 129–149). Washington, DC: U.S. Hemisphere.

Cutrona, C. E., & Russell, D. (1987). The provisions of social relationships and adaptation to stress. In W. H. Jones & D. Perlman (Eds.), *Advances in personal relationships* (pp. 37–67). Greenwich, CT: JAI Press.

Cutrona, C. E., Russell, D. W., Abraham, W. T., Gardner, K. A., Melby, J. N., Bryant, C., & Conger, R. D. (2003). Neighborhood context and financial strain as predictors of marital interaction and marital quality in African American couples. *Personal Relationships, 10*, 389-409.

Danieli, Y., & Nader, K. (2006). Respecting cultural, religious, and ethnic differences in the prevention and treatment of psychological sequelae. In L. A. Schein, H. I. Spitz, G. M. Burlingame, P. R. Muskin, & S. Vargo (Eds.), *Psychological effects of catastrophic disasters: Group approaches to treatment* (pp. 203–234). New York, NY: Haworth Press.

Davenport, C. (2015, December 12). Nations approve landmark climate accord in Paris. *The New York Times*. Retrieved from http://www.nytimes.com/2015/12/13/world/europe/climate-change-accord-paris.html?_r=0

DeSalvo, K. B., Hyre, A. D., Ompad, D. C., Menke, A., Tynes, L. L., & Muntner, P. (2007). Symptoms of posttraumatic stress disorder in a New Orleans workforce following Hurricane Katrina. *Journal of Urban Health*, 84, 142–132.

de Vries, A. L. C., McGuire, J. K., Steensma, T. D., Wagenaar, E., Doreleijers, T., & Cohen-Kettenis, P. T. (2014). Young adult psychological outcome after puberty suppression and gender reassignment. *Pediatrics*, 134(4), 696-704.

Dew, J., & Yorgason, J. (2010). Economic pressure and marital conflict in retirement-aged couples. *Journal of Family Issues*, 31(2), 164–188.

Dezell, M. (2000). *Irish America: Coming into clover*. New York, NY: Anchor.

Di Cesare, M., Khang, Y., Asaria, P., Blakely, T., Cowan, M. J., Farzadfar, F., . . . Ezzati, M., on behalf of The Lancet NCD Action Group. (2013). Inequalities in non-communicable diseases and effective responses. *The Lancet, 381*, 585–597.

Dilworth-Anderson, P., Goodwin, P. Y., & Williams, S. W. (2004). Can culture help explain the physical health effects of caregiving over time among African American caregivers? *Journals of Gerontology Series B: Psychological Sciences and Social Sciences, 59*(3), S138–S145.

Doherty, W. J., Jacob, J., & Cutting, B. (2009). Community engaged parent education: Strengthening civic engagement among parents and parent educators. *Family Relations, 58*, 303–315.

D'Onofrio, B. M., & Lahey, B. B. (2010). Biosocial influences on the family: A decade review. *Journal of Marriage and Family, 72*, 762–782.

Durso, L. E., & Gates, G. J. (2012). *Serving our youth: Findings from a national survey of services providers working with lesbian, gay, bisexual, and transgender youth who are homeless or at risk of becoming homeless*. Retrieved from http://escholarship.org/uc/item/80x75033

Dyk, P. A., & Schvaneveldt, J. D. (1987). Coping as a concept in family theory. *Family Science Review, 1*(1), 23–40.

Edward, K. L., & Warelow, P. (2005). Resilience: When coping is emotionally intelligent. *Journal of the American Psychiatric Nurses Association, 11*(2), 101–102.

Elder, G. H. (1974/1999). *Children of the Great Depression*. Boulder, CO: Westview Press. (Originally published in 1974, University of Chicago Press, Chicago, IL)

Elder, G. H., Jr., & Giele, J. (Eds.). (2009). *The craft of life course research*. New York, NY: Guilford Press.

Elder, G. H., Jr., & Shanahan, M. J. (2006). The life course and human development. In W. Damon & R. M. Lerner (Eds.), *Handbook of child psychology: Theoretical models of human development* (pp. 665–715). New York, NY: Wiley & Stone.

Ellis, B. J., & Boyce, W. T. (2008). Biological sensitivity to context. *Current Directions in Psychological Science, 17*, 183–187.

Erikson, E. (1950). *Childhood and society*. New York, NY: Norton.

Essau, C. A., Lewinsohn, P. M., Seeley, J. R., & Sasagawa, S. (2010). Gender differences in the developmental course of depression. *Journal of Affective Disorders, 127*(1), 185–190.

Evans, E. E. (1957). *Irish folk ways*. London, UK: Routledge & Kegan Paul.

Fiese, B. H., & Wamboldt, F. S. (2000). Family routines, rituals, and asthma management: A proposal for family-based strategies to increase treatment adherence. *Families, Systems, & Health, 18*(4), 405–418.

Fincham, F. D., & Linfield, K. J. (1997). A new look at marital quality: Can spouses feel positive and negative about their marriage? *Journal of Family Psychology, 11*, 489-502.

Folkman, S., & Lazarus, R. S. (1980). An analysis of coping in a middle-aged community sample. *Journal of Health and Social Behavior, 21*(3), 219–239.

Folkman, S., Lazarus, R. S., Pimley, S., & Novacek, J. (1987). Age differences in stress and coping processes. *Psychology and Aging, 2*, 171–184.

Forman, M. H. (Ed.). (1935). *The letters of John Keats* (2nd ed.). New York, NY: Oxford University Press.

Fox, J. W. (1980). Gove's specific sex-role theory of mental illness: A research note. *Journal of Health and Social Behavior, 21*, 260–267.

Fravel, D. L., McRoy, R. G., & Grotevant, H. D. (2000). Birth mother perceptions of the psychologically present adopted child: Adoption openness and boundary ambiguity. *Family Relations, 49*(4), 425–433.

Freud, S. (1915/1957). Repression. In P. Gay (Ed.), *The Freud reader* (pp. 562–568). New York, NY: Norton. (Original work published 1915)

Ganong, L. H., & Coleman, M. (2004). Family resilience in multiple contexts: Introduction to the special section. *Journal of Marriage and Family, 64*, 346-348.

Gardner, B., & Moore, R. F. (1998, September 4). 6 children slain; mother arrested. St. Paul police find victims ages 5, 6, 7, 8, 9, 11. *St. Paul Pioneer Press*, p. 1A.

Garmezy, N. (1987). Stress, competence, and development: Continuities in the study of schizophrenic adults, children vulnerable to psychopathology, and the search for stress-resistant children. *American Journal of Orthopsychiatry, 57,* 159–174.

Garreau, J. (1982). *The nine nations of North America.* New York, NY: Avon Books.

Garwick, A. W. (1991). Shared family perceptions of life with dementia of the Alzheimer's type (Doctoral dissertation, University of Minnesota, 1991). *Dissertation Abstracts International, 52*(5), A1908.

Garwick, A., Detzner, D., & Boss, P. (1994). Family perceptions of living with Alzheimer's disease. *Family Process, 33,* 327–340.

Gates, G. J. (2011, April). How many people are lesbian, gay, bisexual, and transgender? *UCLA School of Law Williams Institute eScholarship.* Retrieved from https://escholarship.org/uc/item/09h684x2

Gelles, R. J., & Cornell, C. P. (1990). *Intimate violence in families.* Newbury Park, CA: Sage.

Gerard, J. M., & Buehler, C. (2004). Cumulative environmental risk and youth problem behavior. *Journal of Marriage and Family, 66,* 702–720.

Gergen, K. J. (1994). *Realities and relationships: Soundings in social construction.* Cambridge, MA: Harvard University Press.

Gergen, K. J. (1999). *An invitation to social construction.* London, UK: Sage.

Gergen, K. J. (2001). *Social construction in context.* London, UK: Sage.

Gergen, K. G. (2006). Back cover. *Loss, trauma and resilience.* New York, NY: Norton.

Getzel, G. S. (2000). Judaism and death: Practice implications. In J. K. Parry & A. S. Ryan (Eds.), *A cross-cultural look at death, dying and religion* (pp. 18–31). Chicago, IL: Nelson Hall.

Glynn, S. J. (2012). The new breadwinners: 2010 update. *Center for American Progress.* Retrieved from https://www.americanprogress.org/issues/labor/report/2012/04/16/11377/the-new-breadwinners-2010-update

Goffman, E. J. (1959). *The presentation of self in everyday life.* Garden City, NY: Doubleday.

Goffman, E. J. (1974). *Frame analysis: An essay on the organization of experience.* New York, NY: Harper & Row.

Goldenberg, H., & Goldenberg, I. (2004/2008). *Family therapy: An overview* (7th ed.). Belmont, CA: Thomason Brooks/Cole.

Gose, P. (1994). *Deathly waters and hungry mountains: Agrarian ritual and class formation in an Andean town.* Toronto, Canada: University of Toronto Press.

Gottman, J. M. (1999). *The marriage clinic: A scientifically-based marital therapy.* New York, NY: Norton.

Gottman, J. M., Carrere, S., Swanson, C., & Coan, J. (2000). Reply to "from basic research to intervention." *Journal of Marriage and the Family, 62*(1), 265–273.

Gottman, J. M., Coan, J., Carrere, S., & Swanson, C. (1998). Predicting marital happiness and stability from newlywed interactions. *Journal of Marriage and the Family, 60*(1), 5–22.

Gove, W. R. (1973). Sex, marital status, and mortality. *American Journal of Sociology, 79,* 45–53.

Gove, W. R., & Tudor, J. F. (1973). Adult sex roles and mental illness. *American Journal of Sociology, 78,* 812–835.

Grant, H. (2015, May 8). *New research shows need to challenge violence supportive attitudes among youth.* Retrieved from http://www.ourwatch.org.au/News-media/Latest-news/New-research-shows-need-to-challenge-violence-supp

Grief. (1993). *New shorter Oxford English dictionary* (4th ed.). New York, NY: Oxford University Press.

Griswold, E. (2016, January 24). Unsettled. *The New York Times Magazine,* pp. 42–49, 62–63, 65.

Guest, J. (1976). *Ordinary people.* New York, NY: Viking.

Hansen, D., & Hill, R. (1964). Families under stress. In H. T. Christensen (Ed.), *Handbook of marriage and the family* (pp. 782–819). Chicago, IL: Rand McNally.

Harburg, E., Erfurt, J. C., Schull, W. J., Schork, M. A., & Colman, R. (1977). Heredity, stress and blood pressure, a family set method—I: Study aims and sample flow. *Journal of Chronic Diseases, 30*(10), 625–647.

Hardy, K. V., & Laszloffy, T. A. (1995). The cultural genogram: Key to training culturally competent family therapists. *Journal of Marital and Family Therapy, 21*(3), 227–237.

Hart, S. L., Hodgkinson, S. C., Belcher, H. M., Hyman, C., & Cooley-Strickland, M. (2013). Somatic symptoms, peer and school stress, and family and community violence exposure among urban elementary school children. *Journal of Behavioral Medicine, 36*(5), 454–465.

Harwood Group. (1999). *Community rhythms: Five stages of community life.* New York, NY: Charles Stewart Mott Foundation.

Hawley, D. R. (2000). Clinical implications of family resilience. *American Journal of Family Therapy, 28*, 101–116.

Hawley, D. R., & DeHaan, L. (1996). Toward a definition of family resilience: Integrating life-span and family perspectives. *Family Process, 35*(3), 283–298.

Hays, J. C., & Hendrix, C. C. (2008). The role of religion in bereavement. In M. Stroebe, R. O. Hansson, H. Schut, & W. Stroebe (Eds.), *Handbook of bereavement research and practice: Advances in theory and intervention* (pp. 327–348). Washington, DC: American Psychological Association Books.

Healy, M. (2015, July 24). You think mass shootings are happening all the time? They are more frequent, data show. *Los Angeles Times.* Retrieved from http://www.latimes.com/science/sciencenow/la-sci-sn-mass-shootings-more-frequent-data-20150618-story.html

Henry, C. S., Merten, M. J., Plunkett, S. W., & Sands, T. (2008). Neighborhood, parenting, and adolescent factors and academic achievement in Latino adolescents from immigrant families. *Family Relations, 57*, 579–590.

Henry, C. S., Morris, A. S., & Harrist, A. W. (2015). Family resilience: Moving into the third wave. *Family Relations, 64*, 22–43.

Hernandez, B. C., & Wilson, C. M. (2007). Another kind of ambiguous loss: Seventh-day Adventist women in mixed-orientation marriages. *Family Relations, 56*(2), 184–195.

Hidecker, M. J. C., Jones, R. S., Imig, D. R., & Villarruel, F. A. (2009). Using family paradigms to improve evidence-based practice. *American Journal of Speech-Language Pathology, 18*(3), 212–221.

Hill, R. (1949/1971). *Families under stress.* Westport, CT: Greenwood. (Original work published 1949)

Hill, R. (1958). Generic features of families under stress. *Social Casework, 39*, 139–150.

Hilmert, C. J., Dominguez, T. P., Schetter, C. D., Srinivas, S. K., Glynn, L. M., & Hobel, C. J. (2014). Lifetime racism and blood pressure changes during pregnancy: Implications for fetal growth. *Health Psychology, 33*(1), 43–51.

Hofferth, S. L. (2003). Race/ethnic differences in father involvement in two-parent families: Culture, context, or economy? *Journal of Family Issues, 24*, 185–216.

Hollander, T. (in press). Ambiguous loss and complicated grief: Understanding the grief of parents of the disappeared in Northern Uganda. *Journal of Family Theory & Review, 8*(3).

Hollingsworth, G. W. (2011). Community family therapy with military families experiencing deployment. *Contemporary Family Therapy, 33*, 215–228.

Holmes, T. H., & Rahe, R. H. (1967). The social readjustment rating scale. *Journal of Psychosomatic Research, 11*, 213–218.

Homans, G. C. (1950). *The human group.* New York, NY: Harcourt, Brace & World.

Hooper, L. M. (2009). Individual and family resilience: Definitions, research, and frameworks relevant for counselors. *Alabama Counseling Association Journal, 35*, 19–26.

Houseknecht, S. K., & Lewis, S. K. (2005). Explaining teen childbearing and cohabitation: Community embeddedness and primary ties. *Family Relations, 54*, 607–620.

Huebner, A. J., Mancini, J. A., Wilcox, R. M., Grass, S. R., & Grass, G. A. (2007). Parental deployment and youth in military families: Exploring uncertainty and ambiguous loss. *Family Relations, 56*(2), 112–122.

Hunter, E. J. (1984). Treating the military captive's family. In F. Kaslow & R. Ridenour (Eds.), *The military family: Dynamics and treatment* (pp. 167–196). New York, NY: Guilford.

The importance of doing what's important to you. (2001). *Harvard Women's Health Watch,* 1.

Jacobson, N. S., & Gottman, J. M. (1998). *When men batter women: New insights into ending abusive relationships.* New York, NY: Simon & Schuster.

Jacobson, N. S., Gottman, J. M., Waltz, J., Rushe, R., Babcock, J., & Holtzworth-Munroe, A. (1994). Affect, verbal content, and psychophysiology in the arguments of couples with a violent husband. *Journal of Consulting and Clinical Psychology, 62*(5), 982–988.

Johnson, J. (2012, October 14). Residents free of fear in former North Place neighborhood. *Athens Banner Herald.* Retrieved from http://onlineathens.com/local-news/2012-10-13

Kane, R. (with Ouellette, J.). (2011). *The good caregiver: A one-of-a-kind compassionate resource for anyone caring for an aging loved one.* New York, NY: Penguin.

Kaslow, F. (2001). Families and family psychology at the millennium. *American Psychologist, 56*(1), 37–46.

Keefe, S. E., & Padilla, A. M. (1987). *Chicano ethnicity.* Albuquerque, NM: University of New Mexico Press.

Keenan, E. K. (2010). Seeing the forest and the trees: Using dynamic systems theory to understand "stress and coping" and "trauma and resilience." *Journal of Human Behavior in the Social Environment, 20*(8), 1038–1060.

Kessler, R. C. (1979). Stress, social status, and psychological distress. *Journal of Health and Social Behavior, 20,* 259–272.

Kessler, R. C. (1983). Methodological issues in the study of psychosocial stress. In H. B. Kaplan (Ed.), *Psychosocial stress: Trends in theory and research* (pp. 267–341). New York, NY: Academic Press.

Kessler, R. C., & McLeod, J. D. (1984). Sex differences in vulnerability to undesirable life events. *Sociological Review, 49,* 620–631.

Kessler, R. C., & McRae, J. A., Jr. (1982). The effect of wives' employment on the mental health of married men and women. *American Sociological Review, 47,* 217–227.

Kiefer, J. J., Mancini, J. A., Morrow, B. H., Gladwin, H., & Stewart, T. A. (2008). *Providing access to resilience-enhancing technologies for disadvantaged communities and vulnerable populations.* Oak Ridge, TN: Oak Ridge National Laboratory. Retrieved from http://www.uno.edu/chart/documents/ProvidingAccess.pdf

Kingsbury, N., & Scanzoni, J. (1993). Structural-functionalism. In P. G. Boss, W. J. Doherty, R. LaRossa, W. R. Schumm, & S. K. Steinmetz (Eds.), *Sourcebook of family theories and methods: A contextual approach* (pp. 195–217). New York, NY: Plenum.

Kiser, L. (2015). *Strengthening family coping resources: Intervention for families impacted by trauma.* New York, NY: Routledge.

Kiser, L. J., Backer, P. M., Winkles, J., & Medoff, D. (2015). Strengthening Family Coping Resources (SFCR): Practice-based evidence for a promising trauma intervention. *Couple and Family Psychology: Research and Practice, 4*(1), 49–59.

Kiser, L. J., Donohue, A., Hodgkinson, S., Medoff, D., & Black, M. M. (2010). Strengthening Family Coping Resources: The feasibility of a multifamily group intervention for families exposed to trauma. *Journal of Traumatic Stress, 23*(6), 802–806.

Kissane, D. (2003). Family focused grief therapy. *Bereavement Care, 22*(1), 6–8.

Kissane, D. (2011). Family therapy for the bereaved. In R. A. Neimeyer, D. L. Harris, H. R. Winokuer, & G. F. Thornton (Eds.), *Grief and bereavement in contemporary society: Bridging research and practice* (pp. 287–302). New York, NY: Routledge.

Kissane, D. W. (2014). Family grief. In D. W. Kissane & F. Parnes (Eds.), *Bereavement care for families* (pp. 3–16). New York, NY: Routledge.

Kissane, D. W., & Parnes, F. (Eds.). (2014). *Bereavement care for families.* New York, NY: Routledge.

Klaus, H. D., & Tam, M. E. (2015). Requiem aeternam?: Archaeothanatology of mortuary ritual in colonial Morrope, North Coast of Peru. In I. Shimada & J. L. Fitzsimmons (Eds.), *Living with the dead in the Andes* (pp. 267–303). Tucson: University of Arizona Press.

Klein, D. M., & White, J. M. (Eds.). (1996). *Family theories: An introduction.* Thousand Oaks, CA: Sage.

Kolar, K., Erickson, P. G., & Stewart, D. (2012). Coping strategies of street-involved youth: Exploring contexts of resilience. *Journal of Youth Studies, 15*(6), 744–760.

Koos, E. L. (1946). *Families in trouble.* New York, NY: King's Crown.

Kotchick, B. A., Dorsey, S., & Heller, L. (2005). Predictors of parenting among African American single mothers: Personal and contextual factors. *Journal of Marriage and Family, 67,* 448–460.

Koutsikou, S., Crook, J. J., Earl, E. V., Leith, J. L., Watson, T. C., Lumb, B. M., & Apps, R. (2014). Neural substrates underlying fear-evoked freezing: The periaqueductal grey-cerebellar link. *Journal of Physiology, 592*(10), 2197-2213.

Kretzmann, J. P., & McKnight, J. L. (1993). *Building communities from the inside out: A path toward finding and mobilizing a community's assets.* Evanston, IL: Asset-Based Community Development Institute, Institute for Policy Research, Northwestern University.

Kriseman, N. (2014). *The mindful caregiver.* Landham, MD: Rowman & Littlefield.

Kübler-Ross, E. (1969). *On death and dying.* New York, NY: Macmillan.

Kübler-Ross, E., & Kessler, D. (2005). *On grief and grieving: Finding the meaning of grief through the five stages of loss.* New York, NY: Scribner.

Kuiper, N. A. (2012). Humor and resiliency: Towards a process model of coping and growth. *Europe's Journal of Psychology, 8*(3), 475–491.

Kwon, H. K., Rueter, M. A., Lee, M. S., Koh, S., & Ok, S. W. (2003). Marital relationships following the Korean economic crisis: Applying the family stress model. *Journal of Marriage and Family, 65*(2), 316–325.

Kwon, S-Y. (2006). Grief ministry as homecoming: Framing death from a Korean American perspective. *Pastoral Psychology, 54*(4), 313–324.

Kyu, L. K. (1984). The concept of ancestors and ancestor worship in Korea. *Asian Folklore Studies, 43,* 199–214.

Landau, J. L. (2013). Family and community resilience relative to the experience of mass trauma: Connectedness to family and culture of origin as the core components of healing. In D. S. Becvar (Ed.), *Handbook of family resilience* (pp. 459–480). New York, NY: Springer.

Landau, J., & Saul, J. (2004). Facilitating family and community resilience in response to major disaster. In F. Walsh & M. McGoldrick (Eds.), *Living beyond loss* (2nd ed., pp. 285–309). New York, NY: Norton

LaRossa, R., & Reitzes, D. C. (1993). Symbolic interactionism and family studies. In P. Boss, W. Doherty, R. LaRossa, W. Schumm, & S. Steinmetz (Eds.), *Sourcebook of family theories and methods: A contextual approach* (pp. 135–163). New York, NY: Plenum.

Laurie, A., & Neimeyer, R. A. (2008). African Americans in bereavement: Grief as a function of ethnicity. *OMEGA, 57*(2), 173–193.

Lavee, Y. (2013). Stress processes in families and couples. In G. W. Peterson & K. R. Bush (Eds.), *Handbook of marriage and the family* (3rd ed., pp. 159–176). New York, NY: Springer US.

Lavee, Y., McCubbin, H. I., & Patterson, J. (1985). The double ABC-X model of family stress and adaptation: An empirical test by analysis of structural equations with latent variables. *Journal of Marriage and the Family, 47*(4), 811–826.

LaVeist, T. A., Thorpe, R. J., & Pierre, G. (2014). The relationship among vigilant coping style, race, and depression. *Journal of Social Issues, 70*(2), 241–255.

Lazarus, R. S. (1966). *Psychological stress and the coping process.* New York, NY: McGraw-Hill.

Lazarus, R. S. (1976). *Patterns of adjustment* (3rd ed.). New York, NY: McGraw-Hill.

Lazarus, R. S. (1993). Coping theory and research: Past, present, and future. *Psychosomatic Medicine, 55*(3), 234–247.

Lazarus, R. S. (2012). Evolution of a model of stress, coping, and discrete emotions. In V. H. Rice (Ed.), *Handbook of stress, coping, and health: Implications for nursing research, theory, and practice* (pp. 195–222). Thousand Oaks, CA: Sage.

Lazarus, R. S., & Folkman, S. (1984). *Stress, appraisal, and coping.* New York, NY: Springer.

Lee, E., & Chan, J. (2004). Mourning in Chinese culture. In F. Walsh & M. McGoldrick (Eds.), *Living beyond loss: Death in the family* (2nd ed., pp. 131–136). New York, NY: Norton.

Leipold, B., & Greve, W. (2009). Resilience: A conceptual bridge between coping and development. *European Psychologist, 14,* 40–50.

Leite, R. (2007). An exploration of aspects of boundary ambiguity among young, unmarried fathers during the prenatal period. *Family Relations, 56*(2), 162–174.

Letiecq, B. L., & Koblinsky, S. A. (2004). Parenting in violent neighborhoods: African American fathers' strategies for keeping children safe. *Journal of Family Issues, 25,* 715–734.

Lewin, K. (1951). *Field theory in social science.* New York, NY: Harper & Row.

Lietz, C.A. (2013). Family resilience in the context of high-risk situations. In D. S. Becvar (Ed.), *Handbook of family resilience* (pp. 153–172). New York, NY: Springer.

Lindemann, E. (1944). Symptomatology and management of acute grief. *American Journal of Psychiatry, 101,* 141–148.

Lipsitt, L. P., & Demick, J. (2012). Theory and measurement of resilience: Views from development. In M. Ungar (Ed.), *The social ecology of resilience: A handbook of theory and practice* (pp. 43–52). New York, NY: Springer.

Lucier-Greer, M., Arnold, A. L., Mancini, J. A., Ford, J. L., & Bryant, C. M. (2015). Influences of cumulative risk and protective factors on the adjustment of adolescents in military families. *Family Relations, 64,* 363–377.

Lukachko, A., Hatzenbuehler, M. L., & Keyes, K. M. (2014). Structural racism and myocardial infection in the United States. *Social Science and Medicine, 103,* 42–50.

Luster, T., & Oh, S. M. (2001). Correlates of male adolescents carrying handguns among their peers. *Journal of Marriage and Family, 63,* 714–726.

Macquarrie, C. R. (2005). Experiences in early stage Alzheimer's disease: Understanding the paradox of acceptance and denial. *Aging & Mental Health, 9*(5), 430–441.

Maes, S., Leventhal, H., & de Ridder, D. T. (1996). Coping with chronic diseases. In M. Zeidner & N. S. Ender (Eds.), *Handbook of coping: Theory, research, applications* (pp. 221–251). Oxford, UK: Wiley & Sons.

Major, B., Quinton, W. J., & McCoy, S. K. (2002). Antecedents and consequences of attributions to discrimination: Theoretical and empirical advances. In M. P. Zanna (Ed.), *Advances in experimental social psychology* (pp. 251–330). San Diego, CA: Academic Press.

Makimura, H. (1996). *Ohaka to kazoku [graves to family].* Osaka, JA: Toki Shobo.

Mancini, J. A., Arnold, A. L., Martin, J. A., & Bowen, G. (2014). Community and primary prevention. In T. Gullotta & M. Bloom (Eds.), *Encyclopedia of primary prevention and health promotion* (2nd ed., pp. 335–351). New York, NY: Springer.

Mancini, J. A., & Blieszner, R. (1992). Social provisions in adulthood: Concept and measurement in close relationships. *Journal of Gerontology: Psychological Sciences, 47,* 14–20.

Mancini, J. A., & Bowen, G. L. (2009). Community resilience: A social organization theory of action and change. In J. A. Mancini & K. A. Roberto (Eds.), *Pathways of human development: Explorations of change* (pp. 245–265). Lanham, MD: Lexington Books.

Mancini, J. A., & Bowen, G. L. (2013). Families and communities: A social organization theory of action and change. In G. W. Peterson & K. R. Bush (Eds.), *Handbook of marriage and the family* (pp. 781–813). New York, NY: Springer.

Mancini, J. A., Bowen, G. L., & Martin, J. A. (2005). Community social organization: A conceptual linchpin in examining families in the context of communities. *Family Relations, 54,* 570-582.

Mancini, J. A., Bowen, G. L., O'Neal, C., & Arnold, A. L. (2015). Relationship provisions, self-efficacy, and youth well-being in military families. *Journal of Applied Developmental Psychology, 40,* 17–25.

Mancini, J. A., Martin, J. A., & Bowen, G. L. (2003). Community capacity. In T. P. Gullotta & M. Bloom (Eds.), *Encyclopedia of primary prevention and health promotion* (pp. 319–330). New York, NY: Kluwer Academic.

Mancini, J. A., Nelson, J. P., Bowen, G. L., & Martin, J. A. (2006). Preventing intimate partner violence: A community capacity approach. *Journal of Aggression, Maltreatment & Trauma, 13,* 203–227.

Mancini, J. A., & Orthner, D. K. (1988). The context and consequences of family change. *Family Relations, 37,* 363–366.

Mancini, J. A., Quinn, W., Gavigan, M., & Franklin, H. (1980). Social network interaction among older adults: Implications for life satisfaction. *Human Relations, 33,* 543–554.

Many Oklahoma grandparents step in to raise grandchildren [Video file]. (2012, September 9). *News9.* Retrieved from http://www.news9.com/story/19496497/many-oklahoma-grandparents-step-in-to-raise-grandchildren

Marshall, N. L., Noonan, A. E., McCartney, K., Marx, F., & Keefe, N. (2001). It takes an urban village: Parenting networks of urban families. *Journal of Family Issues, 22,* 163–182.

Masten, A. S. (2001). Ordinary magic: Resilience processes in development. *American Psychologist, 56,* 227–238.

Masten, A. S. (2007). Resilience in developing systems: Progress and promise as the fourth wave rises. *Development and Psychopathology, 19,* 921–930.

Masten, A. S. (2014). *Ordinary magic: Resilience in development.* New York, NY: Guilford Press.

Masten, A. S., & Coatsworth, J. D. (1998). The development of competence in favorable and unfavorable environments: Lessons from research on successful children. *American Psychologist, 53*(2), 205–220.

Mather, M. (2010). U.S. children in single-mother families. *Population Reference Bureau.* Retrieved from http://www.prb.org/pdf10/single-motherfamilies.pdf

Matsuyama, R. K., Balliet, W., Ingram, K., Lyckholm, L. J., Wilson-Genderson, M., & Smith, T. J. (2011). Will patients want hospice or palliative care if they do not know what it is? *Journal of Hospital Palliative Nursing, 13*(1), 41–46.

McBride, A. M., Sherraden, M. S., & Pritzker, S. (2006). Civic engagement among low income and low-wealth families: In their words. *Family Relations, 55,* 152–162.

McCarthy, J. R., & Edwards, R. (2011). *Key concepts in family studies.* London, UK: Sage.

McCubbin, H. (1979). Integrating coping behavior in family stress theory. *Journal of Marriage and the Family, 41,* 237–244.

McCubbin, H., & McCubbin, M. (1988). Typology of resilient families: Emerging roles of social class and ethnicity. *Family Relations, 37,* 247–254.

McCubbin, M. A., & McCubbin, H. I. (1993). Families coping with illness: The resiliency model of family stress, adjustment, and adaptation. In C. B. Danielson, B. Hamel-Bissell, & P. Winstead-Fry (Eds.), *Families, health, and illness: Perspectives on coping and intervention* (pp. 21-64). St. Louis, MO: Mosby,

McCubbin, H. I., McCubbin, M. A., Thompson, A. I., & Thompson, E. A. (1998). Resiliency in ethnic families: A conceptual model for predicting family adjustment and adaptation. In H. I. McCubbin, E. A. Thompson, A. I. Thompson, & J. E. Fromer (Eds.), *Resiliency in Native American and immigrant families* (pp. 3–48). Thousand Oaks, CA: Sage.

McCubbin, H. I., & Patterson, J. M. (1983). The family stress process: The double ABC-X model of adjustment and adaptation. *Marriage & Family Review, 6*(1–2), 7–37.

McCubbin, H. I., Patterson, J., & Wilson, L. (1981). *Family Inventory of Life Events and Changes (FILE): Research instrument.* St. Paul: University of Minnesota, Family Social Science.

McCubbin, H. I., Thompson, E. A., Thompson, A. I., & Fromer, J. E. (Eds.). (1998). *Resiliency in Native American and immigrant families.* Thousand Oaks, CA: Sage.

McFarlane, W. R., Lukens, E., Link, B., Dushay, R., Deakins, S. A., Newmark, M., . . . Toran, J. (1995). Multiple-family groups and psychoeducation in the treatment of schizophrenia. *Archives of General Psychiatry, 52*(8), 679–687.

McGoldrick, M. (2004). Mourning in Irish families. In F. Walsh & M. McGoldrick (Eds.), *Living beyond loss: Death in the family* (2nd ed., pp. 140–145). New York, NY: Norton.

McGoldrick, M., Gerson, R., & Shellenberger, S. (1999). *Genograms: Assessment and intervention*. New York, NY: Norton.

McGuire, J. K., Catalpa, J. M., Lacey, V., & Kuvalanka, K. A. (in press). Relational rupture: Using ambiguous loss as a process for decentering cisnormativity. *Journal of Family Theory & Review, 8*(3).

McIllwain, C. D. (2002). Death in Black and White: A study of family differences in the performance of death rituals. *Qualitative Research Reports in Communication, Winter,* 1–6.

Mead, G. H. (1956). *On social psychology: Selected papers* (A. Strauss, Ed.). Chicago, IL: University of Chicago Press. (Original work published 1934)

Meers, S., & Strober, J. (2009). *Getting to 50/50: How working couples can have it all by sharing it all.* New York, NY: Bantam Books.

Meyer, I. (1995). Minority stress and mental health in gay men. *Journal of Health and Social Behavior, 36,* 38–56.

Meyer, I. H. (2003). Minority stress and mental health in gay men. In L. D. Garnets & D. Kimmel (Eds.), *Psychological perspectives on lesbian, gay, and bisexual experiences* (2nd ed., pp. 699–732). New York, NY: Columbia University Press.

Mian, A., & Sufi, A. (2014). *House of debt: How they (and you) caused the Great Recession and how we can prevent it from happening again.* Chicago, IL: University of Chicago Press.

Middlebrooks, J. A., & Audage, N. C. (2008). *The effects of childhood stress on health across the lifespan.* Atlanta, GA: Centers for Disease Control and Prevention, National Center for Injury Prevention and Control.

Miller, J. L. (2012). *Psychosocial capacity building in response to disasters.* New York, NY: Columbia University Press.

Mills, S. (2012). Sounds to soothe the soul: Music and bereavement in a traditional South Korean death ritual. *Mortality, 17*(2), 145–157.

Minuchin, S. (1974). *Families and family therapy.* Cambridge, MA: Harvard University Press.

Mirowsky, J., & Ross, C. (1989). *Social causes of psychological distress.* New York, NY: Aldine.

Mishel, M. H. (1981). The measurement of uncertainty in illness. *Nursing Research, 30,* 258–263.

Mishel, M. H. (1990). Reconceptualization of the uncertainty in illness theory. *Image: Journal of Nursing Scholarship, 22,* 256–262.

Mitchell, M. B. (2016). *The neglected transition: Building a relational home for children entering foster care.* New York, NY: Oxford University Press.

Mockett, M. M. (2015). *Where the dead pause and the Japanese say good-by: A journey.* New York, NY: Norton.

Mogey, J. (1964). Family and community in urban-industrial societies. In H. Christensen (Ed.), *Handbook of marriage and the family* (pp. 501–534). Chicago, IL: Rand McNally.

Mondia, S., Hichenberg, S., Kerr, E., & Kissane, D. W. (2012). The impact of Asian-American value systems on palliative care: Illustrative cases from the Family Focused Grief Therapy Trial. *American Journal of Hospice and Palliative Care, 29*(6), 443–448.

Moore, J. L., & Constantine, M. G. (2005). Development and initial validation of the collectivistic coping style measure with African, Asian, and Latin American international students. *Journal of Mental Health Counseling, 27,* 329 –347.

Moore, R. F. (1999, April 10). Police file reveals details on Khoua Her. Life spiraled downward before six children slain. *St. Paul Pioneer Press,* p. 1A.

Moos, R. (1993). *Coping Response Inventory-Youth Form professional manual.* Odessa, FL: Butterworths Press.

Moradi, B., & Risco, C. (2006). Perceived discrimination experiences and mental health of Latino/a American persons. *Journal of Counseling Psychology, 53,* 411–421.

Morgan, J. D., & Laugani, P. (2002). General introduction. In J. D. Morgan & P. Langani (Eds.), *Death and bereavement around the world: Vol. 1. Major religious traditions* (pp. 1–4). Amityville, NY: Baywood.

Murry, V. M., Brown, P. A., Brody, G. H., Cutrona, C. E., & Simons, R. L. (2001). Racial discrimination as a moderator of the links among stress, maternal psychological functioning, and family relationships. *Journal of Marriage and Family, 63,* 915–926.

Nadal, K. L. (2009). *Filipino American psychology: A handbook of theory, research, and clinical practice.* Bloomington, IN: AuthorHouse.

Nadeau, J. W. (1998). *Families making sense of death.* Thousand Oaks, CA: Sage.

Nakamatsu, T. (2009). Conventional practice, courageous plan: Women and the gendered site of death rituals in Japan. *Journal of Gender Studies, 18*(1), 1–11.

Napier, A., & Whitaker, C. A. (1978). *The family crucible.* New York, NY: Harper & Row.

National Alliance for Caregiving & AARP Public Policy Institute. (2015). *Caregiving in the U.S. 2015.* Retrieved from http://www.aarp.org/content/dam/aarp/ppi/2015/caregiving-in-the-united-states-2015-executive-summary-revised.pdf

Navaie-Waliser, M., Spriggs, A., & Feldman, P. H. (2002). Informal caregiving: Differential experiences by gender. *Medical Care, 40*(12), 1249–1259.

Neacsiu, A. D., Rizvi, S. L., Vitaliano, P. P., Lynch, T. R., & Linehan, M. M. (2010). The dialectical behavior therapy ways of coping checklist: Development and psychometric properties. *Journal of Clinical Psychology, 66*(6), 563–582.

Neimeyer, R. A. (2014). Series editor's foreword. In D. W. Kissane & F. Parnes (Eds.), *Bereavement care for families* (pp. xviiii–xx). New York, NY: Routledge.

Neufeld, V. (Executive Producer). (2001, February 28). *20/20.* New York, NY: American Broadcasting Corporation.

Ng, R., Ang, R. P., & Ho, M. H. R. (2012). Coping with anxiety, depression, anger, and aggression: The mediational role of resilience in adolescents. *Child & Youth Care Forum, 41*(6), 529–546.

Ní Raghallaigh, M., & Gilligan, R. (2010). Active survival in the lives of unaccompanied minors: Coping strategies, resilience, and the relevance of religion. *Child & Family Social Work, 15,* 226–237.

Nichols, M. P., & Schwartz, R. C. (2004). *Family therapy concepts and methods* (6th ed.). Boston, MA: Allyn & Bacon.

Nichols, W. C. (2013). Roads to understanding family resilience: 1920s to the twenty-first century. In D. S. Becvar (Ed.), *Handbook of family resilience* (pp. 3–16). New York, NY: Springer.

Norris, F. H., Stevens, S. P., Pfefferbaum, B., Wyche, K. F., & Pfefferbaum, R. L. (2008). Community resilience as a metaphor, theory, set of capacities, and strategy for disaster readiness. *American Journal of Community Psychology, 41,* 127–150.

Norwood, K. (2012). Transitioning meanings? Family members' communicative struggles surrounding transgender identity. *Journal of Family Communication, 12*(1), 75–92.

Norwood, K. (2013a). Grieving gender: Trans-identities, transition, and ambiguous loss. *Communication Monographs, 80*(1), 24–45.

Norwood, K. (2013b). Meaning matters: Framing trans identity in the context of family relationships. *Journal of GLBT Family Studies, 9*(2), 152–178. doi:10.1080/1550428X.2013.765262

Nossiter, A., & Gladstone, R. (2015, November 13). Paris attacks kill more than 100, police say: Border controls tightened. *New York Times* Online. Retrieved from http://www.nytimes.com/2015/11/14/world/europe/paris-shooting-attacks.html?rref=collection%2Fnewsevent collection%2Fattacks-in-paris&action=click&contentCollection=europe&region=stream &module=stream_unit&version=latest&contentPlacement=293&pgtype=collection&_r=1

Nystrom, K. C., Buikstra, J. E., & Muscutt, K. (2010). Chachapoya mortuary behavior: A consideration of method and meaning. *Chungara, Revista de Antropologia Chileana, 42*(2), 477–495.

O'Brien, M. (2007). Ambiguous loss in families of children with autism spectrum disorders. *Family Relations, 56*(2), 135–146.

Oh, H. J., Ozkaya, E., & LaRose, R. (2014). How does online social networking enhance life satisfaction? The relationships among online supportive interaction, affect, perceived social support, sense of community, and life satisfaction. *Computers in Human Behavior, 30,* 69–78.

Okafor, E., Lucier-Greer, M., & Mancini, J. A. (2015, November). *Coping and depressive symptoms: Latent profile analysis of military adolescents.* Paper presented at the Annual Meeting of the National Council on Family Relations, Vancouver, Canada.

Oldehinkel, A. J., & Bouma, E. M. (2011). Sensitivity to the depressogenic effect of stress and HPA-axis reactivity in adolescence: A review of gender differences. *Neuroscience & Biobehavioral Reviews, 35*(8), 1757–1770.

O'Neal, C. W., Richardson, E., Mancini, J. A., & Grimsley, N. (2016). Parents' early life stressful experiences, their present well-being, and that of their children. *American Journal of Orthopsychiatry.* Advance online publication. http://dx.doi.org/10.1037/ort0000140

O'Neal, C. W., Ross, D. B., Oed, M., Lucier-Greer, M., & Mancini, J. A. (2014, March). *Money matters in marriage: Financial concerns, warmth, and hostility among military couples.* Paper presented at the Society for Research in Human Development Conference, Austin, TX.

Ornelas, I. J., Perriera, K. M., Beeber, L., & Maxwell, L. (2009). Challenges and strategies to maintaining emotional health: Qualitative perspectives of Mexican immigrant mothers. *Journal of Family Issues, 30,* 1556–1575.

Papalia, D. E., Olds, S. W., & Feldman, R. D. (2001). *Human development* (8th ed.). New York, NY: McGraw-Hill.

Paré, D. A. (1995). Of families and other cultures: The shifting paradigm of family therapy. *Family Process, 34*(1), 1–19.

Patterson, J. M. (2002). Integrating family resilience and family stress theory. *Journal of Marriage and Family, 64,* 349–360.

Patterson, J. M., & Garwick, A. W. (1994). Levels of meaning in family stress theory. *Family Process, 33,* 287–304.

Pearlin, L. I. (1975). Sex roles and depression. In N. Datan & L. H. Ginsberg (Eds.), *Life-span developmental psychology: Normative life crises* (pp. 191–207). New York, NY: Academic Press.

Pearlin, L. I. (1989). The sociological study of stress. *Journal of Health and Social Behavior, 30,* 241–256.

Pearlin, L. I., & Lieberman, M. A. (1979). Social sources of emotional distress. In R. G. Simmons (Ed.), *Research in community and mental health* (pp. 217–248). Greenwich, CT: JAI.

Pearlin, L. I., & Schooler, C. (1978). The structure of coping. *Journal of Health and Social Behavior, 19*(1), 2–21.

Pena, E. (2003). Reconfiguring epistemological parts: Creating a dialogue between psychoanalyses and Chicano/a subjectivity, a cosmopolitan approach. *Journal for the Psychoanalysis of Culture & Society, 8*(2), 308–319.

Peters, M. F., & Massey, G. C. (1983). Mundane extreme environmental stress in family stress theories: The case of Black families in America. *Marriage and Family Review, 6,* 193–218.

Petkov, B. (2004). Mourning in Jewish families. In F. Walsh & M. McGoldrick (Eds.), *Living beyond loss: Death in the family* (2nd ed., pp. 145–149). New York, NY: Norton.

Pew Research Center. (2014, January 14). Religious hostilities reach six-year high. *Pew Research Center.* Retrieved from http://www.pewforum.org/2014/01/14/religious-hostilities-reach-six-year-high

Picot, S. J., Debanne, S. M., Namazi, K. H., & Wykle, M. L. (1997). Religiosity and perceived rewards of Black and White caregivers. *The Gerontologist, 37,* 89–101.

Pierce, C. M. (1970). Offensive mechanisms. In F. Barbour (Ed.), *The Black seventies* (pp. 265–282). Boston, MA: Porter Sargent.

Pierce, C. M. (1974). Psychiatric problems of the Black minority. In S. Arieti & G. Kaplan (Eds.), *American handbook of psychiatry* (Vol. 3; pp. 512–523). New York, NY: Basic Books.

Pinkerton, J., & Dolan, P. (2007). Family support, social capital, resilience, and adolescent coping. *Child & Family Social Work, 12*(3), 219–228.

Pollard, K., & Scommenga, P. (2014). Just how many Baby Boomers are there? *Population Reference Bureau*. Retrieved from http://www.prb.org/Publications/Articles/2002/JustHowManyBabyBoomersAreThere.aspx

Ponn, A. L. (2001). Judaism. In C. J. Johnson & M. G. McGee (Eds.), *How different religions view death and afterlife* (pp. 145–159). Philadelphia, PA: Charles Press.

Portes, A., & Rumbaut, R. G. (2006). *Immigrant America: A portrait* (3rd ed.). Berkeley, CA: University of California Press.

PSS/WSF Grandparent Family Apartments. (2016). Retrieved from http://www.wsfssh.org/buildings/psswsf-grandparent-family-apartments

Quinlivan, L. (1999, January 9). Khoua Her sentenced to 50 years. St. Paul mother details troubles that led to murdering 6 children. *St. Paul Pioneer Press,* p. 1A.

Radloff, L. S., & Rae, D. S. (1981). Components of the sex difference in depression. In R. G. Simmons (Ed.), *Research in community and mental health* (pp. 77–110). Greenwich, CT: JAI.

Rahe, R. H., Veach, T. L., Tolles, R. L., & Murakami, K. (2000). The stress and coping inventory: An educational and research instrument. *Stress and Health, 16*(4), 199–208.

Rampell, C. (2013, May 29). U.S. women on the rise as family breadwinner. *The New York Times*. Retrieved from http://www.nytimes.com/2013/05/30/business/economy/women-as-family-breadwinner-on-the-rise-study-says.html?_r=0

Reibolt, W. (2001). Adolescent interactions with gangs, family, and neighborhoods: An ethnographic investigation. *Journal of Family Issues, 22,* 211–242.

Reiss, D. (1981). *The family's construction of reality.* Cambridge, MA: Harvard University Press.

Reiss, D., & Oliveri, M. E. (1991). The family's conception of accountability and competence: A new approach to the conceptualization and assessment of family stress. *Family Process, 30,* 193–214.

Riegel, K. (1979). *Foundations of dialectical psychology.* New York, NY: Academic Press.

Riley, J. R., & Masten, A. S. (2005). Resilience in context. In R. D. Peters, B. Leadbeater, & R. McMahon (Eds.), *Resilience in children, families, and communities: Linking context to practice and policy* (pp. 13–25). New York, NY: Kluwer Academic/Plenum.

Robins, S. (2010). Ambiguous loss in a non-Western context: Families of the disappeared in postconflict Nepal. *Family Relations, 59*(3), 253–268.

Robins, S. (2013). *Families of the missing: A test for contemporary approaches to transitional justice.* New York, NY/London, UK: Routledge Glasshouse.

Robins, S. (2014). Constructing meaning from disappearance: Local memorialisation of the missing in Nepal. *International Journal of Conflict and Violence, 8*(1), 104–118.

Robins, S. (in press). Discursive approaches to ambiguous loss: Theorizing community-based therapy after enforced disappearance. *Journal of Family Theory & Review, 8*(3).

Rodgers, R. H., & White, J. M. (1993). Family development theory. In P. G. Boss, W. J. Doherty, R. LaRossa, W. R. Schumm, & S. K. Steinmetz (Eds.), *Sourcebook of family theories and methods: A contextual approach* (pp. 225–254). New York, NY: Plenum.

Rojano, R. (2004). The practice of community family therapy. *Family Process, 43,* 59–77.

Romero, A. J., & Roberts, R. E. (2003). Stress within a bicultural context for adolescents of Mexican descent. *Cultural Diversity & Ethnic Minority Psychology, 9,* 171–184.

Roosa, M. W., Deng, S., Ryu, E., Lockhart-Burrell, G., Tien, J. Y., & Jones, S., . . . Crowder, S. (2005). Family and child characteristics linking neighborhood context and child externalizing behavior. *Journal of Marriage and Family, 67,* 515–529.

Roper, S. O., & Jackson, J. B. (2007). The ambiguities of out-of-home care: Children with severe or profound disabilities. *Family Relations*, 56(2), 147–161.

Rosenblatt, P. C. (2013). Family grief in cross-cultural perspective. *Family Science*, 4(1), 12–19.

Rosenblatt, P. C., & Wallace, B. R. (2005). *African American grief*. New York, NY: Routledge.

Russell, S. T., McGuire, J. K., & Laub, C. (2008). School climate for lesbian, gay, bisexual, and transgender (LGBT) students. In M. Shinn & H. Yoshikawa (Eds.), *Toward positive youth development: Transforming schools and community programs* (pp. 133–149). New York, NY: Oxford University Press.

Rutter, M. (2007). Resilience, competence, and coping. *Child Abuse & Neglect*, 31, 205–209.

Saez, E., & Zucman, G. (2014). Wealth inequality in the United States since 1913: Evidence from capitalized income tax data (Working Paper No. 20625). *National Bureau of Economic Research*. Retrieved from http://gabriel-zucman.eu/files/SaezZucman2014.pdf

Saldana, D. H. (1994). Acculturative stress: Minority status and distress. *Hispanic Journal of Behavioral Sciences*, 16(2), 116–128.

Salvatore, J. E., & Dick, D. M. (2015). Gene-environment interplay: Where we are, where we are going. *Journal of Marriage and Family*, 77, 344–350.

Sandberg, S. (2013). *Lean in: Women, work, and the will to lead*. New York, NY: Random House.

Saul, J. (2014). *Collective trauma, collective healing: Promoting community resilience in the aftermath of disaster*. New York, NY/London, UK: Routledge.

Scherz, F. H. (1966). Family treatment concepts. *Social Casework*, 47(4), 234–240.

Schoen, J. W. (updated April 8, 2010). Study: 1.2 million households lost to recession. *NBCNEWS.com*. Retrieved from http://www.nbcnews.com/id/36231884/ns/business-eye_on_the_economy/t/study-million-households-lost-recession/#.VoqXT5VdGP8

Schoulte, J. C. (2011). Bereavement among African Americans and Latino/a Americans. *Journal of Mental Health Counseling*, 33(1), 11–20.

Schulz, R., & Beach, S. R. (1999). Caregiving as a risk factor for mortality: The caregiver health effects study. *Journal of the American Medical Association*, 282(23), 2215–2219.

Schwartz, S. J., & Unger, J. B. (2010). Biculturalism and context: What is biculturalism, and when is it adaptive? *Human Development*, 53, 26–32.

Schwartz, S. J., & Zamboanga, B. L. (2008). Testing Berry's model of acculturation: A confirmatory latent class approach. *Cultural Diversity and Ethnic Minority Psychology*, 14, 275–285.

Seligman, M. E. P. (1975/1992). *Helplessness*. New York, NY: Freeman. (Original work published 1975)

Seligman, M. E. P. (1991). *Learned optimism*. New York, NY: Knopf.

Selye, H. (1978). *The stress of life* (Rev. ed.). New York, NY: McGraw-Hill.

Selye, H. (Ed.). (1980). *Selye's guide to stress research* (Vol. 1). New York, NY: Van Nostrand Reinhold.

Shapiro, E. R. (1996). Family bereavement and cultural diversity: A social developmental perspective. *Family Process*, 35, 313–332.

Shaw, D., Scully, J., & Hart, T. (2014). The paradox of social resilience: How cognitive strategies and coping mechanisms attenuate and accentuate resilience. *Global Environmental Change*, 25, 194–203.

Shear, M. K., Simon, N., Wall, M., Zisook, S., Neimeyer, R., Duan, N., . . . Keshaviah, A. (2011). Complicated grief and related bereavement issues for DSM 5. *Depression and Anxiety*, 28(2), 103–117.

Shepard, G. H. (2002). Three days for weeping: Dreams, emotions, and death in the Peruvian Amazon. *Medical Anthropology Quarterly*, 18(2), 200–229.

Siemerink, E. J., Jaspers, J. P., Plukker, J. T., Mulder, N. H., & Hospers, G. A. (2011). Retrospective denial as a coping method. *Journal of Clinical Psychology in Medical Settings*, 18(1), 65–69.

Silberman, S. (2007, August). Where is Jim Gray? *Wired Magazine*, 15(8), 130–139, 154–155.

Simmel, G. (1955). *Conflict and the web of group affiliations.* New York, NY: Free Press.

Skinner, E. A., & Zimmer-Gembeck, M. J. (2007). The development of coping. *Annual Review of Psychology 58,* 119–144.

Slopen, N., Non, A., Williams, D. R., Roberts, A. L., & Albert, M.A. (2014). Childhood adversity, adult neighborhood context, and cumulative biological risk for chronic diseases in adulthood. *Psychosomatic Medicine, 76,* 481–489.

Smith, B. R. (2008). 'We don't want to chase 'em away': Hauntology in central Cape York Peninsula. In K. Glaskin, M. Tonkinson, Y. Musharbash, & V. Burbank (Eds.), *Mortality, mourning, and mortuary practices in indigenous Australia* (pp. 189–207). Burlington, VT: Ashgate.

Smith, M., & Davey, M. (2015, November 2). Illinois district violated transgender student's rights, U.S. says. *The New York Times.* Retrieved from http://www.nytimes.com/2015/11/03/us/illinois-district-violated-transgender-students-rights-us-says.html?_r=1

Southwick, S. M., Bonanno, G. A., Masten, A. S., Panter-Brick, C., & Yehuda, R. (2014). Resilience definitions, theory, and challenges: Interdisciplinary perspectives. *European Journal of Psychotraumatology, 5.* Retrieved from http://www.ejpt.net/index.php/ejpt/article/view/25338

Stanley, S., Bradbury, T., & Markman, H. (2000). Structural flaws in the bridge from basic research on marriage to intervention for couples. *Journal of Marriage and Family, 62*(1), 256–264.

Staudenmayer, H., Kinsman, R. A., Dirks, J. F., Spector, S. L., & Wangaard, C. (1979). Medical outcome in asthmatic patients: Effects of airways hyperreactivity and symptom-focused anxiety. *Psychosomatic Medicine, 41*(2), 109–118.

Stevens, K. (2013). The impact of evidence-based practice in nursing and the next big ideas. *OJIN: The Online Journal of Issues in Nursing, 18*(2), 4–14. doi: 10.3912/OJIN. Vol18No02Man04

Stevenson, S. (2015, September 4). 8 predictions about the future of assisted living. *Senior Living Blog.* Retrieved from http://www.aplaceformom.com/blog/2013-8-27-future-senior-care

Stix, G. (2011). The neuroscience of true grit. *Scientific American, 304*(3), 28–33.

Stonequist, E. V. (1961). *The marginal man.* New York, NY: Russell & Russell.

Strauss, M., & Gelles, R. (Eds.). (1995). *Physical violence in American families.* New Brunswick, NJ: Transaction.

Stryker, S. (1968). Identity salience and role performance: The relevance of symbolic interaction theory for family research. *Journal of Marriage and the Family, 30,* 558–564.

Stryker, S., & Stratham, A. (1985). Symbolic interaction and role theory. In G. Lindsey & E. Aronson (Eds.), *Handbook of social psychology* (Vol. 2; pp. 311–378). New York, NY: Random.

Suilleabhain, S. O. (1967). *Irish wake amusements.* Dublin, Ireland: Mercier.

Suzukamo, L. B. (1998a, September 6). History of family turmoil portrait: As mother awaits charges in her children's slayings, a bitter story emerges. *St. Paul Pioneer Press,* p. 1A.

Suzukamo, L. B. (1998b, September 6). Hmong community asks: Why? Local leaders try to find sense in tragic deaths of 6 St. Paul kids. *St. Paul Pioneer Press,* p. 15A.

Swim, J., Clayton, S., Doherty, T., Gifford, R., Howard, G., Reser, J., . . . Weber, E., & Task Force on the Interface Between Psychology and Global Climate Change. (2009). *Psychology and global climate change: Addressing a multi-faceted phenomenon and set of challenges.* Washington, DC: American Psychological Association.

Swisher, R., Sweet, S., & Moen, P. (2004). The family-friendly community and its life course fit for dual-earner couples. *Journal of Marriage and Family, 66,* 281–292.

Takazawa, A., & Williams, K. (2011). Communities in disasters: Helpless or helping? *Perspectives on Global Development and Technology, 10,* 429–440.

Tanner, J. G. (1995). Death, dying, and grief in the Chinese perspective. In J. K. Parry & A. S. Ryad (Eds.), *A cross-cultural look at death, dying, and religion* (pp. 183–192). Chicago, IL: Nelson Hall.

Tchombe, T. M. S., Shumba, A., Lo-Oh, J. L., Gakuba, T. O., Zinkeng, M., & Teku, T. T. (2012). Psychological undertones of family poverty in rural communities in Cameroon: Resilience and coping strategies. *South African Journal of Psychology, 42*(2), 232–242.

Thomas, W. I., & Znaniecki, F. (1918). *The Polish peasant in Europe and America*. Boston, MA: Badger.

Tiu, A. T., & Seneriches, J. S. (1995). *Depression and other mental health issues: The Filipino American experience*. San Francisco, CA: Jossey-Bass.

Tolstoy, L. (1878/2001). *Anna Karenina* (R. Pevear & L. Volokhonsky, Trans.). New York, NY: Penguin. (Original work published 1878)

Trzesniak, P., Liborio, R. M. C., & Koller, S. K. (2012). Resilience and children's work in Brazil: Lessons from physics for psychology. In M. Ungar (Ed.), *The social ecology of resilience: A handbook of theory and practice* (pp. 53–65). New York, NY: Springer.

Tsai, J. L., & Chentsova-Dutton, Y. (2003). Variation among European Americans in emotional facial expressions. *Journal of Cross-Cultural Psychology, 34*(6), 650–657.

Tyshenko, M. G., & Paterson, C. (2010). *SARS unmasked: Risk communication of pandemics and influenza in Canada*. Montreal, Quebec: McGill-Queen's University Press.

Ungar, M. (2012). (Ed.). *The social ecology of resilience: A handbook of theory and practice*. New York, NY: Springer.

Ungar, M. (2013). Family resilience and at-risk youth. In D. S. Becvar (Ed). *Handbook of family resilience* (pp. 137–152). New York, NY: Springer.

U.S. Census Bureau. (2015). *Facts for features (FFF): National Grandparents Day 2015: September 13*. Retrieved from https://www.census.gov/newsroom/facts-for-features/2015/cb15-ff15.html

U.S. Census Bureau News. (January 2015). *Facts for features: Irish-American Heritage Month (March) and St. Patrick's Day (March 17): 2015*. Retrieved from http://www.census.gov/newsroom/facts-for-features/2015/cb15-ff04.html

U.S. Surgeon General. (2001). *Mental health: Culture, race, and ethnicity. A supplement to mental health: A report of the surgeon general*. Washington, DC: U.S. Department of Health and Human Services. Retrieved from http://www.ncbi.nlm.nih.gov/books/NBK44243

Vaughn, B. E., Egeland, B., Sroufe, L. A., & Waters, E. (1979). Individual differences in infant-mother attachment at twelve and eighteen months: Stability and change in families under stress. *Child Development, 50*, 971–975.

Wadsworth, S. M. (2010). Family risk and resilience in the context of war and terrorism. *Journal of Marriage and Family, 72*, 537–556.

Wahlig, J. L. (2015). Losing the child they thought they had: Therapeutic suggestions for an ambiguous loss perspective with parents of a transgender child. *Journal of GLBT Family Studies, 11*(4), 305–326.

Walsh, F. (2002). A family resilience framework: Innovative practice applications. *Family Relations, 51*, 130–137.

Walsh, F. (2012). Facilitating family resilience: Relational resources for positive youth development in conditions of adversity. In M. Ungar (Ed.), *The social ecology of resilience: A handbook of theory and practice* (pp. 173–185). New York, NY: Springer.

Walsh, F. (2013). Community-based practice applications of a family resilience framework. In D. Becvar (Ed.), *Handbook of family resilience* (pp. 65–82). New York, NY: Springer.

Walsh, F., & McGoldrick, M. (Eds.). (1991). *Living beyond loss: Death in the family*. New York, NY: Norton.

Walsh, F., & McGoldrick, M. (Eds.). (2004). *Living beyond loss: Death in the family* (2nd ed.). New York, NY. Norton.

Walter, T. (1999). *On bereavement: The culture of grief*. Buckingham, UK/Philadelphia, PA: Open University Press.

Wei, M., Liao, K. Y. H., Heppner, P. P., Chao, R. C. L., & Ku, T. Y. (2012). Forbearance coping, identification with heritage culture, acculturative stress, and psychological distress among Chinese international students. *Journal of Counseling Psychology, 59*(1), 97–106.

Weiss, R. S. (1974). The provisions of social relationships. In Z. Rubin (Ed.), *Doing unto others* (pp. 17–26). Englewood Cliffs, NJ: Prentice Hall.

Wekerle, C., Waechter, R., & Chung, R. (2012). Contexts of vulnerability and resilience: Childhood maltreatment, cognitive functioning, and close relationships. In M. Ungar (Ed.), *The social ecology of resilience: A handbook of theory and practice* (pp. 187–198). New York, NY: Springer.

Weston, K. (1991). *Families we choose: Lesbians, gay men, kinship.* New York, NY: Columbia University Press.

Wethington, E., McLeod, J. D., & Kessler, R. C. (1987). The importance of life events for explaining sex differences in psychological distress. In R. C. Barnett, L. Beiner, & G. K. Baruch (Eds.), *Gender and stress* (pp. 144–156). New York, NY: Free Press.

Whitaker, C. (1982). *From psyche to system: The evolving therapy of Carl Whitaker.* New York, NY: Guilford.

Whitaker, C. A. (1989). *Midnight musings of a family therapist.* New York, NY: Norton.

White, R. B. M., Roosa, M. W., Weaver, S. R., & Nair, R. L. (2009). Cultural and contextual influences on parenting in Mexican American families. *Journal of Marriage and Family, 71,* 61–79.

Whiteside, K. (2014, April 18). Seeing the world in a different way: Boston survivor copes with physical realities. *USA Today,* p. 3-C.

Wiens, T. W., & Boss, P. (2006). Maintaining family resiliency before, during, and after military separation. In C. A. Carson, A. B. Adler, & T. W. Britt (Eds.), *Military life: The psychology of serving in peace and combat* (Vol. 3). *The military family* (pp. 13–38). Westport, CT: Praeger Security International.

Wikan, U. (1988). Bereavement and loss in two Muslim communities: Egypt and Bali compared. *Social Science Medicine, 27*(5), 451–460.

Wikler, L. (1981). Chronic stresses of families of mentally retarded children. *Family Relations, 30*(2), 281–288.

Wikler, L. (1986). Periodic stress of families of older mentally retarded children: An exploratory study. *American Journal of Mental Deficiency, 90,* 703–706.

Windle, G. (2011). What is resilience: A review and concept analysis. *Reviews in Clinical Gerontology, 21,* 152–169.

Windle, G., & Bennett, K. M. (2012). Caring relationships: How to promote resilience in challenging times. In D. S. Becvar (Ed.), *Handbook of family resilience* (pp. 219–231). New York, NY: Springer.

Yee, J. L., & Schulz, R. (2000). Gender differences in psychiatric morbidity among family caregivers: A review and analysis. *The Gerontologist, 40*(2), 147–164.

Yeh, C. J., Arora, A. K., & Wu, K. A. (2006). A new theoretical model of collectivistic coping. In P. T. P. Wong & L. C. J. Wong (Eds.), *Handbook of multicultural perspectives on stress and coping* (pp. 55–72). New York, NY: Springer.

Zimmerman, M. A., Ramirez, J., Washienko, K. M., Walter, B., & Dyer, S. (1998). Enculturation hypothesis: Exploring direct and protective effects among Native American youth. In H. I. McCubbin, E. A. Thompson, A. I. Thompson, & J. E. Fromer (Eds.), *Resiliency in Native American and immigrant families* (pp. 199–220). Thousand Oaks, CA: Sage.

Zuković, S., Knežević-Florić, O., & Ninković, S. (2013). Adolescents' perception of coping strategies within families. *Ljetopis socijalnog rada, 19*(2), 275–296.

Index

ABC-X model:
    community and neighborhood,
        148, 159
    death experience, 66–67
    family crisis (X factor), 34, 45–50, 67
    in Contextual Model of Family Stress
        (CMFS), 34–50
    linking roller-coaster model, 47–48
    model illustration, 26*f*, 35*f*, 72*f*
    perception (C factor), 34, 43–45,
        67, 129, 148
    resilience, 129–131
    resources (B factor), 34, 43,
        66–67, 129, 148, 159
    stressor events (A factor), 34, 35–43,
        66, 129–131, 148
Able community, 156–157
Aborigines (Australia), 56
Acculturative stress, 14
Acute stressors, 37*t*, 41
Adversity, 129–131
A factor of ABC-X model. *See* Stressor
    events (A factor)
African Americans:
    cost of resilience, 141
    death experience, 58–60
    female-headed households, 20
    personal narrative, 7
    racial discrimination experiences,
        15–17, 58–59
Age of resilience, 131–133
Allostatic load, 141
Alzheimer's disease, 167
Ambiguous gain, 80–81
Ambiguous loss:
    both-and thinking technique, 77–79
    closure myth, 76
    community effects, 75

Contextual model of family stress
    (CMFS), 26*f*, 27*f*, 32*f*, 72*f*
cultural differences, 76–77
defined, 71
discussion questions, 82
effects of, 74–75
family effects, 75
individual effects, 74–75
Internet resources, 86
intervention guidelines, 77–79
linear stage theory, 77
negative capability perspective, 78
paradox of meaning, 76
perceptions of, 76
physical ambiguous loss, 72, 73–74
premise of, 73
psychological ambiguous loss, 72, 74
psychological family, 76, 78
relativity of truth, 77
religious beliefs and, 80
resilience and, 73, 77, 136, 139
summary, 81
theoretical assumptions, 76–77
theoretical characteristics, 72–73
transgender community, 167–168
types of, 73–74
versus ambiguous gain, 80–81
versus ambivalence, 80
versus uncertainty, 80
vignettes, 72
what it is not, 79–81
See also Boundary ambiguity
Ambiguous stressors, 37*t*, 38–39
Anna Karenina (Tolstoy), 1, 10, 26, 172
Approach coping, 107
Asian culture, 60–63
Australia, 5
Avoidance coping, 107